TEACHING
TENNIS
VOLUME 2

TEACHING
TENNIS
VOLUME 2

THE DEVELOPMENT
OF ADVANCED
PLAYERS

Martin van Daalen

To order additional copies of this book, contact:
Xlibris
1-888-795-4274
www.Xlibris.com
Orders@Xlibris.com
755986

I want to dedicate this book to my parents
For encouraging me to be the best I can be

FOREWORD BY LYNNE ROLLEY

(After becoming the number 2 player in the United States, Lynne has focused on her career in coaching. As director of women's tennis for the USTA, she has helped develop many top players, including Lindsey Davenport, Chanda Rubin, and Jennifer Capriati. Lynne was inducted in the tennis hall of fame in 2008 and is now executive director of tennis at La Quinta Resort & Club and PGA West)

Martin Van Daalen has done it again. After his first book *Teaching Tennis Volume 1*, instructing the fundamentals of the game, he has followed it up with a book for the development of advanced players. In this unique book *Teaching Tennis Volume 2*, his clear process shows you how to become a better player, regardless of your level. If you are interested in learning the game and want to ensure you are on track, use his guidance to take a step-by-step approach to success and improvement. He will enable you, as a reader, to coach yourself or others in all the specifics of the game of tennis.

The game of tennis requires technical, tactical, physical, and mental skills, combined with movement, patience, and passion to become a good player. Martin has spent over thirty-five years mentoring players, coaches, and families on how to be successful in this process and will enjoy the ride. In this second book, he takes his fundamental principles to another level by adding all the specifics of the game. There are many basic nuances to high-performance tennis, and Martin pays amazing attention to detail to ensure improvement. Adhere to his advice, drills, and patterns, and your success will soon become a reality.

FOREWORD BY RODNEY HARMON

(Besides being a successful player on the pro tour, and reaching the quarterfinals in the US Open, Rodney Harmon has dedicated himself in becoming one of the top coaches in the United States and a leader and respected speaker in the tennis industry. He was the former USTA men's director, helping many players reach their goals, and is now the head coach of Georgia Tech women's team.)

Martin van Daalen is, without doubt, one of the best developmental coaches in the tennis world. A coach's coach, Martin brings a passion for our sport that is so essential to motivate young players and push them to their very best.

Martin draws on over thirty-five years of playing, coaching, and developing champions to give us the recipe for his secret sauce that has fueled countless players into successful careers in this wonderful game. He starts with an unshakeable belief that if an athlete is prepared to put in the time, he or she will see results. He adds to that his enviable work ethic, preparation, and planning to form the genesis of a winning strategy for producing elite players. Martin adopts the holistic approach to coaching in order to evince the excitement and drive that all serious players must have. Before you can coach an athlete, you must win their respect and their confidence.

I have learned so much about coaching and developing players from Martin, and he is always ready to share his experiences with other coaches. Besides his coaching ability, a unique gift is his joy at spending unlimited time with players to help them grow and mature as athletes, but more importantly as upstanding citizens. A coach can have tremendous influence over a player's growth and maturity during what often is a stressful time. I have seen Martin spend time with players, discussing things that are important in their lives while stressing the importance of hard work, integrity, honesty, and kindness to others.

This book is a great follow-up to his breakthrough first book, *Teaching Tennis Volume 1: The Fundamentals of the Game*, published in 2011. His focus this time is the growth and development of advanced elite players. Martin shares his blueprint for helping these players improve all aspects of their game. He also delves into the cognitive evolution necessary for players to compete and win at national and international levels of competitive tennis. I have no doubt that this book, *Teaching Tennis Volume 2*, will become a tremendous resource for all parents, coaches, and elite players to achieve their ultimate goals.

FOREWORD BY MAGNUS NORMAN

(Magnus was one of the top Swedish players, reaching the finals of the French Open and the number 2 spot on the ATP ranking [2000]. He is now one of the leading international respected coaches who has helped many top players like Thomas Johansson, Robin Soderling, and Stan Wawrinka, each reaching great heights in their careers. He is also partnering in one of the leading academies in the world, Good to Great, located in Stockholm, Sweden.)

I have worked together and alongside Martin van Daalen on various player development projects, and we still keep in contact on a regular basis. I am proud to have Martin as a friend and colleague, to call on for a second opinion of my players, whom I work with on tour. He knows the art of coaching, spending more than thirty-five years working with players of all levels. I really respect his knowledge of coaching with his tactical and technical knowledge being second to none. What I also admire is his way of translating that knowledge to the players he is working with. In my opinion, that is the essence and the art of coaching. His second book, *Teaching Tennis Volume 2*, will assist many coaches in developing their players to the next level and bring more pleasure and satisfaction to their game.

PREFACE

It was my father who introduced me to the game of tennis when I was ten years old. That summer, he took my brother and me to the local tennis club and showed us how to play the game. We practiced often together until we became good enough to compete in tournaments. I played my first tournament when I was twelve and lost to the number one seed. Even though I was very upset, it was at that moment I decided I wanted to learn how to excel in this wonderful sport of tennis.

As a junior, I had a lot of good players to practice with. I also had some great coaches who taught me the basics of the game. Having an older brother helped me to compete and was a driving force to improve. We would spend afternoons at the club playing singles and doubles matches against each other. There was a great tennis culture at our club with players of all ages and styles of play. We loved being there.

Growing up in Holland, I played for the most part in the summer and other sports in the winter. I was fortunate to receive one or two hours of private instruction a week. It took over an hour of travel each way to get there. Practice was never boring to me, so I never minded the travel. From a young age, I was very independent in taking charge of my tennis, making my own tournament schedule and taking care of all the entries. I couldn't wait for the new tournament schedule to arrive each spring and usually had my plan ready for the year that same afternoon! Sometimes my parents drove me to the tournaments, but often I would take the bus or train to get there. I started making notes of my training, my improvements, and the players I played. Taking notes helped me to remember the things that went well and what to improve and the specifics about matches and players. In a way, I became my own coach at an early stage.

I started getting much more serious about my tennis game around the age of sixteen when I became the junior eighteen and under club champion. It sure helped my confidence. With the limited coaching hours, compared to training today, I had to be resourceful in learning the game by reading more tennis books and making notes of my practice sessions. I also started to do a little coaching on the side and enjoyed sharing the information and helping others.

After high school, I attended two years of technical college (mechanical engineering) before I realized how much I missed tennis. Little did I know that the mechanical engineering background would help me tremendously in my coaching career.

Europe has professional training for coaches, and I assigned myself the goal of becoming the best coach I could possibly be. The two years' training was extensive and detailed in teaching tennis. Part of the course is an internship working at a club, under the tutelage of an experienced instructor and coach from the teaching program. Together with the other student coaches, we had to learn by trial and error, how to coach students of different levels. The learning process of teaching and evaluating each other proved to be an excellent training and experience to become a coach.

When I was twenty, I was drafted in the national army of the Netherlands for sixteen months and stationed in Germany. Being in the army made me tougher and much more assertive in dealing with others. With the rank of sergeant, I learned how to lead others with a calm and determined demeanor. (Later on, I would help organize the first "boot camp" for top junior tennis players at the US Marine Corps headquarters in San Diego, directed by Sgt. Maj. Keith Williams.)

After the draft, I continued the coaches' training course and, at the age of twenty-one, became the youngest national coach in the Netherlands at that time. Even then, I started working on a book for myself of training plans for technique, tactics, and mental and physical training.

Taking ownership and initiative was a skill I had already acquired as a junior to use in the development as a teacher and a coach. After finishing the second coaching course for advanced players, I was working at three different clubs with most of the top players in the eastern part of Holland and was (playing) captain of the top team for many years.

I decided I needed more international experience and wrote to the Australian coach Harry Hopman in the United States to request for an internship position at his academy in Clearwater, Florida. The Dutch Tennis Federation granted me a leave of absence to gain international training methods. It was a great experience in coaching and playing with the world's best players at the time. Some of the top players that trained there were John McEnroe, Bjorn Borg, Vitas Gerulaitis, and many other great players from those days. It was a very busy place with up to 250 players training there each week. I trained there myself with Paul McNamee, Kathy Horvath, Jimmy Brown, Andrea Yeager, and many others. Later, I returned to Holland to continue my work with the federation. I applied a lot of the new coaching techniques in working with the players and in playing tournaments myself.

A few years later, when visiting the United States, I was offered a job at Saddlebrook, a tennis and golf resort. They had recently taken over the program from Harry Hopman, who had just passed away the previous year. Working there for six and a half years was very interesting and educational. My task was to work with a variety of top junior players and professionals: Jared Palmer, Ty Tucker, Mary Pierce, Jennifer Capriati, Mark Kratzmann, Shuzo Matsuoka, Pete Sampras, Jeff Tarango, Jim Courier, and too many others to name. During this time, I took on a number of coaching opportunities that meant traveling on the road with top juniors, pro-level players, and federations including the USTA. One of those opportunities was in Japan, working at a club and coaching juniors of the Japanese federation. This training experience was invaluable in learning to cope with various international players, customs, and styles of play.

I was offered a job in Amsterdam as the head coach and director of the Popeye Gold Star tennis academy. I started with only six students. The academy grew rapidly, and within three years, we grew to forty-five students. It was a rewarding achievement to build this academy from the ground up. It was a joy to work and develop this talented group of players. One major accomplishment that I am very proud of during this time was winning the International League for three years in a row.

My next position was the director of women's tennis position for the Dutch tennis federation. It taught me a lot about management and, unfortunately, about the politics in these organization. Even though I did not enjoy this position as much, it was a great learning tool in dealing with players, coaches, parents, and board members. After this position ended, I took on a very promising junior, Michelle Gerards, to train her privately. She made tremendous progress and, at thirteen years of age, won the national indoor championship for eighteen and under. Unfortunately, I was not able to continue her development when I was invited to join the USTA player development program as a national coach and coordinator of the south region (Southern nine states).

I worked for the USTA for eleven and a half years in various positions. Starting off, I worked under Tom Gullickson (director of coaching) and later on under Lynne Rolley (director of women's tennis), and Rodney Harmon (director of men's tennis). As a national coach, I used to travel to many national and international events, with the Grand Slam junior tournaments being one of the main goals of the year. I was always involved with the development of young junior players. Some of those players were Ashley Harkleroad, Alex Kuznetsov, Chase Buchanan, Rhyne Williams, and Ryan Harrison, to name a few. During this time, I was very involved in changing the US junior ranking system to a point system, similar to the one used by the ATP, WTA, and ITF junior ranking. It made sense that juniors in the United States learned the point system, just as they do on the international scene. After some years of testing, it was finally adopted as the national ranking and is now an intricate part of the junior competition and development in the United States. The new system has sparked the competitive spirit in many junior players to play a lot more matches. In addition, it also allows players to check and calculate their own ranking via the Internet. When the USTA commenced their training program in Boca Raton, I was in charge of the player development group of coaches on the men's side. I oversaw the coaches, the development of the players at the academy, and I assisted with the coaching education of the national men's coaches. After working privately for a while, I took the position of director of Player Development in Finland and was able to make an impact to the culture of training and tournament play. At the moment, I am back in Florida in developing players and programs at the Miami Beach Tennis Academy.

The development of advanced players can be a very gratifying experience as a coach. To see your students progress and excel is rewarding in itself. As a coach, parent, or student, this book will assist you to reach your goals to ultimately play at a higher level. May you have as much fun reading it as I had writing it!

Best of luck,
Martin van Daalen

Author: Martin van Daalen (age 21)

CONTENTS

INTRODUCTION

Teaching Tennis Volume 2 is a comprehensive book for players, coaches, and parents about the development of intermediate to advanced players. This is the second volume in a series of three instructional books with specifics to enhance the understanding of methodology and progression in teaching. After the fundamentals of the game are explained in volume 1, readers are able to build on the information of the first book. Volume 3, *Competition*, is for instructing national and international levels of play. For a better understanding of the material, it is beneficial for readers to examine these books in order, starting with volume 1. The series will further assist the reader with the execution and <u>applications</u> in training or teaching the game of tennis.

This second book explains in detail how to instruct yourself, or others, how to become or develop an intermediate or advanced tennis player. It illustrates the progression of the various subjects with many examples of drills and exercises. There are many technical subjects with some tactical, physical, and mental applications of the game. The format throughout the book has specifics on each subject, with common mistakes and how to correct them with practice drills. The goal was to make the book adaptable for everyone involved in the development process (players, coaches, and parents), so each might find an interest and a learning experience.

Players are able to follow this book and improve their game step by step with detailed instructions that fit their game style. There are technical, tactical, physical, and mental tips with examples of corrections, drills, stroke improvements, and different methods of training.

Coaches are able to use this book as a guide to coaching and teaching intermediate and advanced players. It shows the philosophy and methodology to teaching and how to apply these on court with enhanced techniques and examples. This book will help you organize your training in progressions of learning. It also includes some short stories and anecdotes from the author to illustrate the different ways of coaching.

Parents can use this book to either assist their children with coaching or use it as a reference or handbook in solving many issues that arise in the development of a tennis player. It will provide parents with firsthand knowledge of the many issues that coaches and players deal with on a daily basis and how to solve them.

Note: The additional coaching stories show some of the situation that might occur and how to deal with them in an innovative way.

TEACHING AND COACHING PHILOSOPHY

A teaching and coaching philosophy develops over time and with added experience. There are many influences that affect your thoughts on how to teach and coach. Your philosophy is often influenced by the way you used to play as a player or how your coach used to teach you. As a novice coach, you might have an opinion early on in your career, but over time, this might change or get adjusted somewhat. This can be caused by new teaching methods, added experiences, or new styles of play in an ever-evolving game. So be patient and flexible and keep an open mind to new ideas.

Teaching and Coaching

The difference between teaching and coaching is that teaching can be coaching, but coaching is not always teaching. The instruction and learning process is a one-way communication with very little or no input from the student since they lack the knowledge of the subjects. In this case, the student is less experienced and cannot share information with the instructor. For instance, you are taught the fundamentals and the details of the game. A coach is someone that is training and guiding you in tournament play. The instruction and learning process is a two-way communication with the student sharing their input and feedback on the subject. Obviously, the student has to be more experienced to share information on the various aspects of the game. A coach can prepare you for tournament play with training and practice matches. The coach can discuss with the student how to analyze your opponent and what strategy to play. Sometimes the coach can also assist you with the mental side of the game. Most of the time, a coach will accompany you to the tournaments and help you with a game plan and discuss your progress after the match. The communication here is the key.

Philosophy

Although the philosophy of teaching and coaching can change over time, mine has always maintained the same. And I suppose my philosophy does have a background in how I taught myself for most of the time.

My philosophy for teaching and coaching is to instruct the players how to coach themselves, coaching themselves technically, tactically, physically, and mentally in a positive and competitive manner.

As a tennis player, you are most often competing on your own against another player. You are on your own during play, sitting alone on the bench during changeovers and making your decisions on shot choice and strategy. The only times this is not the case is while playing doubles and in team competition. With this in mind, you have to be resourceful, resilient, and competitive in your own mind without relying on help or other outer influences. I personally like to coach players to be independent by instructing them how to solve problems on their own while playing the game. I want them to focus inward and figure out what to do by giving them the background information they need. It might take a little more time for them to digest the material and master this skill, but in the end, I feel you are creating a mature tennis player. This philosophy might not be the same for you, but that is the fun part of coaching. You get to decide for yourself what your teaching and coaching philosophy might be.

Objectives and Vision

Your objectives (goals) as a coach need to be clear from the start. Specific goals are needed to form your objectives. Even a novice coach should have an idea to what he or she wants to accomplish as a coach. Coaches often have similarities in their goals, but to me, the three most common ones are the following:

- To teach and coach students to develop their game
- To show them how to enjoy the game
- To assist young athletes to reach their potential

Your vision starts with your objectives as a coach but expands into how you see yourself develop as a coach with the interaction with players, parents, and others.

Executing Your Philosophy

The challenge in executing the philosophy is being consistent with your beliefs. For instance, in my case, I choose to teach my players to coach themselves. In doing so, I had to take the following steps:

1. *Teach them self-analysis and how to fix their strokes. (Technical)*
2. *Teach them how to make a game plan and how to execute. (Tactical)*
3. *Teach them how to train and maintain their conditioning. (Physical)*
4. *Teach them how to be compete and be disciplined in execution. (Mental)*

The execution of teaching your students to coach themselves takes a little more time. It demands you get the students involved with the process of thinking along with your way of teaching. You have to encourage them to ask questions and propose some problems for them to solve. Only then will they fully understand what you are trying to accomplish.

Whatever philosophy you have, it should find its way back in your teaching of the most important aspects of the game: technical, tactical, physical, and mental. But also it should have its effect on how you organize your lessons. Having your students take ownership of their development is in my mind the highest level of learning in the game. Teaching your students this skill, with the passion and enjoyment of the game, is a most rewarding experience for a coach.

The execution of your philosophy should also be reflected in your training and tournament plan. The training and tournament plan are always linked together and should show the fundamentals and specifics of your philosophy. The fundamentals of the training plan should be split into technical, tactical, mental, and physical segments with specific topics in those areas. The tournament plan is coordinated to the training plan keeping in mind the progression of the lessons. The focus in the matches and tournaments should be in line with the topics of the training plan. The students will show better results in tournaments when they master the topics first in practice and then try them out in tournament play before moving on to the next topic.

Developing an Advanced Player

There is not one way to develop a player. Especially knowing the many pathways players have taken to reach the top. Some have dominated first in the juniors before trying out in pro events. Others will not develop so rapidly and choose a college path. This gives you the option to keep developing but still trying out in pro events. In some rare cases, the players have hardly played any junior events and moved to pro levels fairly quickly. And then there are all the combinations in between. There is not one golden pathway, no standard development that fits everyone. But there are some important steps in the development of a player that can improve your chances of success. Making the right choices can help you with your tennis game in trying to be the best you can be while not forgetting to enjoy the journey in reaching your goals.

What Is an Advanced Player?

An advanced player is not defined by age, gender, or amount of years they have played. It is defined by how well they play and the experience gathered in competition. An advanced player could be a nationally ranked junior or an adult who competes at a regional and national level. Their skill level is high, and they are very serious about their game. They usually train often and compete in many events.

Building the foundation is all about getting the basics right from the start. You don't want to go back and change strokes or grips and waste time in your development. When starting to play tennis, your strokes and style of play are like the "blueprint" of your game. You will follow this blueprint for a good portion of your tennis career. Good and bad habits are formed early on. Mastering the fundamentals can make a great impact on your improvements and future level of play.

A good age to start getting serious about your game is around the ages of fourteen or fifteen. The player will become stronger and start showing their skills. The passion and push has to come from the players themselves. The coach and parents can stimulate their interest, but can't force a player to want it. A good sign of passion is when you see the player start to work harder than others around them and taking initiative to improve.

Find a good coach to teach the advanced skills needed for competition, someone with an interest in developing juniors to advanced players and who has a proven record. As a parent, you need to do your homework and investigate the background, experience, and demeanor of the coach. These factors are important to find a coach that "fits" the character traits of your child. This person has to have knowledge in working with kids and experience in coaching in general. Ex-players have the knowledge of how to play themselves, but don't necessarily possess the coaching and/or development skills (training) to communicate this to others. All these things need to be considered before making a choice on your future coach.

Continuity in coaching is an important factor in the development process. Parents also need to consider this factor before they decide to coach their own child. How long can you fulfill this role, but more importantly, is that the right choice for your child? Many players change coaches if they, or their parents, see other players be successful with another coach. Especially in tennis, the grass seems to be greener on the other side. Making a change in coaching more often makes you lose time in development and, unless really necessary, needs to be avoided. The new coach might start changing the technique of the player and cause a loss of confidence. With every major change in your strokes, you could be looking at a loss of six months or more. This is even more so the case with older players. The longer a player has been trained to play a particular way, the more difficult it is to make changes. Corrections in strokes should only be considered if the current stroke will hamper their development or if they are adamant in making the changes themselves. In the progress of many players, they reach a certain plateau where they stagnate before improving again. This is true for virtually every player and can be very deceiving to players and parents in thinking they are not making any improvements. Only make changes in coaching when you feel the coach has reached their plateau of teaching or when the relationship is breaking down.

Playing other sports (cross-training) can have a positive effect on the physical growth of the tennis game. The different sports train all the various muscle groups needed to create the athletic body to compete at a higher level. For example, if you were playing soccer, it would not hurt your game but stimulate the coordination, strength, stamina, and footwork speed to compete in tennis.

Group lessons or private lessons are individual choices and depend on the goals and interest of the player. Don't take only private lessons early on, unless there are some fundamental things to correct. The interaction with other players is important for competition. Once a player starts to excel and shows passion to become an advanced player, the coach or parents can consider a more specific approach in coaching.

Academies are very popular these days, and many parents decide to enroll their kids every year. If your child is just starting off in learning the game, these schools are not for you. The academies are much more suited for kids that have had a solid base in stroke development and want to play a lot more tennis. The academies are set up to bring many kids together to excel in a competitive environment. For advanced and pro players, this is an excellent environment to improve their game with plenty of practice. If you still want to go in this direction, I would advise the family to move there and to find an experienced coach within the academy to take responsibility for your child's development (think of continuity of coaching).

Regional programs are available in every section of the community. They organize many training opportunities from "quick start" for the novice young players (five to seven years) to training opportunities in the section and regional training centers. In the United States, there are three training centers for the top juniors in LA, New York, and Orlando (to open in 2017). You would do well to call the section office in your section to find out what programs are available for your students.

Grips and strokes are important to learn the fundamentals of the game. Bad grips and strokes can be very limiting to progress, with the limiting factors negatively impacting the execution of the strategy. The fundamentals in building the strokes do have long-term effects. So being taught the proper way early on is a great advantage. There are lots of ways to correct strokes and grips without making it a burden. At an early age, kids usually don't like technique lessons. They are easily bored and can lose their focus. So using a game approach at this age can be a useful method to get their attention. Showing them ways how to improve their strokes to win points will make sense to them. Imagination and inventiveness of the coach is the key to success!

Training for advanced players is organized differently than recreational players. The main factor is the intensity of the execution. Just this one factor alone will increase the improvements and results tremendously. This is further stimulated with more tennis specific condition training (running and movement program, weight training, etc.). The last factor is the focus on strategy and tactics. Learning the patterns of play and more shot choices gives any player more options to combat their opponent. Training these aspects in practice matches provides them with the experience and mental toughness that is required in tournament play.

Weapon development is a necessity for advanced players to pressure the opponents. In watching top international players of today's game, you will notice very quickly that they have one or two big weapons (sometimes even more). Most weapons are constructed from well-developed strokes that are not only reliable in consistency, but also have the ability to apply pressure through power, spin, or tempo (or all of them combined). They are able to set up the rally to use their weapons effectively to force mistakes or to make outright winning shots. However, the weapons can also be a tactical, physical, or mental ability. Most young intermediate players will already start showing signs of possible weapon development. As they mature, it will become evident to coaches where to seek the weapon development for each individual player. Let there be a natural progression of weapon development rather than forcing one on them. This method will create more confidence and commitment through ownership.

The proper level of play in tournaments should be adjusted to the motivation and intensity of the player. Playing a tournament level where you can win matches helps to gain confidence through accomplishment. Not every child can be a champion from the start. Let them be their own motivator and wait for indications from them how serious to take the game (passion for the game). The player has to be the leader in this process, not parents or coaches. The win-loss ratio is an important factor for progress and improvement. (A good win-loss ratio minimum should be 2 to 1.)

Have a development plan to organize your training and tournament schedule. The plan is an outline to develop their game that fits their style of play from technique, tactical, mental, and conditional aspects. There should be a list of strengths and weaknesses and how to improve those with short and long-term goals. It should also contain the organization of when to play, when to train, but most importantly when to rest! This plan needs to be made together with the player, coach, and parents. Make it simple and realistic, and make sure you stick to it! Everyone should have input and agree to the plan. Usually, the original and simple plans are the best ones to execute.

Philosophy of teaching is important for a coach to develop a player. You might be a parent who is trying to coach your child or an experienced coach, but it is imperative to develop a philosophy of coaching to become a coach with a "big picture" vision. As a novice coach, there will not be sufficient experience to develop a specific philosophy of teaching or coaching, but you can develop it over time. There are a variety of factors that play a role in this process. It can be something you are very passionate about or what made an impression on you when competing yourself. It is also possible that it could change over time. Whatever it might be, try to implement it in your lessons as your style of coaching.

Communication is probably the most important in building a good relationship. As a coach, this is the foundation and a necessity in any form of teaching. As a parent, communication is fundamental, not only with your own child, but also with the coach, other parents, other competitors, and maybe other kids within your own family. Communication with the coach should be one of respect and letting the coach do his job. Good communication in getting along with the other parents, coaches, and competitors is imperative to not creating rivalries and stress between the kids. Try to lower anxiety and animosity among them and stimulate a healthy competitive spirit. Finding the right balance in staying down-to-earth and stimulating a child is not an easy thing to do, once they starts winning a lot. It is important for kids to understand that even if they can play a decent game of tennis, life does not change in communicating with others and treating everyone with respect. This attitude within the family will help, later on, to establish a normal relationship. Having a down-to-earth feeling will help bring stability to their life.

Talent Identification

When we talk about a tennis talent, we most often recall how this player hits the ball or how the spectacular shots were produced. It might be accentuated in the gracefulness of the strokes, the fluidity of the movements, or the effortless appearance in continually hitting winning shots. Age also seems to play a large role in how we define talent: the younger the player, the more we are impressed by their skills. There are obvious examples of players that developed at a young age: Pete Sampras, Andre Agassi, Steffi Graf, Andrea Yeager, Roger Federer, Rafa Nadal, Martina Hingis, Kim Clijsters, Maria Sharapova, Jennifer Capriati, Serena and Venus Williams, and many others. Even today, there are some young players breaking through to the top 100 of the ATP and WTA rankings. I remember watching a sixteen-year-old Richard Gasquet at the US Open, and his talent, skills, and results up to that point were quite evident.

I watched a thirteen-year-old Martina Hingis play one of the Dutch girls I was coaching for the federation in the first round of the French open junior event. You could see the obvious talent she had in anticipating tactical situations and moving forward to knock off the volley when needed. She went on to win the tournament and became one of the youngest competitors to win a junior grand slam. But there have also been many examples of "late bloomers," especially those that went to college first or needed more time to physically and mentally mature.

Martina Hingis

I was coaching at the Roland-Garros junior qualifying event, and one of the American juniors was playing a sixteen-year-old Novak Djokovic.

If you would have asked me then if he was going to be the number 1 player in the world, I would have said, "No way." Not that he was not up to par, but at that time, there were many young juniors that looked just as good or even more promising. From this point forward, he made great strides to improve his physical conditioning, smoothed out his sometimes failing ground strokes to strong weapons on both sides, changed his diet, improved his serve and return to weapons as well, and has much improved attacking and defensive skills, to becoming a dominating player of this generation of players. So was this talent or great coaching and player development, or was it plain hard work and dedication? Maybe in his case it was all three. I have also seen some highly skilled players at a very young age that I thought for sure would succeed, but they never seemed to reach their potential.

So what are the factors that determine a talented player to become successful? It is not only the technical aspects that play a role since all better players hit the ball well. There are also the physical, tactical, and mental aspects to consider. Good analysis of a student is important to identify talent. But with so many players striking the ball so well in today's tennis, how do you determine what makes someone stand out above the rest? There are several aspects of the game that can determine the talent level of a player:

1. *Fundamentals of the strokes*
2. *Footwork and movement on the court*
3. *Pattern development to exploit a weakness of the opponent*
4. *Reading the game and anticipation of situations*
5. *Consistency of performance under pressure*
6. *Shot selections in tactical situations*
7. *Weapon development to dominate the opponent*
8. *Attitude and character to succeed*
9. *Work ethic in training and matches*
10. *Passion for the game*
11. *Age to skills and results ratio*
12. *Decision making for development*

1. *Fundamentals of the strokes*
   The basics or fundamentals of the strokes provide the foundation to consistent reproduction of these swings. Just like building a house, the foundation needs to be solid without any cracks or pieces missing for it to function properly and efficiently. The quality of the swing production shows the talent level.

2. *Footwork and movement on the court*
   Movement and recovery are essential to good footwork. It requires the skills of speed, coordination, agility, flexibility, balance, and endurance. The fine motor skills come into play when making adjustments with the feet in coordination with trajectory, speed, and spin of the ball. The different court surfaces also require different skills in footwork and movement.

3. *Pattern development to exploit the weakness of the opponent*
   Understanding the possible patterns in any given situation and how to counter those takes many years of experience in match play. Some players will understand the patterns better than others with an intuitive feeling on how to use them. Making the right shot choices for each tactical situation is sometimes a natural talent, but can also be taught as a skill.

4. *Reading the game and anticipation of the situation*
   When playing matches, it is imperative to "read" the opponent's body language in movements and strokes to predict their shots. It is also possible to recognize the patterns, trajectory, speed, and spin of the ball in order to prepare for a good response. The eyes have to be trained to read this information in a split second. The player can then use this information in combination with past experiences of playing points and matches. Talented players with natural "reading" abilities recognize game styles, patterns, and trajectories much faster and will have an advantage over other players with quicker responses to each situation.

5. *Consistency of performance under pressure*

It is possible to be consistent in practice but still struggle to maintain the same performance in pressure situation or point/match play. Players become proficient in matches when practicing specific point situations on a regular basis. This is why it is so important to also play points whenever possible in practice.

6. *Shot selection in tactical situations*

Making committed decisions with shot choices or strategies will improve the point and match play. Being clear and confident will assist the player to make faster decisions. Being unsure or doubtful of the shot choices will cause the player to lose time in executing the stroke and possibly lead to unforced. The decisions making also pertains to mental and organizational talents: what tournaments to play, how to train, how to control your attitude, and how to communicate with others. These factors become crucial in the development of an advanced tennis player.

7. *Weapon development*

Playing defensively requires just as much skills as playing offensively. Both can be considered weapons. However, in today's tennis, most players have several weapons they can attack or defend with. These can be determined by certain strokes, but it can also be a physical, strategic, or mental ability. Most players have a good serve and one or two other weapons. Weaknesses can, and always will be, exploited fairly quickly. Talented players will quickly find ways to score points with their weapons over and over again. They are able to use these weapons to dominate their opponent.

8. *Attitude and character to succeed*

The mental attitude of a player can define their confidence and determination. The body language is a telltale sign of the state of mind and the confidence level. Talented players most often portray a positive attitude and belief that shows in their posture and movement. They have a winning attitude and never give up.

9. *Work ethic in training and matches*

Hard work in training and matches always pays off in the long run to develop your game and to succeed in tournaments. It develops the natural stamina and toughness needed in today's competition. Talented players will understand pretty quickly that it takes more than fancy strokes and footwork to become successful; it also takes hard work, determination, and perseverance.

10. *Passion for the game*

As players become more successful, they understand the commitment and hard work it takes to succeed. The only way to get through this is to love the game with a passion that makes all the sacrifices worth the efforts. Talented players show the passion through an obsession and enthusiasm to learn anything about the game.

11. *Age-to-skill ratio*

The age of a player and the rate of skill development is also a component in determining the talent level of a player. There have been some clear examples of young players developing at a much faster rate than others. Not all top players you know today have reached their current position with all the skill levels listed above, and the rate of development and/or timing of development will vary from player to player. In some cases, they have developed by using some of the skills to their utmost potential. With hard work and dedication, it is possible to develop the remaining skills.

12. *Decision making for development*

In order to develop at a faster rate, it is necessary to make good choices concerning training, coaches, tournaments, communication, and organization. The ones that do well in this skill will have a higher chance of success in their development.

Definition of a Talent

First of all, we have to understand that it takes great skill to play tennis. It usually takes two years just to master the game in the sense of hitting rallies. From a physical standpoint, it requires great coordination, flexibility, endurance, and speed. And then you still need to gain considerable strategy experience with patterns and styles of play before you start winning matches or events. With playing more sectional and national competition, the mental game comes into the equation as well. As you can see, it takes a lot of talent in just reaching a national

Novak Djokovic

level (let alone playing at an international or pro level). All junior players competing at a national level should be considered "talented" just because of the skill level of the game. It is out of this pool of players that top players emerge. Everyone's definition of a top player is different and might change over time. This can range from top 100, top 50, or even top 10. This depends largely on each person's personal point of view and their experience in the game. For a top player to emerge on the scene, it takes a lot of things to happen at the right time. I can't count the times I have been a witness to talented players not making it to the top. Or in other cases, the player makes it to the tour level but through a variety of circumstances, drops back down. Everything has to fall into place in the right sequence of events, from having the right start, creating good fundamentals of the strokes, winning matches or events at the right time, having the funds to finance the national and international travel and coaching, to getting the proper guidance and coaching at every level. Only then, with a little luck, a new star will be born.

> ## *Myth in tennis: If a young player is talented, they will become a top player.*

It is one thing to become a talented junior; it is an entirely different objective to become a successful pro player. After a junior player reaches an international level and makes the transition to the pro events, you actually find out if they are able to sustain the progress and stabilize the results over several years. Some players reach that level at a very young age, whereas others take a more steady climb through the rankings. There is no one way to success, and there are no guarantees. Just because you are a talented player does not mean you will be ensured a career as a pro player. And even if a player does reach this goal, it is even harder to stay there! A career in tennis is a risky business, filled with lots of ups and downs along the way. It takes years of investment, commitment, and a lot of perseverance to even have a chance to reach the entry level of pro tennis. Tens of thousands of young, promising, and talented players are on the road every year between fifteen and twenty-five weeks, all chasing their dream of becoming a top player. A study done a few years ago by the ITF showed that only 50 percent of the top 10 juniors in the world reach the top 100 in the pro rankings. The rewards can be very high if you are successful. But the reality is that only a hundred men and women are making a decent living on the pro tour. Small odds for a chance at a career in tennis!

Alex (Sasha) Zverev

(Here at age fourteen while preparing for the junior Orange Bowl boys 14 in Miami. Currently ranked 20 ATP, October 2016. He always worked hard and did not solely rely on his talents)

Pitfalls of Talented Players

For over more than thirty years of coaching, I have seen many talented players fail to reach their goal in becoming a top player, even when the opportunities were there from the start. There are some common aspects that play a vital role in the development of a player, but in the end, it comes down to smart decision making by players, coaches, and parents. Some of the common mistakes made are as follows:

1. Telling a talented player he is talented. This usually leads them to rely on their talents too much instead of working hard on all aspects of their game, especially their weaknesses. There are many instances where a talented player will lose to a player that "outworks" them. It also is common to see a young player work less hard once they turn pro since they feel a sense of accomplishment and want to rest on their laurels or rely on their talent.

> *Hard work beats talent when talent does not work hard!*

2. Pushing them beyond their physical and mental capabilities. As parents and coaches, we often forget that it all started with enjoyment of the game. It is a good lesson to learn that hard work leads to results, but pushing them beyond their limits can lead to overtraining and loss of drive and passion for the game.
3. Choosing the proper coach at each level of the game. Just like in school, there are teachers for elementary and higher-level coaching. Finding the right coach to bring them to the next level can be crucial to their development.

4. Choosing the proper developmental pathway. Knowing where you are in your development and the choices you make can determine your career. Some need to go the college route when there is no clear indication they are mentally or physically ready to start a pro career. Your ATP or WTA ranking is a good indicator to the path you should follow.

5. Keep doing what works for you. Just like in any match, never change a winning game! I can't count the times I have seen players fail once they started their pro career by making too many changes. Turning pro usually happens during the transition period between junior and playing more pro events. This transitional phase is difficult enough without having to deal with equipment and/or coaching changes. This can often lead to a loss of confidence at a time when the player needs it the most.

A True Talent

So what is a true and real talent? Talents are available in every level of the tennis sport. However, as far as I am concerned, talent is just an opportunity to greatness, but it can be heavily overrated when relied upon too much.

A true and real tennis talent is a player who is driven by their opportunities and passion for the game in making the right decisions in becoming the best they can be. These decisions are not just limited to how hard they train on every aspect of their game, but also to making smart decisions during matches and events, knowing when to make changes in their game, choosing the right people to guide them, and in making any sacrifices to reach their goals.

METHODOLOGY TO TEACHING

What is methodology of teaching? The words indicate a method of teaching, but it is much more than that. To get a good understanding, we can look at the two definitions below:

- *An organized system to teaching*
- *A study of organized systems and principles to teaching*

We could simplify and combine them as follows: a systematic approach to teaching tennis in a simple and logical order to stimulate and enhance the learning process.

For example, you would not start teaching a topspin forehand or a topspin serve to a beginning junior. Without a good order of teaching, the player will easily get frustrated since the topics are not yet within their skill level, experience, and racket control. Without a method and progression, students will become very inconsistent with their strokes and haphazard with their ability to play the game in a strategic way.

With this in mind, we can identify a few important aspects to methodology of teaching:

1. **Systematic approach to teaching.** This means that coaches have to prepare and execute their lessons with a method that creates order and an understanding of the material that enhances the learning curve of each student. Start by organizing the groups and private lessons by competency levels and prepare each lesson with topics of learning according to a progression, organizing your lesson content with a warm-up, learning phase, practice phase, and point play. This will help students to master the subjects and progress more rapidly. Prepare each lesson and write some key points for each phase of the session. Finish each period with a cooldown and recap of the lesson, emphasizing the key points. Preparation also means thinking ahead about how many courts and teaching attributes you are going to need. A systematic approach to teaching with preparation and organization of your lessons will instill an attitude of professionalism that will not go unnoticed by your employer, students, and parents.

2. **Logical progression order.** Go from easy to more complicated topics. Teach the basics first before moving on to more complicated subjects, and keep it as simple as possible with each next step of learning. In your enthusiasm to teach, it is easy to get distracted from the goals of your lesson plan and teach topics that are too difficult for your students. Don't confuse students with too much information so they can concentrate properly on each subject of learning. Make sure they master each subject with sufficient skill before moving on to the next subject. In my efforts to push students to higher levels of excellence, I have made these same mistakes by introducing subjects to intermediate and advanced players that were above their skill level. An example of this is illustrated in the following story when teaching my own son Tom.

The Running Forehand

In teaching the running forehand to my thirteen-year-old son, I learned a valuable lesson in not teaching the specialty shots too early.

On a sunny weekend, we were practicing Tom's ground strokes at the Gold Star racket club in Amsterdam. He was hitting the ball very powerfully that day, and I was impressed with his efforts. He asked me to teach him the running forehand, and since he was doing so well, I decided to oblige him.

I took him through the paces in explaining the technical specifics of the stroke. He took to it like a duck to water and pretty soon was enjoying the extra capabilities of his newfound stroke. We practiced it some more before trying it out in point play. To my great surprise, Tom started to run slower every time I played a wide ball to his forehand. I yelled out him, "Run faster!" and "Set up early!" but he kept on slowing down with his footwork. It was then that I understood what he was doing. He was slowing down his footwork to create a running forehand. Like all young players, he liked to hit the flashy shots and was making a deliberate attempt to only hit that shot. It took me some time to make him understand that this shot should be reserved for extreme situations and should not be created on purpose. Many years later, we often talked about this funny incident with fond recollections. Even when we hit some balls today, he loves the running forehand.

This is a good example where the intentions were correct, but where logic and understanding of proper tactical execution should prevail. It should fit within the progression of the student for them to progress instead of regress.

Even if a student asks you to teach something, it is up to the coach to decide if they are ready for this subject. A better solution is to challenge them by teaching it only when previous skills are mastered first.

3. **Master the skill.** Don't move on to the next topic until the student has mastered the skill to a degree of excellence and confidence. Too often, we as coaches will be impatient to teach at an ever-increasing pace and move past the point where the students are able to comprehend the subject matter or become confused and lose confidence in the execution. A good measure is to repeat the exercise several times and to try it out in points. If you observe the same quality of the execution in repeated practice and match play, it is safe to move on to the next progression or subject. Keep repeating the subjects from time to time to maintain confidence and the skill level of each individual topic.

4. **Repeat learned skills.** Keep repeating the topics to keep up the confidence and skill levels of each subject. Repetition of skills is often overlooked in an effort to learn new things. We might try to advance too fast and too far in the progressions. Reconfirming the confidence of the execution is the only way to keep up the skills learned in the past. The brain controls the strokes and body movements. Repetition and training will reinforce the neural pathways that control the coordination of all muscle groups. Over time, these movements become automotive habits. With an enhanced automation, students can trust the execution of their strokes and become more efficient. This enables players to focus on strategy and tactics.

By following these simple rules of teaching, your student will have a much better understanding of the game, master the skills more quickly, maintain the execution under pressure, and play freely with more confidence.

A systematic approach to teaching and coaching has some further details. There are three aspects to consider:

- New subjects
- Corrections
- Improvements

Martin van Daalen

1. **New subjects.** The progression of learning with new subjects is about finding the right order of exercises and drills to make the learning process as smooth as possible. This will enhance confidence and consistency. It is imperative to choose easy and simple drills to take away any doubts and/or fears in the execution so the student can build on those skills with confidence. Sticking to the four steps above from systematic approach to logical competency order, mastering the skill, and repeating the practice are points to keep in mind.

2. **Corrections.** This particular progression is a change of implementation in order to correct a mistake in execution or to enhance the execution. This method is the most complicated since bad habits and automotive actions take a long time to correct by "reprogramming" the brain and reconstructing the neural pathways responsible for automotive actions. Before you make a correction, make sure that the corrections are really necessary and not based on personal preference of the execution. The corrections might not improve the student at all and might even stall their progression. There are several steps you have to follow to ensure that what you are about to teach is going to remedy the error. Here are the steps to follow:

   - Analysis
   - Error detection
   - Correction
   - Postanalysis

   A. You start by making an *overall analysis* of the subject matter. This method will narrow down the area in which to look for errors of execution. It will also give you a wider view in case it is caused by more than one factor.
   B. The *error detection* is the crucial part of the correction. Making an initial mistake in error detection will lead to more complication in corrections.

C. *Corrections* need to be made with a progression of learning that stimulates the learning process. Explain what you are about to change and why. Furthermore, describe how you want to make the changes and give a demonstration. This process will facilitate the students to fully understand the task at hand.

D. The *postanalysis* is a feedback for you to make sure that the correction was the right one and that the error has been corrected properly. Make sure to give some positive and constructive feedback to your students.

3. **Improvements.** Practice of a formerly practiced subject helps to improve the confidence of the player and enhance the consistency. Improvements will not occur when making major changes in the execution. They occur with stimulation and minor adjustments of the subject in practice with a systematic approach to ensure a smooth transition from what was taught in the past. The following method will provide the most improvements:

A. Repetition of the old subject
B. Practice until confident
C. Enhance and improve for automation
D. Feedback from point play and tournaments
E. Training subjects from match-play feedback

Automation of the strokes and patterns is the ultimate goal for every player. Once they can rely on automated actions and reflexes, they will have more time to focus on the actions of the opponent and the strategy they want to follow. This methodology of training will provide the largest possibility of success and create confidence and consistency.

From Basics to Advanced Tennis

Basic Strokes

There are some basic strokes a player must learn in order to play the game. These can vary according to the age of the player and their level of play:

Beginner ➡ Intermediate ➡ Advanced ➡ Professional

In learning the game of tennis, there are four basic strokes. As the skill level enhances, the *volley* can be added later to that repertoire. All these four basic strokes have to work in unison with each other in order to be effective in playing the game well:

- *Service*
- *Forehand*
- *Backhand*
- *Volley*

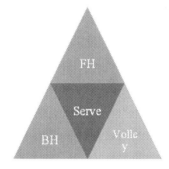

When starting the game, keep it simple with just the first three. Don't add the volley until the student has mastered the ground strokes and short balls and the transition to the net is required.

As students progress to advanced players, there are two more strokes that are added to the basic strokes:

- *The return*
- *The overhead*

The return is similar to forehand and backhand but is a specialty shot in its execution. It is the most neglected stroke in practice but represents half the games played. It is also crucial in breaking the serve from the opponent in winning the match.

The volley becomes a stroke to attack the opponent by shortening the response time. The volley, if used appropriately, becomes an added weapon for the advanced player to prevent opponents from running down balls and forcing them to hit passing shots under pressure.

The overhead or smash is the stroke to finish off the points at the net or in case the opponent tries to hit a lob over the net.

The Four Pillars of Tennis

The basics of tennis have its origin in technical, tactical, mental, and physical aspects. These four components, also called "the four pillars of tennis," are the cornerstones of the game. They all play an intricate part in the development and teaching of each student and should be taught with each component in mind. The components are interconnected with another and have implications on the level of execution.

- *Technical*
  The mechanics form the specifics of the swing to reproduce consistent and reliable strokes. They are built from a coordinated effort of footwork and the stroke in delivering the racket head in the proper position through the contact point. The stroke controls the ball flight in speed, spin, and trajectory.

- *Tactical*

  Development of the strategy and tactics is accomplished by proper execution of a game plan. It takes experience and understanding of the strengths and weaknesses of the opponent. This also requires taking advantage of your own strengths and guarding against your weaknesses. The shot choices and patterns of play enable you to outmaneuver your opponent to gain an advantage.

- *Mental*

  Controlling the emotions during practice and match play will enhance the player's performance with a calm and determined thought process. Staying calm enhances the focus for better shot choices and playing with controlled aggression to manage the points with initiative.

- *Physical*

  Learning how to train and use your physical ability to gain an advantage on your opponent in point and match play. A player can do this with endurance, power, balance, speed, flexibility, recovery footwork, and tempo of play.

The best way to introduce and teach these topics is by showing the relationship of the components and how they work together. For example, a tactical pattern can drive a player to a technical adjustment. Or a physical play can lead to a technical adjustment.

Examples:

1. *With the opponent hitting high balls to the player's backhand, the player can make a technical adjustment by backing up and hitting the ball at a lower contact point or make a tactical adjustment by running around and using the forehand instead of the backhand.*
2. *With the opponent attacking the backhand of the player, the player can make a tactical adjustment by hitting the ball up the line. The opponent will often choose to hit cross-court to the player's forehand.*

The player can also make a technical adjustment in using the slice to slow the ball down.

With the opponent hitting wide balls, the player can make a technical and tactical adjustment in returning the ball high with topspin to gain time to recover and neutralize the situation.

Teaching Order

There is a logical order and method to introduce and teach tennis subjects to your students. This is especially true for technical aspects, but the same goes for tactical, physical, and mental aspects. Whenever you are teaching technical aspect, always keep in mind the tactical implications. It is important your students understand the same concept. An example would be when teaching the service action; consistency and placement have a large impact on the response possibility of the opponent.

Technical teaching order with tactical applications:

1. Consistency
2. Depth
3. Direction (change of direction)   **Progression**
4. Spin
5. Power
6. Tempo

As you can tell by the order of teaching above, the subject matter is from simple to more complex and from basic to specific. In teaching students, always try to find a progression that follows a method and logical order.

Tactical Situations

The methodology in teaching tactical situations is similar to teaching strokes. The coach can use the same technical order in teaching the tactical situations. The tactical situations are in the same logical order of teaching from easy to more complex:

1. Baseline play
2. Serve and return
3. Net play
4. Approaching the net
5. Playing against the net player

Physical Aspects

There are a lot of physical aspects that come into play when training this sport. It requires a lot of practice to excel to advanced levels but will have a large effect on your game. The physical teaching aspects are as follows:

- Endurance
- Strength
- Flexibility
- Coordination
- Speed
- Balance

The teaching order is not necessarily set, and subjects can be trained individually and in accordance to the students' needs after a physical analysis. Many of these aspects can be trained on court during the tennis training. For advanced players, off-court training can further stimulate the progress in match play and tournaments.

Off-Court Training

Specific physical aspects can be trained individually or as a group with the use of on-court drills while focusing the subjects. Off-court training can be performed in the gym or on the playing surface you intend to play matches on.

• Gym training (strength training, plyometrics, endurance, flexibility)

• Movement training   - Lower body (specific footwork, speed, agility)
                       - Trunk (stomach and lower back)
                       - Arms and shoulders
                       - Combination movements (all of the above)

These last aspects are more specific in nature. Although endurance, strength and flexibility are trained here, the focus will be more on coordination, speed and balance.

Mental Aspects

Mental aspects can be taught as habits and routines, but they are difficult to learn when they are not inherently available. The determination or passion has to drive the person to acquire these mental traits. If bad mental attitudes and routines are ingrained in the character of a person, they are hard to shake unless they themselves make the effort to change. Therefore, learning mental skills has to start at a young age by teaching them in a playful and competitive structure. When looking at mental aspects, there are three main aspects to consider:

A. Emotional mental aspects (trainable aspects)
B. Intrinsic mental aspects (less trainable aspects)
C. Reasonable mental aspects (trainable aspects)

The emotional parts are trainable with cooperation of the student and include aspects like nervousness and excitement, fear, pressure, and aggression. The feelings of the player are very much involved in playing tennis, and coaches should be aware of these.

The intrinsic or inherent mental aspects are less trainable since they are mostly driven by the character traits of a player in combination with accomplishments and results. These intrinsic aspects include motivation, drive, determination, willpower, discipline, and confidence. These mental aspects can be improved over time with positive feedback and improvements in the emotional and reasonable mental aspects.

The reasonable mental aspects come from the thought processes of a player. The player can make decisions on intensity and method of thinking that enhances the toughness in match play. Some of these reasonable aspects include concentration, discipline, routines and habits, problem solving, and stress management. They are all trainable mental skills that are needed to succeed at an advanced level of play.

International Team Championships (Fourteen and Under)

The international team championships for boys and girls 14 and under are held each year in the Czech Republic. The 2004 boys team reached the semi-final. From left to right: Chase Buchanan, Martin van Daalen (coach), Blake Davis, Devin Britton. All of these players were successful in playing national and international junior events and went on to college. Devin and Chase have also played on the ATP circuit.

Gender Differences

Teaching boys and girls (men or women) is not so different in content but more so in the delivery of the subjects. As a coach, or parent, the communication becomes important in teaching and coaching boys and girls. There are some distinct differences in physical and psychological factors that have an influence on how to teach or coach a player and when and how to communicate with them. Let's look at some of these differences:

Physical Differences

Blood and circulation are different in the sense that women have 30 percent less hemoglobin. These are the red blood cells that transport the oxygen through the body. Therefore, the oxygen supply (read energy supply) will also be 30 percent less.

At the start of a menstrual cycle, 25 percent of girls are afflicted with an iron deficiency. The iron content in the blood determines the amount of oxygen (energy) that can be transported through the circulatory system. With women generally having smaller blood vessels, the circulation of blood will also be affected. This results in a "cold" feeling.

A woman's body temperature fluctuates over the course of a menstrual cycle. This again can have an effect on the circulation, especially during competition in extreme hot or cold temperatures.

Muscles and fat in the body are different with men and women. The muscle growth is mainly stimulated by testosterone. This is generally 10 percent higher in men than women. This results in women normally having 20 percent less muscle mass. However, when strength is measured in lean body weight, this percentage is somewhat reduced. Testosterone also produces wider shoulders in many body structures.

Estrogen is produced in much larger amounts in women than men and results in wider hips and a larger amount of fatty tissue. Women generally have 20 to 26 percent fat tissue, whereas men have 15 to 20 percent. This relates to the proportion of muscle and fat in the body and the correlation between body mass and energy supply from muscle tissue.

Bone densities are also different with women generally having smaller, less dense bone structures. The growth of the bones in girls starts normally two years earlier than boys due to the female hormones. It is not uncommon that twelve- and fourteen-year-old girls are taller than boys of the same age.

Sweat production is more prevalent with men than women. Men also start sweating earlier during activity. This can be advantages for men in extreme hot weather in cooling the body down, but can lead to dehydration problems with extended activity.

Physical performance comparison between men and women indicate that men have an advantage because of greater muscle mass, heart and lung capacity, and aerobic capacity. This gives men (boys) generally more strength, power, and speed. Women have the advantage in flexibility and buoyancy (swimming).

Psychological Differences

Prior to puberty, boys and girls play sports for the same reasons: they want to have fun!

Being together as a group, competing against each other, and mastering skills in sports are important to them. Boys and girls interact and express themselves differently in their sport of interest. Let's examine some of the psychological differences.

Interaction between boys and girls of the same sex is different with girls acting in a more cooperative, sharing manner while boys interact in a competitive, individualized, and egocentric manner. They also try to maintain their gender styles of interaction in dealing with the opposite sex. These differences become even more apparent during puberty. These interactions need to be taken into account in coaching and communication.

Self-esteem differs in boys and girls as they mature. Studies have shown that 60 percent of girls are happy with "the way they are" in elementary school while that number drops to 29 percent of girls in high school (physical appearance becomes more important). As children progress through schools, boys do better than girls since they feel better about themselves. Girl's self-esteem, opinions about their own sex, and scores on standardized test can also decline. Girls place a much larger value on what others think than boys do.

Values are related to self-esteem issues to the extent of the relationships. Because girls place a greater value on what others think of them and how they fit within the group, considerable satisfaction is gained from the relationships that they form on a team. Girls see their teammates as friends, so team chemistry is very important to female athletes. Girls tend to hold grudges longer, which will influence their interaction with each other and negatively influence team chemistry. Boys, on the other hand, view their teammates as people they play sports with, no more, no less. Boys tend to be more individualistic. Boy's teams function well even if the players are not friends and can put their personal relationships on hold when competing. Girls place their performance in the context of team performance. Boys, however, have a tendency to externalize their performance from that of the team and are more likely to place the blame on others for the team's performance than to take responsibility themselves.

Motivation to play and train for a sport can be different for boys and girls. In general, boys play sports for the individual need and competition. They are attracted to the individual benefit from their effort and work. On the other hand, girls tend to be motivated by pleasing others. Showing how their hard work affects the rest of the team motivates them. Because girls are more relationship oriented, it is important, as a coach, that you separate how you view the player as a person, from their activities and abilities on the playing field. Motivating girls is very strongly tied to the coaches' relationship with them. If you do or say anything that negatively affects your relationship with them, you may have difficulty motivating them. The leadership style that you use to motivate men and women are distinct. Girls need to know that they a have connection with the coach and that the coach cares about them personally, whereas with males, the consistently successful men coaches usually have strong personalities who lead with a powerful presence and will. When leading males, a coach has to convince them that his vision is correct, whereas with women, they are at least willing to consider a coach's vision and try it first before judging. With males, you do not need a personal relationship as long as there is respect.

Behaviors of how parents, teachers, and coaches treat boys and girls vary with gender. This treatment changes over time as children mature. For each age group, there are very specific expectations concerning the behaviors of each gender and from the people that instruct them. Here are some examples. Boys are generally expected to be independent and are played with more roughly. Girls tend to be treated more delicately and gently. Girls are rewarded for their looks while boys are often more rewarded for their physical performance.

Some Examples of Coaching Differences

BOYS are trained to the following:	GIRLS are trained to the following:
Stand out and strive to be no. 1.	Fit in. Standing out gets you banned.
Achieve directly.	Be cute and reach goals indirectly.
Be tough physically and emotionally.	Be tender; toughness means bitchy.
Bulk up physically.	Slim down.
Be task orientated, solve problems.	Be relationship oriented.
Be single-minded.	To juggle problems, be methodical
Achieve a straight line path to success.	Successful life is full of curves, detours.
Go for it and to let go.	Hold back. Be reserved. Look good.
Master the external world.	Master the inner world: feelings.
Winning is more important.	Relationships are more important.
Trust and logic.	Trust, feelings, and intuition.

Tips in Coaching Gender

• *Take into account the physical and psychological differences when coaching.* Know your players individually and treat them accordingly, even in a group situation. To be a good coach means to adjust your demands and demeanor from player to player. Sometimes physical demands will be the same between boys and girls, especially at a younger age. How you convey your information to both genders can be similar in teaching technique but different in teaching delivery or mental attitude. Example: girls can take comments personally or are concerned how much you like them, whereas boys are more concerned about their performance.

- *Know the characteristics of your players when communicating information.* Know how your player reacts to different ways of teaching and communication. Individual players learn in their own specific way. Students learn visually by seeing an example, auditorily by explaining the topic, or sensorially by feeling the stroke and/or movement. This in combination with the specific characteristics of the player in mental and emotional attitude toward teaching and competition helps the coach in choosing the proper tone, demeanor, and delivery.

- *Establish a relationship.* With men, obtaining the information is most often the main objective. The relationship can improve through communication, but that is not a necessity. Girls and women value the relationship and communication more before trusting the source of the information. Getting along together is a necessity.

- *Keep the information concise.* Men have less patience in listening to long-drawn out explanations. They like you to sum it up right away in bullet points and are less interested in why. Therefore, in teaching boys, it would do you wise to tell them why first and then sum up how to do it. *Women would like you to explain why more.* Girls like to be convinced why one way is better than the other.

- *Men like an authoritative demeanor.* But don't confuse this with being patronizing. The demeanor of the coach needs to be forceful and confident in delivery without talking down to the player or making them feel inferior. *Women like a soft-spoken gentler approach.* The coach needs to watch the tone of his or her voice and to be sensitive of their word choice, all this without losing the urgency of the message.

- *Women need a lot more praise and conformation than men.* They want the coach to let them know they are doing well and compliment them more often when they play well. Young boys still need praise whereas men are interested with the process of practice in competing and comparing their accomplishments with others.

- *Women take criticism more personally than men in directions or corrections.* Girls and women are much more sensitive to criticism and see it as a form of betrayal. Men are less sensitive to criticism

Martin van Daalen

and take it less personally. The coach can avoid this by always starting with a positive remark before mentioning the correction: "That looks much better, let's see if you can make it even better by doing it this way." You can also wait for a proper execution and then immediately make a comment, such as "I really like how you did the execution that way." This last method works really well in making corrections without long explanations.

- *Women retain information better the first time than men. Men need repetition.* Boys are much easier distracted and have more trouble focusing with long explanations. They can lose track of the purpose of the drills and get confused. In coaching a mixed-gender group, a coach will do well to repeat in short what the main points were at the end of an explanation. Another method is to ask players to repeat the explanation. This usually makes the whole group pay attention to the explanation, knowing they could be called on next. Boys also need more repetition with rehearsal of drills and execution of strokes, patterns, and strategies. Memory is an important factor to play well, so focus and paying attention to instruction are key. Generally, girls also have a better muscle memory and coordination at a younger age. This all helps in retaining the execution over a longer period of time. *(In 2007 and 2008, I spearheaded a "US Marines boot camp" for six top US tennis boys. One of the first things they learned, the hard way, is to pay full attention and focus on what is said by the drill sergeants. The end result was astonishing and showed that boys can learn to pay attention and focus really well. It just took more "persuasion" and effort to get them to that level.)*

- *Girls mature sooner than boys.* This shows physically. (Think about the girls' menstrual cycle starting between thirteen and fifteen. Boys usually have their hormones "kick in" between the ages of fifteen and eighteen.) Girls also mentally and emotionally mature sooner than boys. (Think about how they behave on court in matches.) This has its effect on how girls approach match situation at a younger age. It is therefore not so surprising that girls turn pro at a younger age!

- *Women are willing to try new subjects directly. Men are more stubborn.* Once you have established the relationship with women, they will be very willing to try new subjects with strokes, techniques, or strategies. You have to earn their trust first. Boys, on the other hand, are generally more stubborn in trying new things unless they see their peers perform the subject. This stimulates them to copy and perform the subject in a competitive way. At a younger age, this psychological factor can be useful in having boys practice together in groups. As boys mature, they become much more mature in trying new subjects.

- *Girls generally have better coordinative skills than boys at a younger age.* This is not surprising if you think about how boys try to show off their power in hitting the ball increasingly harder. In using more than 60 percent of maximum power in strokes, the coordination will be adversely affected. (See graph below.) With less muscle mass and power available to young girls, they will more naturally seek their coordinative skills and timing to strike the ball. This often results in girls striking the ball more "cleanly" and with more efficient power transfer at a younger age.

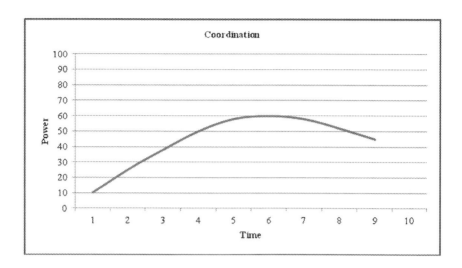

(As you can see illustrated in this graph, the coordination decreases in using more than the 60 percent of the maximum power available. Also, the duration of play or the amount of repetitions of strokes plays a role in coordination decreasing over time.)

Teaching Methods

The Learning Process

There are many ways to teach tennis and still keep it interesting. An experienced coach will use several methods to keep his students focused and physically challenged. This can be very helpful when students are not responding to one specific training method. Students learn by the information provided to them and the method of reception they use to receive this information. Keep in mind that they learn and obtain information in different ways or with a combination of the following:

Auditory Hearing (learn from hearing what you explain)
Visually Seeing (learn from seeing an example)
Sensory Feeling (learn from feeling the action)
Intuitive Instinctive (learn from a natural instinct how to perform)

Students might respond to one of these senses of learning alone or a combination of two or more. Every student is different in that respect, and it benefits you, as a coach, to pay attention to how your students learn most efficiently. In the learning process, there are several ways to transfer information:

- *Teaching auditory*
  The actual teaching is explaining what to do and how. The explanation should consist of (1) what to do, (2) how to execute it, and (3) the duration of the exercise.

- *Demonstrate*
  The demonstration should indicate how to perform the action in specifics with an example. You can perform this as the coach or have your students do it.

Martin van Daalen

- *Manually directing*

  This is a teaching method where you physically touch the racket, the person, or both together to guide them through the proper action.

- *Visualizing*

  This method requires thinking about the motion or action as if watching a film. Closing your eyes helps this process in "seeing" the action in your thoughts.

- *Assignment*

  Giving an assignment helps the students to coach themselves once they are on the court playing a match. This method trains the task solving needed in competition. You can do this either with a closed-end exercise (the drill stops at the end of the task) or open-end drill (playing out the point once the task is performed).

- *Discussion*

  The discussion should be with a question-and-answer session that should be a "two-way" conversation between coach and student. These discussions also help establish better relationships and communication between coach and student.

Different Teaching Methods

In teaching different players, there are several methods. Each method has a philosophy in approach and execution that requires some practice. Not every player will respond to each training method so it is up to the coach to find out what way will have the best response and result.

- **The Rhythm Method**

  This method of teaching uses the rhythm of the stroke and the timing of the bounce of the ball with the contact point. The coach uses this method to stimulate timing in order to improve technique and consistency. Besides those advantages to this method, it is very useful in creating smooth and relaxed strokes to improve fluidity and efficiency.

- **The Balance Method**

  The balance of the body before, during, and after the stroke will influence the execution of the stroke. The balance method of teaching uses these three balance points in the swing to stabilize the stroke and improve consistency in performance. This can be performed with and without the recovery footwork as long as speed and tempo are adjusted. This method improves the preparation of the strokes, the overall balance, and the recovery of the strokes.

- **The Contact-Point Method**

  The contact points of the strokes are the most determining factor of the trajectory and direction of the ball. This method is fundamental in showing the mechanics of the stroke and is a reference point in the "key positions." (See "Technical Training.") It can improve the timing of the strokes and greatly influence the technical training and quality of performance.

- **The Combination Method**

  This teaching uses a combination of two or all three of the methods to improve the strokes. A combination of these methods can improve overall performance or a certain aspect of a stroke. If a player does not respond as well to one method, you can try another or a combination. Being flexible in trying different methods to suit your student will improve and cut down the learning process.

- **Reference Training Method**

  Using different aspects of the game to improve another can have stimulating effects on the performance. When trying to make changes, players often relate much better when realizing the tactical, physical, and mental advantages to their game. They will make a larger effort and adopt changes more easily.

  A good example of this type of training is illustrated in the next story in working with Jared Palmer. I was still a young coach at the time when I was working with him privately at the Saddlebrook Resort.

Teaching Technique with Strategy

I had been working with Jared Palmer when he was still fifteen, and we spent some time that spring on his baseline strokes. He wasn't really interested in making changes to his technique, and I had tried for some time to better his topspin forehand. He had an "Eastern forehand grip" at the time, and I was trying to convince him to use a "Semi-western grip" to add more flexibility to the wrist to create more topspin and with the contact point more out in front.

I explained to him the advantages and technical details of the stroke, but I could see that he was not convinced and wasn't really trying his best to make a change. As soon as we came to the point play, he livened up instantly. So I decided to take a different approach to teaching.

I started the next lesson by introducing a game to him. We were going to play a baseline game where he was only allowed to use topspin and I would try to beat him with slice strokes only. I challenged him that I would beat him with my slice shots only. His face lit up with anticipation because he loved to play points.

What he did not anticipate was my strategy. I played my slice to the backhand where his topspin would be ineffective and short cross to the forehand where it would be difficult for him to get under the ball with his Eastern forehand grip. The ball would pop up, and I could attack him deep again. He would run across the court much more than anticipated. After losing the first match, he looked confused and wanted to play again. The same result was repeated twice after that, and we sat down to talk about it. After some debating, we came to the same conclusion that he needed to improve on his topspin forehand for it to be more affective. After that exercise, Jared was much more willing to work on that stroke to improve the technique, and he went on to win many tournaments that summer. This was a good example of how to use a strategy to teach a certain technique and to make it clear to a student how one part of the game can improve another. Jared went on to be a highly ranked pro player and an excellent doubles player. He also was part of the Davis Cup team. I still run into him at the Grand Slam events when playing senior doubles, often winning the title.

Teaching and Coaching Styles

There are many ways to deliver subjects when teaching and coaching students. Most of it will depend on the character and teaching style of the coach. The teaching style will play a large role in determining how you teach subjects and how you organize practice and competition. The methods you use will also reflect how you deal with players and communicate with them. Your role as teacher and/or coach can largely influence how the student experiences the sport and how they make decisions. Most coaches have one of the three most common teaching or coaching styles:

- **Command style**
  In this particular style of coaching, the coach makes all the decisions. The student has to follow the commands. The style adopted here indicates that the coach is assuming all knowledge and experience to be available to him or her and that the role of the student is to listen and comply.

- **Submissive style**
  With this coaching style, coaches give minimal instruction or guidance and don't intervene in organizing practices or activities. This style lacks in competence and is too casual in meeting the responsibilities of a coach.

- **Cooperative style**
  The coaches share the decision making with the players. They do have a leadership role but like to guide the students into making the goals set forth by themselves in a cooperative manner. They understand that young athletes cannot mature without learning about their responsibilities and making their own decisions. This style of coaching has the best chance of developing successful coaches and players.

Coaching Philosophy

To become a good coach, you have to develop a coaching philosophy. This philosophy is developed over time as you gain more experience in teaching and coaching techniques, organization, and problem solving. If you have never coached before or are adopting the coaching responsibilities as a parent, this task can be difficult. You should take time to gain some experience first. The three aspects that influence your philosophy are as follows:

• **Your coaching style**

Your philosophy of coaching will be influenced by the interaction with players.

• **Your vision as a coach**

How you see yourself as a coach plays an important part in your philosophy.

• **Your coaching objectives**

The objectives or goals that you set for yourself in obtaining the gratification and satisfaction in your role as coach influence your philosophy.

Creative Coaching

Sometimes you have to become creative in your coaching style by adapting to the player and the situation at that particular moment. In the coaching story below, you can find one of those situations from my own experience. This method is not something that will work with anyone, but it is something I tried after failing many times to convince the player to try out my advice on this subject.

Defeating the Comfort Zone

I had been coaching Ashley Harkleroad for three years, and we were at an ITF event in Denmark. She had been playing with an extensive "vibrasorb" in her strings for some time to dampen the vibration in the racket. The one she was using was the most extreme one used on the market and had to be woven in between the string. It not only dampened the vibration but also decreased a lot of the flexibility of the string.

I had been trying for some time to convince her to do without a vibration dampener or at least try one that was not so extreme. My reasoning was that she lost a lot of the power and spin to her strokes by using this device. She wouldn't even try it out in practice or matches, and I knew it would take a lot of effort in getting her out of her comfort zone before she would experiment. Then finally one day, I got my chance.

Ashley was playing in the quarterfinals in Arhus, Denmark, and having a tough time winning her match when her string broke. It was her favorite racket, and she asked me if I could take it to the stringer to have it restrung. She continued the match, and as soon as her racket was ready, I put it back on the court for her to use but left out the vibration dampener!

She picked it up and started playing with it, and I was surprised she didn't notice that it was not in her strings. She played the first point and hit the ball for a winner past her opponent. She looked in shock at her racket and then at me. I just shrugged my shoulders. She asked me what happened to her dampener, and I just shrugged my shoulders again. She continued playing and actually liked how the string felt every time she struck the ball. She ended up winning quite comfortably in the third set. She never used that contraption again after that match!

Now of course that was risky to do what I did, but I had to try. And in the larger scope of her development, it was well worth the risk. She was only fifteen years of age and still had a long way to go. Ashley went on to become a great player on the WTA tour. She has since retired and started a family, living in California. Years later when I caught up with her in Indian Wells, we had a good laugh about it.

Ashley Harkleroad

Martin van Daalen

The Makings of a Successful Coach

Becoming a successful coach depends largely on your goals, character, work ethic, and passion for this profession. Many factors come into play with your development as a coach, part of them being your education and knowledge of the sport. However, there are also some special skills needed to become successful:

- **Coaching philosophies** are the basic principles and beliefs from the coach in the teaching of students. The coaching objectives, the coaching style, and vision of the coach will influence how this philosophy develops over time.
- **Knowledge of the sport** is the information you have acquired through educating and experience over time. Coaches have to learn the specifics of the sport in all aspects of the game: technical, tactical, physical, and mental aspects. But it also has to include knowledge of the history and rules of the game, how tournaments are organized, the specifics of the different surfaces and how they are manufactured, the equipment and how they are manufactured, etc.
- **Playing skills** can help you understand how difficult it was when you were learning the game and what it took to improve to a higher level. Playing at a high level, or even a professional level of tennis, can help you in educating others if you are able to acquire teaching and coaching skills. Great playing skills can assist you in showing others how to do things, but that is just a demonstration and should not be confused with teaching or coaching skills.
- **Teaching and coaching skills** start with educating yourself in the teaching and coaching techniques by following a coaching education course. These courses are available in many countries organized by the national federations. In the United States, there are also some private organizations that offer coaching educations of different levels. You can also improve your teaching skills by watching other experienced coaches. An internship with an experienced coach can be a great learning tool. Just by being in

that environment, you will pick up methods on how to deal with students in the various situations. Reading books on the different topics of coaching will greatly improve your knowledge to work with different levels of students and how they learn the game. Talking to other coaches and sharing information is very valuable in comparing experiences. Traveling to tournaments with your players improves your interaction and communication with players, parents, organizers, and other coaches. It keeps you up to date with the new developments in tennis and creates a bond with your players.

- **Analytical skills** are invaluable to every coach. You have to gain experience to read the games of your student in various ways. There are many coaches that can teach the basics of the game to their students but are unable to see any defects. You have to train your eyes to focus on the overall picture before looking at the details. These aspects can be technical, but also tactical, physical, and mental. The "reading" skills of a coach should be able to identify the problem areas. Once you have made an analysis, you have to know what comments or corrections to make and when to introduce them to your student.

- **Motivation** is not only necessary for players, but also for coaches. You might have all the skills and knowledge, but still lack the motivation to use them the appropriate way. Just think about that student we all have seen that has all the talent, but not the motivation to put in the effort to make it work. How did you feel about that player? Did you not think it a waste? The same goes for becoming a good coach. Motivation means making it your priority to do whatever it takes to improve and develop yourself to your best ability. The key is to develop a passion for teaching and coaching that transcends to your players. Students often follow their coaches' example.

- **Empathy** is the ability to show compassion in thoughts and feelings toward others. Successful coaches understand what their students are going through. By using your own feelings as a young player, you could understand the different emotions players have in playing the game. Sometimes it will be the joy of winning, but it also can be the emotions of frustration and anger in learning the game. Coaches with empathy listen to their students and understand their feelings. They don't talk down to them or belittle them, as they know by experience how this feels. Showing empathy to your students makes them feel you respect their efforts, and in turn, they will respect you as a coach.
- **Professionalism** in your career shows the ethical way you conduct yourself as a teacher, a coach, an educator, and as a person. The honor and respect you earn is reflected by how you execute your job and how you treat players and others in communication, organization, and interaction.
- **Organizational skills** are required in any coach in order to be successful. Managing a club, pro shop, tournaments, or practice all requires organizational skills from the coach. Being decisive, logical, neat, and expedient helps you to perform all these tasks with ease and shows off your professionalism in execution.
- **Communication** is probably the most important skill of a successful coach. Without good communication, it is hard to get your point across in talking to players, parents, organizers, club members, other coaches, etc. You constantly have to hone your skills in order to create a pleasant environment for everyone involved.

Communication

Communicating with others is a necessity with organizing, your lessons, and coaching. Developing these communication skills starts with one as a young player and develops over time as an adult, coach, or parent. Being a parent can improve the experience in dealing with kids and/or teaching kids. As a coach, you can use this training/experience with your students. There are several reasons why communication fails. Some of these are the following:

- The information might be wrong for the situation.
- Your verbal and nonverbal skills are insufficient to get the message across.
- The person is not paying attention.
- The person lacks adequate listening skills and/or misinterprets the message.
- The messages are inconsistent and confuse the person.

Improving Your Communication

There are certain ways to improve your communication skills, and it starts by being a good listener. You cannot communicate well without really hearing what the other person just said to you. You might not fully understand the content. We all know these persons that just ramble on and cut you off midsentence or raise their voice to get their point across. Here are some points to improve your communication skills:

- **Good listening skills** will improve your communication skills. Coaches can be poor listeners when they are caught up in their next "command" or assume they know already what the person is going to say (disrespect of the information), not only hearing what the person has to say, not interrupting them, reacting too quickly, and answering emotionally, but also actively thinking about the content of the message, its meaning, and the complications to your answer. Training your listening skills will greatly improve your relationships.

- **Credibility of your message** is contributed to the belief you have in that person's message or demeanor. That belief will be influenced in how you feel about their knowledge of the subject, if the message is true or not, if there is a distortion of the facts, and how the message is delivered. Your credibility as a coach will improve by adopting a cooperative style of coaching; by being knowledgeable in your expertise as a coach; by being reliable, fair, and consistent; by expressing warmth, friendliness, acceptance, and empathy; and by using positive ways of communication.

- **A positive approach to communicating** emphasizes praise to encourage desirable behaviors and to strengthen confidence. This, unlike the negative approach that uses criticism and punishment and increases the athletes' fear of failure, lowers their self-esteem and undermines your credibility as a coach. In many sports movies, the coach is often (wrongly) portrayed as a very tough and demanding person that shouts and criticizes. In communicating with people, try first to find a positive comment before trying to criticize or correcting the problem in a constructive way.

- **High-information messages** is the information provided in very specific terms how to execute an action the correct way. Telling a person that they are doing something wrong still does not correct the problem. They need precise information on how to correct the problem. Good communication does not mean to judge but to provide the correct information to fix the problem and to help them succeed.

- **Consistency of the message** avoids confusion or distrust. When a coach sends mixed messages in content or explanation, it will confuse the students. Sending mixed messages can undermine teaching. This can occur when teaching emotional control of a student. When coaches react emotionally to situations, students might follow that example. The same confusion is the case in discussing the fitness level of a player while not staying in shape yourself. Failing to keep your word is another inconsistency of message that can be taken harshly.

- **Improving nonverbal communication** is created through body language. With two-thirds of all communication being nonverbal, you can imagine how important this is. People are very sensitive to messages that are transmitted nonverbally much more than verbal messages. Improving these forms of communication takes practice in recognition and execution. There are five different forms of nonverbal communication:

1. **Body motion** includes all the gestures and movements of the entire body that indicate a certain message during communication.
2. **Physical characteristics** of yourself or others, like weight, physical condition, odors, attractiveness, clothing, hygiene, etc. They communicate the importance that person has to physical appearance.
3. **Touching** a person by patting them on the back or putting an arm around their shoulder to comfort them are appropriate touching behaviors that communicate positive reinforcements. Make sure you don't overdo this action as well.
4. **Voice characteristics** are the pitch of the voice with the rhythm, resonance, and the inflection. It is not always what you say but how you say it that conveys the real message. Sometimes it can mean just the opposite by how it is delivered.
5. **Body position** is defined by the personal space between people and how you hold that position. Respecting someone's personal space is just as important as how you hold your position (Example: turning your body position and giving someone "the cold shoulder.")

Learning to improve both verbal and nonverbal forms of communication can be a great tool in establishing and maintaining relationships as a coach and in your private life. Without these necessary skills, it will prove very difficult to teach or coach players at any level of play.

> The skills in communication are reflected
> in the art of listening.

Communication as a Coach

The way you interact with your students, parents, colleagues, and other people involved in the tennis sport will have a great effect on your success as a coach. Learning good communication skills will often enhance the learning curve of your students. With less confusion, they will better understand the tasks and be more committed to the execution of the topics. It will assist you to organize and function more efficiently and be clear about your goals and philosophy. Be patient and informative when you are explaining how you would like to get the job done. The tone of your voice (voice characteristics) and body language will become very important tools to deliver your message correctly.

Adjust Your Teaching and Communication to Your Students

When a student is having trouble performing a certain exercise, keep in mind that they might not have understood it properly, that the drill is not appropriate for their level, that they learn differently (visually), or that the method of teaching does not appeal to them. How you interact with students will greatly show your communication skills as a coach. Some coaches might never change the explanation or the exercise and show their frustration in their body language and tone of voice. This will only increase the stress level and frustration of their students and decrease the level of understanding and learning. Young kids especially can be very sensitive to the form of communication and will show this in their behavior.

Reporting and Demonstrating Your Plan with Parents

When communicating with parents, it is important to know the goals of the student and the parents. This starting point will give you an indication of how serious they are about the performance of their child. In talking with parents, list the things that are going well (positive) before mentioning the topics that need improvement. (By the way, this is not much different than coaching students.) It cannot be all negative comments just to stress how much work still needs to be done. Giving parents an appropriate report with a short list of priorities for improvement (developmental plan) will demonstrate a plan on how to proceed forward.

Be Clear and Informative with Colleagues and Organizers

When communicating with colleagues and organizers, it is important to reveal your goals and expectations. This way, you can avoid any confusion or confrontations. Always try to be professional, polite, and to the point. Make notes of your conversations in your agenda so you have some bullet points and a record for future reference.

The way you communicate as a coach will resonate with your surroundings. A calm but determined voice and demeanor instills confidence and commitment to your message. Players will be inclined to follow your instructions much quicker. Parents will have more confidence in your methods of teaching, and you will gain much more respect from colleagues and organizers.

Keys to Good Communication Skills

Good Listening Skills

- Be actively ready to listen to the message.
- Keep your focus on the message.
- Do not interrupt and let them know that the message is heard.
- Ask questions to make sure the message is understood correctly.
- Use respectful body language to confirm a positive reception.

Effective Verbal Messages

- Be sensitive with your responses.
- Understand the person's situation and point of view.
- Be respectful, straightforward, and compassionate.
- Try to be positive rather than negative with your message.
- Be consistent, reliable, and fair with your comments.
- Make the messages clear and to the point.
- Keep your voice enthusiastic and vibrant.
- Make your message encouraging for the future.

Effective Nonverbal Interaction

- Always maintain eye contact.
- Show a positive and interested body posture.
- Touch the student on the shoulder to get their attention.
- Stay engaged and focused on this interaction (no multitasking).
- Show a good personal example.
- Be aware of your voice characteristics.

Communication as a Parent

The interaction and communication from parents with others can have a large impact on the progress of their child and enjoyment of the tennis game. Some of the most important factors for success are how parents interact and communicate with their child, coaches, and other parents and players. This sets the tone and perception of the game, but also creates a relaxed and satisfactory working environment. Children set their own goals on the level of intensity of the training. In order to create passion for the sport, it has to be their decision, not the parents, on how much they want to train and play. Passion is created when the drive comes from them rather than from the parents or the coaches. Parents will know when their children are enjoying the sport when they themselves ask to do more, not less.

Coaching your Child with Success

No matter if you have a coach for your child, as a parent, you will always be involved in some part of the training and competition. You might not always realize it, but the moment you make a comment on the practice or a match that was played, you are already coaching. The content of the communication and the method of delivery can be of great influence to the progress and enjoyment of your child. If you have hired a coach for his expertise and knowledge, try to make your comments stimulating and supportive. Otherwise, it will undermine the instructions and directions of the coach and possibly create conflicting ideas with your child.

In trying to help your child, it can be difficult to find a good balance between pushing them to excel and enjoying the experience. Players have to learn to create their own passion from within instead of using yours as a parent and/or coach. Even more so with parents, children will be sensitive to the body language and tone of the instruction since

Martin van Daalen

they associate it to the way parents reprimand them. Making training and competition an enjoyable experience for both parents and child is the key to a healthy relationship and a gratifying experience. Your patience, word choice, timing of the comments, and body language will be crucial. As parents, we are more impatient with the progress and attitudes of the players than a neutral person might be. Players learn faster when in a calm environment. If the word choices are too direct, too frequently repeated, and not systematic to the progressions of learning, players will easily become frustrated. Players have to learn to use their own memory instead of yours as a parent and/or coach. By letting them make mistakes, you provide them time to improve and gain confidence in each progression. By pressuring them too soon, you are basically going from step 1 to 10 without the proper progressions in between. Children can read you more than you think. They will be able to tell if you are happy, excited, or frustrated very easily, and you should always keep this in mind when coaching your child. Hiding your emotions when coaching matches will be the biggest challenge of all, so your emotions don't become a distraction for your child.

Parent Communication with Coaches

The communication from parents with a coach can assist in the level of confidence and commitment of your child's training. Parents can have a positive but also a negative influence on the relationship between the coach and their child. Proper discussions should consist of an inquiry and feedback as to how your child is responding to the training. It is not always wise to talk to the coach about training progress and matches in front of players. Observing the training and match play can be difficult without making any comments. It is very easy to interfere with the training and method of coaching without knowing the goals of the coach for that session. Too much interference, comments, or derogatory remarks can undermine the relationship with the coach. It can easily be perceived as criticism in their method of coaching and might have an indirect effect on the relationship between the coach and your child. Understanding your role in this relationship and how to communicate as a parent is instrumental to the progression, success, and enjoyment of your child's sport.

Parent Communication with Other Parents, Players, and Coaches

Many parents, players, and other coaches can be very sensitive to remarks made by other parents and players. Just knowing this fact should make you aware of your message in speaking to other parents, players, and coaches. Keep your comments positive and neutral about training and competition without making any additional comments about the performance of the opponent. This way, no ill feelings and/or stigmas are created toward other parents, players, and coaches. These will increase the pressure in playing other players. There is no need to create additional tension in competition.

Communication as a Player

Players need to learn how to communicate with parents, coaches, and other competitors. The players that communicate better are able to keep things clear and control situations to create a good training and playing environment. This leads to increased opportunities to learn and improve at a faster rate. The listening and focus skills of players play a large role and influence the comprehension of the topics and execution and performance in the drills, exercises, and match play. Asking questions and discussing problems is part of the communication and is necessary to understand the full range and complexity of the strokes, strategy, patterns, and the physical and mental aspects.

Assertiveness is an important aspect in the communication of advanced players. It will assist the player to take charge of difficult situations and show confidence in dealing with each confrontation. Players have to stand up for themselves in speaking up right away when making line calls, keeping track of the score, and dealing with questionable decisions of referees. As players mature, they have to take increased responsibility for their organization of tournaments and scheduling, training, practice partners, doubles partners, etc., and making these decisions with ease.

Parents and Coaching

My mother used to drive me to most of the tennis tournaments when I was still a junior. As a parent, she would watch the matches and not say anything, not even to cheer me on. In fact, she would not make any facial expressions at all. Because of this method, I was never distracted and was able to concentrate on the task at hand. My thoughts stayed on the court and on my opponent. I never realized until I was coaching myself how valuable that was to me.

I was sixteen years old and playing an open tournament in the south of Holland that particular afternoon. I was in the heat of the battle against an experienced player three times my age. He was trying every trick in the book to get me distracted by making remarks and by talking to me during the changeover. He obviously did not want to lose to a junior. When he saw that it was not working, he took it to the next level and started making dubious line calls. I protested, but there was no referee. Finally on the third one, I stopped and protested again about the bad line call. Finally, I looked over at my mother on the side of the court and said, "Did you see that call?" Her response was simple: "I can't say." This answer threw me off since I had expected my mother to defend me in this situation. I became frustrated and mad and ended up losing that match in a close third set.

On the way back home, my mother would usually talk about all other subjects except tennis. Whenever I lost, like this time, I would not say anything and would still be boiling inside with frustration. After ten minutes of listening to her talk about all other subjects, I finally said to her, "Why would you not say anything? Did you not see he was cheating me? Did you not see that call?"

Her answer was "Yes, I did see the ball, but I am not the referee and I am not allowed to make that call, especially not as I am your mother! You did not lose the match because of those bad calls, you lost the match because you got mad and distracted." I was perplexed at first, but later I realized she was right. That was exactly what had happened. I would have to learn to deal with it differently in the future.

These experiences as a junior taught me some valuable lessons as a coach about parents and coaching:

- When parents are coaching their child, be even more careful about cheering and supporting your child. Players are more sensitive to remarks and body language from parents and easily distracted in playing their match. Their focus will be on you instead of the execution of the strokes and the strategy.
- When coaching your own child, give them more time after the match before discussing the match, especially when they just lost. Preferably you should wait for them to ask questions. Children are more sensitive to remarks from their parents, but will except it more easily when given time to think about it. More importantly, they will accept your suggestions more readily when they ask for your opinion rather than when it is provided unsolicited.

Organization

The planning of a practice session is important for the organization of your lesson and the development plan you have set out for your student. Without planning, it is very easy to stray from your goals and intentions and end up just hitting balls without a purpose. A good preparation will convey your professionalism and intention to detail. In making your lesson plan, you should consider the following:

- **Number of students**

  To organize your lesson plan, you need to know the number of students attending. The number of students can influence the topic of your lesson or the materials you need. Are the students going to play with each other, with you, or are you going to feed the balls to them?

- **Level of play**

  Knowing the level of play is imperative in choosing the proper lesson content. It needs to be appropriate to the skill level of the students. If the content is too difficult, frustration could be the result and maybe even discourage them from trying. With the material being too easy, they will become bored and lose interest very quickly. The level of play is also important in pairing players together with the same skill set. This helps you, as a coach, but also in pairing students in competition and having your lessons run smoothly.

- **Surface**

  There are four types of surfaces that are very common to players and coaches alike: hard courts, clay courts, grass courts, and carpet (indoor). When organizing your lesson, take in consideration the surface you are practicing on. Coordinating the lesson content with the surface can assist you in their performance of technical, tactical, and mental aspects (confidence). Training of footwork and strokes also can be specific to a particular type of surface with styles of play.

- **Weather**

  The weather conditions often have an effect on the performance of the players. With extreme heat or cold, you have to take precautions with sufficient breaks. Make sure water is readily available at all times. (*Note: It is possible to become dehydrated in windy, colder conditions without students noticing. Adjusting the lesson content to the weather conditions can be very helpful in teaching your students how to deal with these conditions.*)

- **Equipment**

  Visualizing a target area can enhance the results of your students. You can also use a line or barrier over the net to cross over or under. Equipment is instrumental in enhancing the performance of your students. There are many companies available to purchase these online. Be prepared and organize the equipment ahead of time. This will save valuable time and keep your lessons flowing smoothly.

- **Safety**

  The safety of the students should always be a primary concern when you are practicing or playing matches. You always want to keep the practice area free of loose balls or equipment your students may trip over. Make sure your exercises or point play stays within the limits of the practice area so your students have less chances of injuring themselves on any obstacles.

Martin van Daalen

Lessons Types

Group Lessons

Group lessons (or team training) are a great way to teach advanced tennis players. It creates a competitive environment in which students often excel more rapidly (especially younger players). In this setting, players can learn from others with fewer expenses. Private lessons can be a benefit when trying to work on specific topics. *Academy-style training* is the same format as group lessons, but it is organized daily with sometimes multiple training sessions each day. This style of coaching can be beneficial if the student is technically stable and passionate about their game.

Private Lessons

Private lessons work best in conjunction with group training. It allows players to maintain contact with their peers while providing them with additional opportunity to excel through competition. A good time to consider private lessons is when a player is showing passion and a talent for the sport that goes beyond a recreational level. The general cost for private instruction can range from fifty to eighty dollars, but can also be much higher when working with an experienced or high-profile coach.

Match Play

There are several ways to organize match play. First, you have to determine your goals for development. It can be to improve a stroke, but it can also be a strategy, a pattern, or to improve specific movements. After determining the number of students and courts available, you can practice topics in either singles or doubles. During match play, students have the opportunity to experiment and "self-coach" by giving them subjects to practice. Instead of providing the answers right away, ask students for feedback so you can enhance their knowledge of the game. This method teaches students how to apply the learned topics in point play so they can master these before using it in tournaments. The ultimate goal of a coach should be to teach your students how to play the game.

Visual Training Lessons

The viewing of matches, training, or instruction videos can be very inspirational and beneficial to the learning process (especially to the students with visual learning abilities). These lessons are an excellent substitution on a rainy day and a valuable asset to your teaching. Focus equally with your comments on technical, tactical, physical, and mental aspects when viewing these images. It will open their eyes and minds to the wide range of topics to train and skills to master in their own game.

Coaching Sessions

Tournaments or team events are the testing ground of learning. This is where you get to view the results of the training. For the players, this is the reason they practice and play the game. For coaches, it is an excellent feedback to the development of the students. It is very important for coaches to watch their students in this final stage of the process so they can see if training methods are working or if adjustments need to be made. This is also a valuable time for actual coaching during preparation, match play, and feedback of the match improvements.

DEVELOPMENTAL PLAN

As competitors start taking the game more seriously, they will develop a passion for the game. They practice with more intensity and spend time on their own improving their game. This is when coaches need to communicate on a developmental plan. This plan should be engineered by the coach in cooperation with players and parents. A coach can derive short- and long-term goals by looking at the strengths and weaknesses of the technical, tactical, mental, and physical aspects. The plan should be realistic to the capabilities of the student so that improved confidence and goals are achieved in the chosen path. Then you can make a training plan, a tournament plan, and a periodization plan. Make sure everyone fully agrees to the plan and has had ample input to the content. This way, there would be no confusion later on. Usually, the original and simple plans are the most successful. Here is an outline of a developmental plan:

A. **Strengths and Weaknesses**

The coach can make a proper evaluation of the strengths and weaknesses for a student. These aspects should not just cover the strokes but also all aspects of the game: technical, tactical, physical, and mental. That way, you have a more realistic picture of what to work on and making training priorities for the short-term and long-term goals. The strengths and weaknesses should be evaluated to the following: the level of the player, their age, physical and mental development, and their playing experience.

B. **Goal Setting**

To achieve results, it is important to know what the goals are. Obtaining a clear picture of your goals will motivate the student and the coach to reach that objective. These goals have to be reasonable and reachable to push you forward to your next target. They have to be a challenge to the player and cannot be too easy or too difficult. If it is too easy, players will become bored and disinterested in the topic or become demotivated to work hard. If the target is too difficult to reach, players will become frustrated and lose confidence in their abilities. Once the goals are met within a reasonable time frame, they will feel the accomplishments. It will enhance confidence of a player and make them feel in charge of their own improvements. It becomes their game! Whenever you set goals, it is helpful to use a guideline or a method. Goal setting is best performed by using the "SMART" method:

• **Specific** • **Measurable** • **Attainable** • **Relevant** • **Time frame**	Using the SMART method ensures the goals to be very specific to the student. There is a clear picture of the direction of development with measurable short- and long-term attainable target setting.

There are different types of goals to consider when making a developmental plan. They all have their own specific purpose.

Outcome Goals

These are goals that set the target on winning certain events, matches, or obtain a certain ranking. These particular goals are most common with players and parents since they are often results oriented. However, focusing on results alone can increase the pressure when the goals are set too high and stall or even decrease improvements. It takes the focus away from how to play the game, and the score becomes a self-imposed pressure. Especially with players who are not as confident, it is crucial to have performance and process goals rather than outcome goals. When choosing the targets of these outcome goals, be careful not to reach too high. It is easier to reset a new goal once it has been reached than to restore confidence once it has been damaged.

Performance Goals

These particular goals are set with a certain execution in mind. There are many different forms of execution. It could be the performance of a certain stroke, reaching a higher percentage, a specific strategy, or the physical output in intensity during a match. But it could also be an improvement in mental control with a change of attitude. All these are performance goals that can be obtained under the guidelines of the "SMART" method. These goals can be set for practice or a match situation in a short- or long-term plan. Using these specific targets can be very stimulating to players and are often experienced as a challenge rather than added pressure, especially if the targets and timeline are chosen appropriately.

Process Goals

To achieve measurable success of performance, it is essential to have a method or a process. This process is a step-by-step approach to perform a skill, a strategy, or a tactic. The process goals provide you with a method on how to reach the targets with a specific outline. All these process goals help the player to feel and think their way through the execution to ultimately reach automated functions. Reaching this performance level will enhance a player's confidence and ability to execute under pressure.

Short and Long-term Goals

Besides immediate goals in practice and in matches, it is important to make a plan for improvements and targets for the future that cannot be obtained instantaneously. We can divide these in short- and long-term goals, according to the difficulty in learning and/or priorities.

Short-term goals should be the priority subjects for the student, from a strengths-and-weaknesses perspective. Short-term goal setting depend on the specific problem areas of each individual player. The objective is to stabilize and/or improve the subjects. Short-term goals should be scheduled in a time period from three months to a year. These are usually not complex changes or adjustments and can be successfully accomplished in a shorter time span. This could be a technical adjustment that needs to be addressed before moving onto specialty shot or the tactical application of the stroke. It could be a physical problem, but be aware that those usually take more time to improve.

Long-term goals are more complex systems of learning and therefore take more time to develop. They should be scheduled over six months to two years' time span. After that period of time, the coach should make a new developmental plan. (Best update it each year.) The time frame depends on the complexity of the subject and/or the time needed to acquire experience in this subject. Other factors could be physical strength and improvements in speed that influence the technical and/or tactical capabilities. The growth, maturity, and discipline of the player also play an important role in the speed of learning.

These goals results in three plans:
1. Training plan
2. Tournament plan
3. Periodization plan

1. A training plan will give an outline of the content and specifics of the training with an individualized approach for each player.
2. A tournament plan will provide a tournament schedule that is based on the amount of training and ability of each player to obtain the best results in matches.
3. A periodization plan is a schedule of training, designed for better performance during specific time periods throughout the year.

We will examine these plans individually in the following pages.

Martin van Daalen

Strengths and Weaknesses
(Example)

Player : Date : Coach :	
Strengths	**Weaknesses**
Technical - Forehand - First Serve - Net Play	- Backhand - Second Serve - Return
Tactical - First Strike Capability - Patterns - Weakness recognition	- Consistency - Shot choices - Patience
Physical - Strength - Speed - Change of direction	- Endurance - Flexibility - Coordination
Mental - Aggressiveness - Determination - Competitiveness	- Patience in execution - Fear of losing - Confidence - Focus

Analysis of Strengths and Weaknesses

After completion of the strength and weaknesses form, you can make some conclusion (analysis) of this player. The bullet points in each box are telltale signs of the "makeup" of a player; it shows how he or she performs in all four aspects of the game. Let's examine the example of this player more closely:

Technical

This particular player has a strong forehand, first serve, and good net play. These strokes indicate an aggressive player with good weapons. Certain strokes are less developed (backhand), possibly since this player might be running around the backhand more often to strike with the stronger forehand. This can be a habit developed over time to cover up the weakness of the backhand or the backhand has become weaker because the player has relied more on the forehand. Good net play is a logical continuance in finishing off the ball after the point has been set up. Weapon development in players becomes more visible when strength and speed increase in their game.

Tactical

In looking at the strategy, this player has an aggressive style of play and likes to put the opponent on the defense. It indicates a "first strike" capability with short rallies. This can be an advantage in creating errors from the opponent but can also create errors when being impatient and forcing the situation too much. The patterns will be designed to force the opponent in a defensive position. This style of play creates many opportunities to take advantage in hitting winners or forcing the opponent to make errors. As long as there is patience in building the rallies and developing consistency for the long rallies, players can be very successful with this game style.

Physical

The strengths of this player show that the components are very suitable for this game style. However, some of the components obviously need to be improved in order to play stronger opponents. The game style does not automatically train some of the weaknesses that are visible in a player. The longer rallies will promote a more fluid and coordinated effort and automatically improve the endurance overall. The flexibility of the footwork needs to be improved to coordinate with the strokes and perform under pressure.

Mental

Sometimes the aggressive and competitive nature can drive players to become impatient and too anxious to score the point rather than letting the point develop and unfold on its own. When a player is winning, they will think less, and points will add up quickly with the coordination flowing more naturally. As soon as things don't run smoothly, they can lose focus, and their game can unravel very quickly. It is easy to lose confidence when thoughts of losing become more frequent. For these types of players, it is important to think proactive and ensure they stay patient and on task. Their focus should be on the process of how to create the patterns and shot selections rather than on winning or losing.

Short-Term and Long-Term Goals
(Example)

Player : Date : Coach :	
Short-term goal	**Short-term goal**
Technical - Improve backhand consistency - Improve second serve target - Improve backhand return	- Improve backhand power/spin - Improve kick serve - Add slice backhand return
Tactical - Improve overall consistency - Patterns	- Improve shot choices and targets - Improve and add to patterns - Improve offensive tactics
Physical - Start a running program - Develop a stretching program - Improve coordination - Rhythm drills	- Interval training - Dynamic warm-up routine - Endurance/rhythm drills
Mental - Aggressiveness - Determination - Competitiveness	- Patience in execution - Fear of losing - Confidence - Focus

Martin van Daalen

Analysis of Short and Long-Term Goals

The short-term and long-term goals provide coaches with a priority list of topics. With the short-term goals ranging from three months to a year and the long-term goals ranging from six months to two years, coaches have a good plan for the future. Topics might overlap each other somewhat with the possibility to train both at the same time.

Technical

The first priority would be to improve the basic consistency of the backhand and the return of serve. These two aspects alone will assist their game in confidence. They will feel more relaxed about their strokes since they can rely on their backhand without the urgency to produce winners with the forehand. There will be a buildup of the rallies. After these goals are developed, it is possible to move to the long-term goals with the development of specifics.

Tactical

With the improvement of the consistency and automation in the strokes, players are able to watch the strategy and tactics much more. They will shift their focus from their side of the net, with the execution of their strokes, to the other side of the net and what the opponent is doing. This change of focus will occur when players mature and become more confident. This will open long-term opportunities to develop patterns of play, different shot choices, smart target development, and offensive tactics.

Physical

With players already possessing good physical qualities, it is possible to develop weaker physical areas. In the short term, it is advisable for advanced players to start a running and a stretching program to develop some good routines and a base. As they improve and start feeling the effects in practice and matches, it is possible to improve the specifics with on- and off-court drills and routines. As players mature, the length of the matches are extended or shortened according to the physical capabilities of a player. For example, a fourteen-year-old might have much longer matches at a national level than at a local level. At sixteen years of age, this can change as the power improves and points become shorter.

Mental

The mental training is usually the most difficult to improve. The first few years prove to be very important to instill good mental habits. Young players are able to focus for a shorter period of time, but the best juniors are able to focus longer and achieve better consistency at an early age. Improving consistency alone will force them to focus longer and improve multitasking capabilities, a necessity in playing matches. Point play will provide feedback on all the aspects and improvements. It provides valuable information on improvements and shows weaknesses. Playing practice matches with different scores can alleviate many fears. Players need to learn not to focus on the scores, but on the task at hand with the strategy and tactics. By practicing different starting points in games (1-3, 3-1, 3-3) or points (15-30, 30-15, 30-30), you can create an urgency of how to play these crucial and pinnacle situations. Players will become used to these situations and how to deal with them with focus and confidence.

Training Plan

In order to make a training plan, you need to gather all the information available to make a proper analysis. Look especially at the level of development in relation to their age, concerning technical, tactical, physical, and mental aspects. Also consider their strengths and weaknesses in relation to their playing experience, taking into account their character, motivation, training activity, and talent level. Communication with the player and/or parents is imperative to the goals and direction of a good plan. Here are the most important factors to consider:

- **Age.** You need to take the age of the student(s) into consideration in any plan. You would not train the same way with a fourteen-year-old as with an eighteen-year-old. The subject matter needs to be appropriate to the age and skill level from the players concerning technical, tactical, physical, and mental aspects and the duration of the training.

   Example: When having a fourteen-year-old hit with older and stronger players, they could develop injuries or develop technical problems. The speed could cause them to hit many balls late and start muscling the ball in trying to keep up. Patience is the key!

- **Gender.** The subject matter is mostly the same in coaching different genders. But remember that girls develop quicker and are more mature at a younger age. Girls start playing stronger events, and injuries can be a side effect.

   Example: Girls turn pro on average two to three years before boys do. With this in mind, your training plan needs to be adjusted with a specific approach and focus on strategy and physical development.

- **Playing experience.** The skill level and match experience are important factors to consider before organizing a training plan. As a coach, you do not want to jump ahead too far and introduce material the players are not equipped to execute. On the other hand, if the subject matter is too easy, the students will become bored and not try as hard. The key is to find the correct balance in topics to keep their interest and motivation for improvement.

Example: A player without much match experience won't win as many matches than an experienced match player. This affects the training plan in training activity and intensity and the tournament plan in scheduling.

- **Strengths and weaknesses analysis.** A good analysis of strengths and weaknesses, in relation to the points mentioned above, assists the coach and players in staying "on task" with the plan. Otherwise, it becomes so easy to get sidetracked and jump from topic to topic in training. A good coach will spend more time on the weaknesses that need improving. At the same time, try to maintain or strengthen the strong points in the student's game, creating a training and tournament plan with progression of new subjects and repetitions or improvement of old subjects.

Example: Sometimes you can focus too much on one stroke that the stronger stroke starts suffering (example: backhand forehand). Improving the strengths promotes confidence in training the weaknesses.

- **Training activity.** This activity needs to be twofold in training intensity and training frequency (how many training sessions per week). The progression and intensity of a training plan depends on the subject matter and improvements in prior lessons. The intensity of the training can be the quantity of training or the level of intensity during training. If necessary, adjustments can be made at any time to ensure progress and avoid overtraining.

Example: Your training plan needs to be appropriate/realistic to the amount the training (activity) and tournaments the player is performing each week. Without proper balance of activity and rest, players can tire easily. The results could decline, and confidence will be undermined over time.

- **Tournament plans.** The intensity and subject matter needs to be coordinated with the tournaments and/or competition from the student. Nearing competition, the intensity of the training might be higher, but duration will be shorter. The training should be focused on strategy and mental preparation rather than technical issues.

Example: Closer to the competition, you want players to become comfortable with the execution of the strokes (automation) so they can focus on strategy. Consistency under pressure is established through footwork, patterns, and shot choices. Coaches can adjust the training plan to enforce these factors and increase confidence.

- **Character and motivation.** These two factors come into play concerning the intensity and commitment of both the player and the coach to a training plan. In order to have the most improvements, players should take ownership of their game in convincing the coach of their commitment to improvement. Character and motivation become the driving force to performance in competition.

   Example: The passion for the game and motivation to train hard should not just come from the coach but should show in the character of the player in driving the coach. Players often will exhibit this by starting to train on their own in developing their game and improving each time you see them. The player has to want it more than the coach!

- **Goals from the student.** It is important to know the goals from your student. These goals can be outcome goals, performance goals, or process goals. Most players are results oriented. The coach needs to investigate the goals first from his students, inform them of other goals available before making a training and tournament plan.

   Example: A player's goals can differ from his coach. This can heavily affect the motivation, effort, and outcome of the training and tournaments.

- **Financial.** There can be much cost involved in training and tournament play. This can be an important factor in making a training plan. Most often, parents and players are not aware of the cost involved in coaching advanced players. Coaches can play an important role in assisting to receive financial assistance from sponsors, local clubs, state and national associations. Making a budget of all the cost makes it clear how to proceed with your plan for all parties involved.

Example: Training an advanced player has many expenses. Think of the cost of courts, lessons, travel, hotel, food, and miscellaneous expenses when traveling. This can be even more if international travel is involved with salaries and expenses. The total cost can get up to f $30,000 a year. In this case, try to look at all possibilities of financial assistance and sponsoring in your training plan.

Training Plan Content

The content of the training should be methodical and logical in progression. A good mix of topics is advisable to ensure that you train an all-around player. (It also keeps it much more interesting for your students.) All the topics should be integrated with technical, strategically, physical, and mental aspects to provide a sound education of the game. It is also possible to use one aspect to teach another; for instance, using a tactical aspect in justifying a certain technique. The training content is constructed from information that is gathered from various assessments:

1. Analysis — Technical, tactical, physical, and mental performance
2. Short-term plan — The short-term plans with corrections and improvements
3. Long-term plan — Long-term plans with a vision and philosophy for each player
4. Corrections — Adjustments needed for improvement
5. Lesson plans — Feedback from the lesson content for future training

Corrections

This should be a list of subjects that need correction (short and/or long-term) but more importantly a plan on how to correct them. How you are going to improve something is crucial. For instance, to improve the topspin forehand of a player is different for player A from player B. Being precise on what actually needs to be improved to that stroke for that specific player is the key. After that, you need a way to deliver the correction with a method of correction! (See correction form below.) To determine the correction is not as easy as it seems. Some technical issues can be hidden and are not always detected with the "naked eye." Using slow motion from video can be a very helpful tool.

Correction Form (Example)

Subject	Needs Improvement	Method
Technical		
Topspin forehand	Contact point	Square off shoulders
Tactical		
Backhand slice	Trajectory/target	Aim for a specific target
Physical		
Baseline footwork	Recovery	Stepping out left and right

This form shows some examples of subjects, the improvements needed, and the method of correction used. Obviously, there are many methods to solve the problem. Finding the right one that fits that specific player is the key.

After gathering the information from the evaluation of the player, the coach combines the information in one training plan form. (See training plan form.) In the training plan form, you can decide on what day you want to practice the subject and how you want to deliver the subject with a certain method. The method of teaching should be consistent in the transfer of the messages to the students (communication).

Martin van Daalen

Training Plan Form
(Example)

Week	Day	Subject	Impr/correct	Method
1	**Monday**	FH +BH consistency	Technical	Contact point method
	Tuesday	Service + return	Tactical	Shot choice/ targets
	Wednesday	3rd ball situation	Tactical	Shot choice
	Thursday	FH+BH patterns	Physical	Footwork/ recovery
	Friday	Net play	Technical	Contact points
	Saturday	Point play	Tactical/ mental	Focus on execution
	Sunday	Off	-	-
2	**Monday**	FH+BH topspin	Technical	Trajectory
	Tuesday	Point play	Technical/ tactical	Execution/ shot choice
	Wednesday	Serve + return	Technical	Contact/footwork
	Thursday	Volley	Technical/ physical	Closing on the net
	Friday	Approach + volley	Tactical	Patterns
	Saturday	Point play	Tactical	Tournament
	Sunday	Point play	Tactical	Tournament
3	**Monday**	Off	-	-
	Tuesday	BH slice	Technical/ tactical	Defensive/ drop shot
	Wednesday	Kick 2nd serve	Technical/ tactical	Trajectory
	Thursday	Drills	Physical	Stamina/footwork
	Friday	Point play	Tactical/ mental	Third ball situation

Documentation

Once a plan is clear, coaching a player will become much more structured in not only teaching technical subjects, but also training tactical, physical, and mental aspects. By documenting the plan and making notes on future training plans, the following step is easy to make—a lesson plan. The lesson plan contains the notes of the topics and specifics of your training for that day.

Lesson Plans

Group Lessons

A good method to train advanced player is through group instruction (2–4 players). With everyone being about the same skill level, they don't feel the odd one out. Players like competing with each other, and they can learn a lot from seeing other examples. May it be good or bad examples, this is invaluable experience for a competitor to improve. In a group, you can observe how players deal with the same problems of execution or copy good example from others. Group lessons can expedite the learning process.

Private Lessons

It becomes time to consider private lessons when a player wants to work on specific topics and shows a passion that goes beyond the normal drive or work ethic. When they are still young, it is best to take private lessons in combination with the group lessons. This way, they keep contact with their peers and still provide them with an opportunity to excel. As the advanced players become more proficient, private instruction is best performed with other players from the same level or with hitting partners. This will push players competitively, physically and mentally.

Match Play

After determining your goal of the practice, you can introduce match play to test the improvements for singles or doubles. In your match play instruction, have your students focus on one or two topics. This will help them later on in tournament play in making decisions and coaching themselves. You can either give them a strategy or pattern to execute, or it could be the use of a stroke. But it also could be the focus on a mental aspect of the game in learning rituals to stay calm or pressure point play. This last topic can be introduced with different starts of the score in games or points. (Start the set at 2 or 3 all. Start the game at different scores: 15-30, 30-15, and 30-30. Replay the first three games of the set several times, play tiebreakers.) These pressure-point situations simulate stressful match situations and how they influence performance and execution. Coaching competitors on how to deal with these can be very beneficial to their success in matches.

Lesson Plan (2 hours)

1. **Warm-up**   10 min.
2. **Technical part**   30 min.   - Part A (learning)
3. **Tactical/mental/physical**   40 min.   - Part B (practice)
4. **Point play**   30 min.   - Part C (execution)
5. **Recap and stretching** 10 min.

Even though this is the basic format for a lesson plan, be aware that you can change the main topic at any time. For example, you can make the tactical part of your lesson plan the main topic (Part A) and have part B and part C (or a combination) be about how to apply it. This change of main topic is necessary to make the students aware of how important the tactical, mental, and physical aspects are and also how it all fits together.

Warm-Up

The purpose of a warm-up is to prepare physically and mentally for practice session or tournaments. It not only loosens up and stretches the muscles but also gives the student a heightened sense of awareness, needed for a higher level of performance. It should start with some slow running, followed by specific footwork exercises that are geared toward the tennis game (hops, skips, side steps, lunges, etc.). The intensity can be increased with some sprints. You want players to be able to sprint from the first point on in preparing for matches. Some dynamic stretching and static stretching is important as well to prevent injuries as much as possible. The warm-up in hitting the ball should be the same as if they prepare for a match. They go through all the strokes, starting off slow but reaching match speeds at the end. Warming up too slow will cause a slow start in the match. This is a common mistake made by juniors in an effort to make themselves feel "comfortable" before the match.

Technical (Part A)

This section of the lesson is the main learning phase. The subject matter can be a new topic or part of a sequence in a learning process. Preferably, they are organized in a progression from easy to more difficult in a logical order (methodology). It can also represent a repetition from a prior lesson that needs more practice or a follow-up for the following subject. Note: In teaching the technical subject, keep in mind that you can substitute a tactical subject in this part A. Sometimes it makes it easier to explain the stroke production by showing how it is used in a point or match (tactical). When teaching this section, try to explain the topic as precisely and concisely as possible. Keep the intensity high in concentration by giving them sufficient feedback in short breaks.

Tactical, Physical, Mental (Part B)

This section should represent practice phase of part A. After learning the subject matter in part A, you would want the students to apply it. The practice should show they understand the information and how to use it in match situations. Note: This section of the learning process is usually totally forgotten or left out. It is not uncommon to see coaches spending much of the time on technique and very little time on tactical development, let alone any mental training! Young players especially don't enjoy technical training. However, the more you can help them achieve better results, the more they will appreciate your technical input. Teaching all aspects of the game produces more balanced players.

Point Play (Part C)

Competition is the ultimate goal of all players and provides feedback of their practice. Make it fun and entertaining for all involved, and mix up the games with a wide variety of competition. Rotating the opponents around increases the competition between players. Regardless of their strength, it gives everyone a chance to learn from each other.

Recap and Stretching

While they are stretching, you can recap on the most important points of the practice. You also can get some feedback on the lesson with some questions. It is also a great time to make any announcements on the next lesson time, dates to remember, sign-up dates for tournaments, etc.

Lesson Plan (Example)

Name: Player A Date: Time:	
Warm-up:	- Run around the court - Skips, side steps, lunges, etc. - Stretching
Part A (Teaching part): Topspin forehand	 - Teaching how to swing up - Closing the racket face - Make use of higher net
Part B (Application part): Topspin forehand	 - Play rally over a higher net - Play topspin in service box - Play angle shots
Part C (Point play):	- Play points by using high topspin - Play points and create an angle
Recap:	- Technical points on topspin - Tactical advantages of topspin

Making Notes

Making notes of specific instructions to your students can be very useful. The same goes for making notes on the lesson's analysis, performance, and instructions. Documentation of instruction is instrumental when teaching and coaching large number of players with individual corrections. This will improve consistency of the message received by each individual player.

Tournament Plan

A tournament plan is made after all information is gathered concerning their ranking, tournaments played in the past, and the goals of the player and the parents. In creating this plan, there are two different types of goals to consider:

- **Performance goals**
  These goals can include subjects to improve strokes, strategy, and physical or mental aspects during competition.

- **Outcome goals**
  These goals are focused on trying to win a match, a certain tournament, or even to win a certain number of rounds and matches. It also can be a certain ranking goal.

These goals result in a detailed tournament schedule. The schedule needs to be a semiannual or annual plan that includes all the tournaments throughout the tennis season. In making the schedule, both outcome and performance goals should be added.

Scheduling

The scheduling of tournaments needs to be geared toward the development and goals of the student. The number of tournaments and level of the events is important to gain as much experience during play but also to improve your ranking. Every competitive player should strive to play three levels of events: (1) the lower level to win tournaments, (2) the middle level to be competitive (at least quarter finals), and (3) the higher level to gain experience. To achieve the goals from the student, you need to select a priority of future events and then work backward through the tournament calendar to make it work. An example could be to play the US Open junior event. Then plan the tournaments in such a fashion to improve the ranking to gain entry into the event.

Level of Events

There are several different levels of tournaments that are suitable for advanced players:

18 and under:
1. Sectionals/ nationals
2. ITF/ETA junior events
3. Open events
4. Future events (pro)

19 and over:
1. Open events
2. Future events
3. Challenger events
4. Tour events

The open events are prize money tournaments held in almost every state and are open to every level and age. These events are an excellent training ground for young advanced players to gain experience in play. (Note: To maintain amateur status for college, only accept expenses and fill out official expense form from the tournament director.)

Rule 1: A good rule of thumb in scheduling events is to never move on to the next level of major competition until dominating in the level they are competing in.

Rule 2: A win-loss ratio to keep in mind is at least 2 to 1, but preferably a 3 to 1 ratio in order to keep confidence high (very important with juniors).

Quantity of Events

The number of tournaments is related to the development program and the level of play. In playing lower-level events, a player will play many more matches than higher-level events. The coach also needs to consider playing fewer events when making major changes, giving a player time to get adjusted to the changes in practice matches before trying those in actual tournaments. In general, the players should play two or three tournaments in a row to acquire a rhythm of play and then practice two to three weeks before playing other events again. A good mix between practices and tournaments will improve results and confidence.

Martin van Daalen

Week To gauge the frequency (	National	ITF/ETA juniors	Pro events	Practice
1				Home
	Local event			
2				Home
	Designated			
3				Home
4		ITF event		At event
				At event
5			Pro event	At event
6				Home
	Local event			
7				At Event
			ITF event	At Event
8				Home
	Designated			

In organizing the scheduling, always keep in mind the following:

1. **The age of the player** needs to be appropriate for the tournament. Keep in mind that the age limit is the age you have for the entire year at international junior events.
2. **The ranking of the player** and the entry level of the event go hand in hand. Check the "cut-off" and rankings from last year to find out if entry is a possibility.
3. **Qualifying events** are another possibility to enter (watch dates). They also provide extra practice and match play.
4. **Event dates** are important to see that events don't overlap. This is more important when entering qualifying events with several events played in a row.

5. **Entry dates** are usually three to four weeks prior to the tournament. But they can vary in time, so make a note on the tournament plan of the entry dates.

Periodization Plan

This is a plan to gauge the volume of training with frequency, intensity, and duration of the training. It can be planned quarterly, semiannually, or annually. This is crucial for three reasons: (1) this method achieves the most optimal training program, (2) it creates a "peak" performance at the desired events, and (3) it avoids the player from overtraining.

1. **To gauge the frequency (per day and/or per week) of the practice.**
   With frequency, we mean the number of practice units per day and/or per week. The more training units per week, the more the duration needs to be adjusted. The intensity might decrease over time if duration is maintained.

2. **To gauge the intensity of the practice.**
   With the intensity, we mean the level of energy and effort. With a higher level of intensity, the less frequent you can schedule training units or the duration will have to be adjusted.

3. **To gauge the duration (time) of the practice.**
   With the duration, we mean the time of the practice units. With a longer practice time, the frequency of the training units will need to be lowered and intensity might be affected over time.

By adjusting the volume (frequency, intensity, and duration) of the training, you have the ability to create different types of training. They can be divided in training phases:

Martin van Daalen

1. **Preparation phase**

   In this phase, the coach tries to work on the fundamentals (technical) of the strokes and build up the basic endurance and strength of the player. There will be some match play, with the focus on basic strategies, patterns, and shot choices. (Frequency and duration is high; intensity is medium.)

2. **Precompetition phase**

   In this practice period, there is more specificity of training with the focus on strategy and mental aspects. There is more match play, as competitors get closer to competition. (Frequency and duration will decrease to medium and intensity increases to a high level.)

3. **Competition phase**

   In this phase, there is only specific training with the full focus on tactical and mental preparation drills. There are only short, intense practice sessions with more point play. (Frequency is low; duration and intensity is high.)

4. **Recuperation phase**

   This period is an active rest phase to recuperate physically and mentally before the next practice or precompetition phase. In this period, it is helpful to play other sports in a relaxed fashion or some light physical exercise. (Duration is low at first and medium later; frequency and volume are low.)

Training Compensation

With the body exerting energy through training, the body will adjust during the rest period with supplying more energy during training than previously was available. This cycle of enhancement is called training compensation or "super compensation" (see graph below). If the training units follow each other too fast without proper rest for the muscular and nervous system, the reverse will be the case, with less energy available. If this cycle is repeated many times, it can lead to "overtraining."

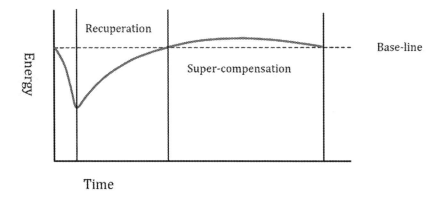

Overtraining

Training in the recuperation phase will cause the energy level to stay below the baseline. The overcompensation of energy will not occur, and the baseline or capacity will be at a lower level. In repeating this cycle too many times, a player might reach a state of "overtraining." Undertraining will prevent you from reaching a peak performance, but overtraining can lead to illness and injuries due to fatigue. There are some signs of overtraining that you need to recognize:

- Chronic fatigue
- Irritability
- Less interest in tennis
- Weight loss
- Slower reflexes
- Reduced speed, strength, or endurance
- Poor performance

As a coach, parent, or even as a player, you need to be aware of these symptoms. If you suspect there is a form of overtraining, it is wise to talk about this as soon as possible. In communicating with players, they will let you know when they feel tired or stale. The best remedy is to lighten the training, play some other sports, find some other interests, or to give the player some time off.

Overtraining

Training in the recuperation phase will cause the energy level to stay below the baseline. The overcompensation of energy will not occur, and the baseline or capacity will be at a lower level. In repeating this cycle too many times, a player might reach a state of "overtraining." Undertraining will prevent you from reaching a peak performance, but overtraining can lead to illness and injuries due to fatigue. There are some signs of overtraining that you need to recognize:

• Chronic fatigue
• Irritability
• Less interest in tennis
• Weight loss
• Slower reflexes
• Reduced speed, strength, or endurance
• Poor performance

As a coach, parent, or even as a player, you need to be aware of these symptoms. If you suspect there is a form of overtraining, it is wise to talk about this as soon as possible. In communicating with players, they will let you know when they feel tired or stale. The best remedy is to lighten the training, play some other sports, find some other interests, or to give the player some time off.

Periodization Plan

Year						TRAINING AND COMPETITIVE SCHEDULE				

Player :				Date of birth				Primary Coach		

Wk begin	TOURNAMENT	PHASE 1 Rating	TRAINING	Rest	TECHNICAL	TRAINING CONTENT TACTICAL	PHYSICAL	MENTAL	Volume

Wk begin	TOURNAMENT	PHASE 2 Rating	TRAINING	Rest	TECHNICAL	TRAINING CONTENT TACTICAL	PHYSICAL	MENTAL	Volume

Coaching and Development

As a national coach, I have taken many groups of players through the developmental stage from juniors to pro level. It is a very enjoyable and gratifying experience to see them all progress through different phases. The toughest part was to find the proper level of tournaments to play. They needed to be challenged with competition but still have enough matches to improve their game and gain confidence. A good win-to-loss ratio for matches would be 2 to 1 or even 3 to 1. However, in this learning process, there is no substitute for winning tournaments! There is a certain point when juniors need to make a "breakthrough" to advance to the next level in juniors. This happens again several times when breaking through to the international level of juniors and pros.

Below, you will find one of those experiences of the boy's group. I supervised this group from the time they were thirteen years of age through eighteen years of age.

Breaking Through

For many juniors, there are several moments that require a breakthrough to move on to the next level. This was also the case for the boys' group I was working with as a national coach for the USTA.

I started taking the top fourteen-year-old boys to the lowest-level ITF tournaments, and they were giving each other a hard time on who would have the most points. Of course, this would change at almost every other event, but it did help the competition and fire everyone up in striving to be the best. A negative factor to this competition was the focus on the points versus the focus on their game! The teasing from the boys was relentless and caused a lot of anxiety with players without points. However, when they eventually did get their first points, it changed everything for them. It made them mentally stronger with many wins in tournaments.

The breakthrough moments are twofold, one at the fourteen- and fifteen-year-old mark when playing national events and ITF events. The second period is usually at the sixteen- and seventeen-year-old mark, when the physical aspects start to kick in. After this point, there is a transition from junior to beginning pro events (future and challenger events). This was also the case with Sam Querrey who joined the group at age sixteen, winning the national tournament at Kalamazoo and winning a wild card for the US Open Junior event. He made the most of it by narrowly losing to Andy Murray in the quarter final after leading in the match. Murray went on to win this event and has now several Grand Slam titles. Sam has been a top 20 player on the tour and just recently beat Novak Djokovic in the quarter finals at Wimbledon (2016). Winning the top international junior events can significantly assist the confidence in players turning pro and making the transition, but it is no guarantee of success. The transition to the pro level is the most difficult and should not take too long to prevent doubts to creep in. Players go through several periods of stabilization of their game before making a jump to a higher level of play.

ANALYSIS OF TENNIS PLAYERS

As players become more advanced, an extensive analysis is very helpful to complement the developmental plan for instructions and corrections. Due to the various techniques and multiple styles of the play, the complexity of instructions and corrections increases. It takes much experience and "a good eye" to find the proper methodology and approach to training the fundamentals, let alone the specialty strokes. A good analysis will give you a better base to provide instructions and corrections for improvements.

Analysis Goals

An analysis of a player can have different purposes. It is not only to determine the errors for correction from a technical point of view, but also involves the tactical, physical, and mental aspects of the game. The different analysis goals are as follows:

- **To determine the level and quality of a player.** This is important for the method of instruction needed to improve the student. It is also a factor for pairing players together with the proper level to optimize the training.
- **To determine the strengths and weaknesses for improvement.** A coach has to examine how their game has been developed within their style of play. This in relation to the technical, tactical, physical, and mental aspects. Most often these last three are overlooked in the analysis or dealt with too late in their development. Just keep in mind that with advanced players, it is usually not the strokes that are holding them back in their development. More often, it is the tactical, physical, and mental aspects that need improvement in execution during matches.

- **To detect the errors for correction.** When a player experiences a problem during play, it can be a simple instruction to correct an error. However, it can also be a deeper lying issue that causes a problem in their game. Learning how to conduct an analysis is crucial in preventing errors with instructions and corrections.

Aspects that Can Influence the Analysis

There are several factors that influence the decision making of a coach. Hopefully, they eventually lead to an accurate analysis. These factors are the following:

- *The experience level of the coach.* It takes years of experience and a good eye to make a good analysis. The knowledge of all the aspects of the game and coaching various players helps, but even then, you still have to know what to look for!
- *The time frame of the analysis.* Making sure that what you are trying to analyze is studied at the correct time frame during the execution. You can easily look at the wrong aspects when not focusing on the proper subject. Also, make sure to analyze with similar ball trajectory conditions so you can make some comparisons.
- *Observing all aspects of a player.* For example: by observing a technical aspect for analysis, it is important to observe the player as a whole. Tactical, physical and mental aspects of their game will influence the execution of the stroke with their personal style and can lead to an inaccurate analysis.
- *The personal style of a player and from the analyst.* Always consider the personal style of the player in making an analysis and make sure to leave your own personal style of play out of the equation. It is very easy to be influenced by your own style of play in making your students play like you. Just remind yourself how many different styles of players there are, and respect them all.

Types of Analysis

There are several types of analysis that can be made. Having a method will reduce the chance of making mistakes and pinpoints the problems for correction. The analysis or observation should not be limited to practice, but also be continued through match play and off-court training. As a coach, it will provide you with a much better picture of your player. There are three types of analysis to consider:

A.	Preanalysis	- Made at the start of the practice or exercise (This method is mostly used to enhance a subject during practice with the intent to make corrections or improvements.)
B.	Continued analysis	- During point play and match play (This method is used to make mental notes of the instructions and to communicate these later with the student.)
C.	Postanalysis	- After the correction is made (This method is used to check if the corrections hold up over time and the students keeps executing the subject correctly.)

Error Detection

When making an analysis, you might come across errors in technical, tactical, physical, or mental execution. It might just be one error that is detected, or there might be several in the same execution of the action. There are two types of these errors:

Primary errors. These are errors that are basically the root of the problem in executing the action. Sometimes the primary error is hard to detect with multiple errors being a factor. This is where experience and knowledge of the fundamentals can be crucial.

Secondary errors. These additional errors are often created by the primary error(s). It is very common to see players develop secondary errors in an effort to stabilize other errors in their execution, sometimes even to the point of becoming a personal style.

It is important to determine the difference in these two types of errors in order to focus on correcting the primary error first before tackling the other errors!

In order to make proper error detections, coaches should study the basic fundamentals and key positions of players. This will provide you with the best chance in making an accurate analysis of the possible errors and also in determining the method of correction.

Methodology of Analysis

Step 1: *First determine your goals, as a coach, and those of the player and/ or parents* before making any analysis. There is no need for an extensive analysis if no changes are desired by the player and parents other than to improve and play the game within their style of play. Preferably, your goals have to match those of the player and parents.

Step 2: *Determine if your analysis is based on fundamentals or on a personal style* of *the player.* This can be of influence in making a proper analysis that is not based on your personal preference as a coach. It is very easy for coaches to fall in a pattern of making an analysis that leads to corrections based on personal preferences. However, it is possible that this is not suitable for that particular player. Changing strokes or making corrections needs to be based on the execution and productivity, with their own personal style of play. Knowing the differences between the fundamentals and style of play are important for a correct analysis.

Step 3: *Stabilize the technique first before making an analysis.* Before you can make any analysis or corrections, you need to stabilize the strokes or situation first in order to get a correct analysis of the player. The follow-through on the strokes is usually a "dead giveaway" on the stability of the stroke production. It will usually indicate that the grips and/or the contact points are not correct. Even in observing a tactical, physical, or mental situation, it is difficult to make a correct analysis when players are not hitting strokes out of stable positions. Questions will arise if the execution was meant to be like that or if it was just a one-time occurrence.

Step 4: *Observe the subject of interest one aspect at a time.* Trying to get the whole picture of the player is the primary focus, but after the general observation, you have to break it down into parts. Break it down in technical, tactical, physical, and mental parts before looking at the specifics of the each subject.

Step 5: *Determine primary and secondary errors.* By making a determination on the root cause of the problem, you can eliminate making additional and unnecessary correction that could make things worse rather than better. Once you have found the primary error, you can make a plan on how to correct this and the secondary problem.

Step 6: *Make sure to do a postanalysis.* This postanalysis is performed to make sure that the analysis was correct and the problem was resolved. It is also to see if the proper corrections were used and if they held up over time.

As you can see, there are several steps you need to take in order to make a correct and complete analysis. This method organizes your analysis in a logical order and increases the chance of making correct observations and decisions for improvements.

Technical Analysis

In making a technical analysis of strokes, you need reference points in the execution of the stroke. That way you can make comparisons to basic fundamentals. These reference points represent certain recognizable positions of the body and racket and are called as follows:

The Key Positions

1. Ready position
2. Backswing
3. Loading
4. Forward swing
5. Contact point
6. Follow-through
7. Recovery

> **1. Look at the whole stroke.**
> **2. Check contact point with grips.**
> **3. Look at all key positions.**

The key positions are basically the same, but can vary from player to player due to grips that lead to different contact points, racket trajectory, ball trajectory, foot stance, the individual style, and intended stroke of the player (think of topspin, slice, etc.).

Before you can start looking at specifics, it is a good idea to look at the whole stroke. This will give you an overall impression how the player is hitting the ball. It will show the consistency and balance of several strokes in a row (repetitive stroke). This is important to see if there is a consistency in the error(s) so you can make an informed decision on primary or secondary errors of the stroke. Then you can look at the specifics of the stroke (key positions) next. I would advise you to start with the contact point in combination with the grip. The reason I like to start this way is because they often dictate all other key positions. The different grips will dictate the contact point of the stroke with the angle of the fingers and wrist on the grip handle. The grip will also dictate the backswing, followed by the swing path of the forward swing and the follow-through. (Note: It is not uncommon for students to have improper contact points and unrelated swing paths for the grips they are using.)

After making an analysis of the grip and contact point, it is possible to look at other factors of the stroke. Some coaches like to follow the key positions from the stroke starting with the ready position and finishing with the recovery. Others like to start with the follow-through or the balance of the swing before moving on the other factors of the key positions. It doesn't really matter what sequence you use in checking all the key positions as long as you cover them all to eliminate any subsequent or secondary errors. Find out what method you like to use most in detecting the errors.

It is necessary to take all these factors in consideration in making a proper analysis. In the next paragraph, we will look more closely at some of the specifics of the stroke and how they affect each other:

- Affect of grips on the contact points
- Affect of grips on the swing path
- Affect of the style of a player on strokes

The grips will affect the contact point and racket trajectory. A continental grip has the contact point to the ball closer to the body than a western grip (see pictures below). The distance to the contact point at the side of the body is also affected by grip choice.

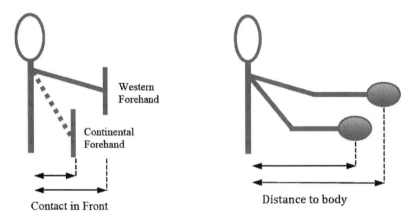

The specific grip used by the player will also influence the trajectory of the arm and racket due to the angle of the hand and the wrist on the racket handle. This position of the hand shapes the path of the racket in the backswing, the hitting phase, and the follow-through. For example, with an eastern grip, the swing path will be more flat oval in shape while with a western grip, it will be more circular oval in shape (see below).

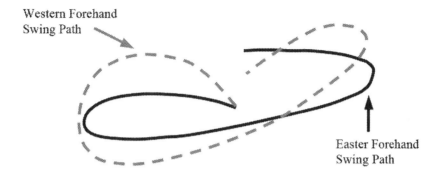

Western Forehand
Swing Path

Easter Forehand
Swing Path

The contact points will affect the rotation of the body and shape and direction of the swing. The contact points can vary quite a bit in tennis strokes due to the height, spin, and trajectory of the oncoming ball. Players have to adjust the feet to find a suitable contact point to make impact with the ball in front of the body. Besides the grips, the shot choice will have great influence on the contact point. This in turn will affect the amount of forward rotation of the body and the shape of the racket trajectory. For example, a low-struck slice backhand will have different key positions than a high-struck topspin backhand. With a low slice backhand the body position will stay more sideways, whereas with a high topspin backhand, the hips and shoulders will be rotating forward. It is important to understand these differences in making an accurate analysis.

The individual style of the player will have a great influence on the swing path and key positions of the stroke. The individual style of a player will change the swing path, the body rotation, and the contact points with the ball. A good example is the difference between the forehands of Pete Sampras, Roger Federer, and Rafael Nadal. They all have their own style in hitting great forehands and developed these as weapons in their game. Even though they have similarities in their forehand grips, the execution looks totally different. Let's examine their forehands closer.

In the early years, Pete used to hit his forehand more out in front of the body while later the contact point was less in front, with a more bent elbow at contact. His backswing was generated by bringing his elbow back and slightly upward. This caused the top of the racket to drop under the elbow before rising up again at the end of the backswing. The backswing was extremely relaxed to create a loose follow-through and maximum racket head speed. This method requires exceptional timing of the ball. In comparing Sampras, Nadal, and Federer's backswing, they have some commonalities in the use of the elbow but still are very different in swing path and execution.

Both Federer and Nadal have a more circular backswing, with Nadal strongly cocking the wrist in the backswing. Sampras would use a combination of S-shaped and oval-shaped backswing to generate a whip action in the forward swing. Federer and Nadal are more similar with their forehand contact points, but have totally different swing paths. Think of Nadal sometimes finishing with his follow-through on the same side above his head. Sampras would use this follow-through as well in later years when hitting running forehands. When analyzing players, keep in mind these individual styles and look at the consistency, reliability, and effectiveness in making judgment.

Analysis Experience

In the next paragraph, I will share a coaching experience that I had in working with Pete Sampras. We were practicing the volleys, and I was trying to look at his movement at the net. My analysis was that he was not moving enough in practice. I was trying to explain to him how the technique is different from hitting balls close to him and the ones he has to reach for. In general, this is the right thing to say to players, but I had not taken into account how much the feel and consistency of reproducing the shots speaks to his approach of gaining the confidence for his volleys. He definitely surprised me with his responses, but even more so with his actions in tournaments!

The Action Photo

I spent many days practicing with Pete Sampras in Saddlebrook, and that day, we happened to be working on the volley. In preparation for Wimbledon, we were going through the routines at the net. First, I played the balls more closely to him, but then played them somewhat farther away. I noticed that he was not moving on some of the balls at all and tried to spur him on. I stopped practice and came up to the net to discuss this with him. Pete's reply was "I don't need to practice those wide ones as long as I have the feel on these close to me. Once I have the feel, I will know how to hit the other ones." I was about to start an explanation when I stopped to think. Who am I to make him do it any different when he has obviously been very successful in the past with his volleys! Pete had by then reached the number 3 ranking in the world and was dominating the tennis world, and specifically the grass courts with his serve and volley game. We finished our practice and sat down to chat for a while, and I decided to give it one more try to convince him of the differences. I brought up a story on one of the practice sessions I had seen on video from Boris Becker. The film showed how Boris practiced the wide volleys by diving on a thick mattress and learning how to roll around and recover for the next ball. Pete was listening to this and laughed as though he thought this to be ridiculous. So I asked him, "You know, come to think of it, I have never seen you dive for a ball like that." His answer was short: "Never needed to."

That year at Wimbledon, Pete was playing a close match in the finals with his opponent, pushing him to his limits. I was at home watching the match on TV and was enjoying every minute of it. At the end of the set, there was a pinnacle moment where you knew one of these guys had to do something special to win the rally. Pete closed in at the net when his opponent hit a great passing shot that looked to be a winner. It was at that time that I nearly jumped out of my seat, in amazement, to see Pete dive horizontally to hit the volley for a winner! He went on to win this match for another Wimbledon title.

The next week, after some time off, he came walking in for another practice session. I congratulated him on his win and then he smiled faintly and said, "Did you see it?" I knew right away what he meant, and we both laughed. Sometimes you just don't think a player is paying attention and then he surprises you! Also, I had to realize that certain players have the talent to make certain corrections on their own. The picture-perfect horizontal dive made the front cover of tennis magazine. I knew the photographer, and later on that year, Pete was presented with a larger copy at the US Open. I wonder if he still has it.

Tactical Analysis

A tactical analysis is totally different from a technical analysis. With a tactical analysis, the reference points lie in the tactical applications of the game. In many cases, the technical, physical, and mental aspects influence the execution of the tactical aspects due to limitations or errors of a player. There are some fundamental points that generate the tactical ability of a player:

- **The Tactical Experience**
  As players gain experience in point play and matches, they increase their tactical skills in learning how to play the game. There is no shortcut to this experience, and it takes many years to obtain the tactical insight. As a coach, make a note of the tactical experience of a player before you make a tactical analysis. Be patient and don't assume they know all you might know as a coach.

- **The Tactical Style**
  The individual tactical style of a player is determined by how the player uses his or her strokes to their advantage with one of the following styles of play:

  A. The aggressive baseline player
  B. The serve and volley player
  C. The all-court player
  D. The counter puncher
  E. The defensive player

The analysis consists of determining the specific style of players, taking into account their age and the skill level of their style of play. Keep in mind that it takes younger players (12-16) more time to develop their style of play.

- **The Tactical Positioning and Status**

  Each ball in a rally should be struck with a tactical objective in mind. Players play a different way from a specific position on the court. The tactical positioning can give you several advantages or disadvantages concerning the next ball. Finding the proper tactical positioning requires good footwork and an understanding of the tactical situations and tactical status. When executed correctly, it will put you in the most favorable position to reach the next ball with multiple-shot choices. There are three types of tactical status:

  1. Offensive
  2. Defensive   ━━━━━▶   Tactical Positioning
  3. Neutral

  The analysis of the tactical positioning should focus on the place of recovery after the shot in combination with tactical status and situation. The analysis of tactical should occur by observing the player's shot choices in combination with the tactical position and tactical situation during point play.

- **The Tactical Situations**

  Every exchange of strokes is developed from a specific tactical situation. These situations are specific to the positions of both players and the shot choices executed from those positions. There are five basic tactical situations:

  1. The serve and return
  2. Baseline play
  3. Approaching the net
  4. Net play
  5. Playing against the net player

All these tactical situations are not mastered and executed the same at every level of play. Each player has their preferences and qualities in performing these tactical situations. The analysis is to find these qualities and judge their capabilities and consistency in execution from each tactical situation.

- **The Shot Choices**

Every tactical situation has various shot choices. Each player has to decide on what stroke to produce, depending on previous experiences in the same situations. There are certain factors that influence the shot choices in the score of the match and the player's tactical, physical, and technical ability. With many options available, there are good and bad shot choices. The good shot choices are strokes executed with the correct tactical status (neutral, offensive, defensive) in mind, in combination with the appropriate trajectory, speed, and spin choices. Bad shot choices are most often experimentations under difficult and pressure situations (score). Competitors with little experience or low confidence are prone to make rash decisions or high-risk shot choices under these circumstances. Confidence in execution plays a vital role in the success rate of pressure shots. Winning the pressure points in matches takes practice, experience, and discipline to make shot choices with a high success rate. The analysis of the shot choices is best observed in the tactical status, the execution, and the discipline of the strategy and tactics during tournament and match play.

- **The Patterns**
Players have their own preferences in developing a pattern of play during a rally. The objective is to gain a tactical advantage by outmaneuvering the opponent. They usually learn through trial and error what patterns work best for them, going by their own knowledge of their strengths and weaknesses. More experienced players have a better understanding and recognition of their patterns than less-experienced players. The analysis of these patterns should

be based on their proper use in building the point by exploiting the opponent's weaknesses and using their own strengths. The quality is also determined by the knowledge and execution of the patterns.

Physical Analysis

In order to make a proper physical analysis, you first need to observe all the components that can influence the physical ability and capabilities of a player. The most important elements that decide the physical makeup of a player are the following:

- **Coordination**
- **Stamina**
- **Strength**
- **S peed**
- **Flexibility**
- **Balance**

> The relationship between these components is different for each individual player. Percentage-wise, they can vary in the physical makeup of every player and possibly also be responsible in determining their strategy and playing style. Even though they are genetically influential, they are not limited and trainable to a certain degree.

Coordination is, percentage-wise (about 60 percent), the largest component of all the physical components that regulates the timing of the strokes. The physical components have to work together to create proper contact with the ball at the correct place and distance to the body. When performed well and efficiently, it produces a fluidity of motion that improves timing and contact with the ball. In analyzing the coordination, look for the fluidity in the physical components. You can observe these qualities in the movement and positioning of a player, the consistency and timing of the ball with proper contact points, and the smooth follow-through and balance during the stroke production.

Stamina of a player is determined by anaerobic and aerobic energy usage of the body and the efficiency thereof. The anaerobic energy comes from short bursts of energy (short rallies). The aerobic energy is produced with long rallies and determined by the duration of the points, but more so the duration of the match. The level of stamina, or conditioning of a player, can be contributed to the capabilities of both these factors. Keep in mind that many anaerobic repetitions can transfer in to aerobic energy usage. Analyzing the stamina of a player is not just how long they can last in matches, but also how often a player can reproduce strokes with intensity, consistency, and accuracy.

Strength has become an important factor in the modern tennis game. Players are hitting the ball harder with more spin and tempo. Racket and string technology has played a large role in allowing players to swing faster while still controlling the ball flight. Weight training has taken a larger role in the weekly training routine of top players. This form of training not only increases strength, but can also improve speed and can guard against injuries. The strength analysis of players can be measured by their accomplishment in weight training, but also in the explosive speed and acceleration of movements and strokes. If used incorrectly, weight training can be counterproductive for tennis players. This occurs when using heavy weights with less repetitions, resulting in muscle mass. Too much muscle mass in the wrong areas of the body (chest and arms) can negatively affect the flexibility and speed of the motion.

Speed is defined by how fast the movement is within a certain time frame. There are several forms of speed that determine how fast a player can move: quickness of action, change of direction, and velocity of movement. All these motions can be trained separately or in combination with the other components.

- *Quickness of action* refers to the speed and motion from arms and body during the hitting phase with the ball (fast body actions).
- *Change of direction* is the speed of agility from a player while slowing down the movement, turning, and accelerating in a different direction.
- *Velocity of movement* is the maximum speed of the player in running from point A to point B.

Due to the specific physical makeup of each individual player, not all are able to attain every type of speed. Every individual has a certain percentage "fast twitch fibers" and "slow twitch fibers" in their muscle structure. They largely determine the level of speed generated in the muscles. This percentage will regularly set a limit on the speed factor of that particular muscle, but still can be trained to a certain degree. Testing the speed of a player is not difficult. The analysis can be made with a series of speed tests that include all three factors of speed mentioned above. Be aware that sometimes a player is fast in the tests, but not while holding a racket in their hand. Practice, commitment, experience, and the mental attitude of a player can strongly influence the improvements of speed.

Flexibility is defined by the range of motion of the joints through the elasticity of the muscles and ligaments. In order to maintain flexibility, it needs to be trained regularly but has some major benefits to tennis players. It has positive effects on the fluidity of movement and the strokes, especially in pressure situations. It will also improve agility, balance, and recovery footwork in difficult situations. Physiologically, it provides less friction in the joints and therefore less effort in performing the motion. This aspect will increase endurance and efficiency in long-lasting matches. Less friction will also benefit speed of movement and speed of the strokes. Increasing speed takes less effort with a larger range of motion, a better elasticity in the muscles, and less friction in the joints. Analyzing flexibility is accomplished by observing range of motion of the movement and the quality of the strokes. The ease of movement and the fluidity and balance of the strokes are good indication to the flexibility.

Balance of strokes and movement provides a player with stability. Without balance, it would be very hard to coordinate strokes and footwork to hit the ball with any kind of control. Balance needs to be maintained before, during, and after the stroke for it to be effective. If any of these three components is out of sync, it will immediately have a negative result in the execution of the stroke and movement. Whenever a player loses balance, the body responds by trying to restore the balance with a quick reaction. We can observe this in players with unfinished strokes and "jerky" movements. Coaches can analyze this during matches, but this is often recognized in practice. When analyzing, be aware that besides a balance problem, it also could be a deeper-lying technical, physical, or even mental issue. Make sure to eliminate the other factors first before coming to a final conclusion.

Mental Analysis

Making a mental analysis of a player can be difficult and misleading. There are so many factors that come into play, and it takes time to come to the proper conclusions on the mental abilities of a player. As a coach, I personally like to use a list of most important mental aspects. This list makes it easier to come to an informed decision and avoids leaving out or forgetting any aspects of the mental analysis:

1. **Goals**
2. **Passion for the game**
3. **Work Ethic**
4. **Competitiveness**
5. **Execution under Pressure**

Analyze these components in this order to get the proper decisions and to avoid skipping any steps and elements in making your final conclusions.

Goals of a player will offer you a good indication what they expect from themselves or from you as a coach. The goals are a starting point, and they drive all the other factors. They help cultivate the passion of a player. It will become their game to take ownership of in the future. The goals also help a coach in making a proper training and tournament schedule for practice and matches. The communication of these goals needs to be clear to students and parents in order to avoid disappointments, to achieve an optimal training environment, and to make a good analysis.

Passion for the game can be exhibited in many ways. It can result in students practicing many more hours on their own; they never seem to get enough of playing the game. It can also result in a hunger in learning. Reading books about tennis is a form of passion for the game. It usually creates a tremendous drive in training harder and trying harder to win in matches. Whenever you see players lose mental control during practice and matches, it also says something about their level of passion for the game. It doesn't mean they have less or more passion for the game, they just don't know how to handle or channel that energy in the right direction for it to be effective. The passion for the game can have positive and negative effects on results in practice and matches. It can also drive players to eventually overcome any negative effects and obstacles in turning their game around and eventually becoming one of the greats in the sport. There have been many examples in the past of famous players who have struggled in the beginning of their career before finally becoming the legendary player we know today. Analyze the passion of a player by questioning them, and their parents, on the goals and expectations for the future. Communication and close long-term observation of their attitude and spirit during practice and matches will give you a good indication of their passion for the game.

Work ethic is the amount of energy and effort of a player on a daily basis. A good work ethic is a discipline that is learned and acquired over time. It drives tennis players to push themselves to train harder with a willingness to make sacrifices to accomplish the results they dream about. It can be a learned or self-taught discipline, depending on the examples delivered by coaches, parents, or their peers. It is not very difficult to recognize a good work ethic in tennis players. Just pay attention to their on- and off-court behavior, how hard they are willing to work, and what they are willing to sacrifice to reach their goals.

Competitiveness is the fighting spirit of a player. You can see it in their attitude in constantly looking for a way to win during point play and competition in general. In order to be successful, they strive for perfection through their drive, determination, willpower, and the resilience to overcome obstacles. These obstacles can be technical, tactical, physical, or mental problems that occur during point play. Whatever they might be, the level of competitiveness is determined by how well a player fights to win, stays on task (focus) without distraction, and enjoys the challenges that might come their way. The quality of these three aspects determines the amount of the competitiveness.

Execution under pressure is the most difficult component to acquire for players of any sport. With tennis being such an individual sport, players have to rely on themselves to control their emotions. In doubles play, it is possible to discuss the strategy with your partner. With the responsibility being divided between both partners, emotions usually don't run so high. It is one thing to play a practice match at your local club; it becomes a totally different experience when playing in a stadium-audience environment. Most professionals experience this on a regular basis. If the emotions are too high, it will influence the execution of the player. Sometimes they generate a positive stimulus that drives the performance under pressure. But most players will experience the opposite effect and tighten up under pressure. The footwork will slow down, and the timing of the strokes will decline. Learning how to channel this energy in a positive way is the actual skill to perform under pressure. Coaches and parents can easily observe the difference in a player's performance since you have seen their average performance level in practice sessions and other events.

Conclusions

Coming to the correct conclusions at the end of your analysis can be a difficult task when you are not organized properly. The many components can lead to confusion. Here are some points to assist your analysis:

1. Determine what you want to analyze.
2. Stabilize the situation for proper analysis.
3. Analyze the whole situation first.
4. Break it down in separate components.
5. Make a list by writing it down.
6. Eliminate possible side issues.
7. Make a final conclusion on the analysis.
8. Do a postanalysis after making the corrections.

If you follow this list in order, you have a larger chance in reaching the correct analysis. Be organized and document your findings. After your conclusions, make a game plan on how to correct the problem before communicating these with your student.

TECHNICAL TRAINING

Fundamentals

In teaching the basic strokes, we have to determine the fundamentals (essential aspects).

Fundamentals are the basic principles to which every player has to adhere to hit the stroke effectively. For example, the contact point is a fundamental. Players have a stroke-specific contact point that correlates to their grip for it to be effective and reliable with consistency. There are no exceptions to this rule. That's what makes it a fundamental for the stroke.

Style

This is a personal expression of the stroke. Many players have different styles in hitting the ball, starting as a junior. (Although Roger Federer has a similar style to Pete Sampras, as he modeled his game after Pete's as a junior, they still have a very distinctive style and there are some differences in how they both strike the ball.)
As long as it adheres to the fundamentals, it can be effective and efficient.

Key Positions

The key positions are like a freeze frame point during a stroke that indicates a certain part of the stroke. They all have an important impact on how the stroke is performed.

These key positions make up the fundamentals of the stroke.

1. Ready position
2. Backswing
3. Loading
4. Forward swing
5. Contact point
6. Follow-through
7. Recovery

Every player has key positions though they might not be performed in the same way. These variations in performance determine the efficiency and style of the stroke that makes each player unique. They are the positions to look for errors in the stroke production! The errors in the key positions are not necessarily because they differ from the norm since there are different ways and styles in hitting the ball.

It is an error when the key positions don't fit with the grips used with the type of stroke played, the wrong key position point is used in that particular stroke, or when one or more key positions breaks down during the stroke production. To study the key positions properly, you need to videotape the stroke production. Make sure to take several shots from the same stroke to see if they vary. Also, take the shots from different angles (side, back, and front) to make sure the body from the player does not block your view of the stroke.

Improvements and Corrections

After an analysis is made, it is possible to make a training plan on how to proceed from this point forward. This training plan consists of improvements and/or corrections of the subjects. Improvements are incremental increases of performance and the next step in a progression of learning. Corrections are changes made in the execution of the subjects when they are not performed correctly. There are instances when the failure of execution is very clear and corrections are needed right away. Others might not be so clear due to style, age of the player, and their level of play. In these cases, it is advisable to take this in consideration before making changes. For example, a player that has been using the same strokes and style for many years will have tremendous trouble making corrections and changes to their game. They might actually digress in execution and feel much more anxious about their performance than before. Here are some guidelines:

1. **The player is executing correctly.**
   In this instance, it is not necessary to make corrections, and the coach can focus on the improvements of the player according to a progression of learning. The coach will continue to make positive comments on the execution and only introduce new subjects that will increase the level of performance. Never change a winning game!

2. **The player is not executing correctly but is still successful within their style.**
   Depending on the goals of the player, in combination with their age, level of play, and style, it is possible to make a decision for corrections or not. The coach has to communicate with the player to either make a change or to improve the execution within their style of play. The decision should weigh heavily with the player.

3. **The player is not executing correctly.**
   After explaining the problem of the execution, it is possible to make the corrections needed. No matter what correction it is, both parties have to agree. The coach will try to create a progression of learning from easy to more complicated within the competency level of the player. The progression is a step-by-step approach in which the player is ensured of improvement before moving on to the next progression. Positive feedback will improve confidence in the changes.

Improvements to the technique of the strokes are best accomplished by following a methodology and progression in the exercises. The methodology is determined by the system used for improvements or corrections. The progression is determined by the series of exercises you devise, from easy to more complex.

By using this step-by-step approach, it is possible to increase the performance while maintaining confidence in the execution. It is important to make sure that the skill is mastered before moving on to the next step in the progression. If coaches move too fast from step to step, students will lack the time to properly train the skill. It is also difficult to retain the information and the learned skills and might slowly decline over time. Provide them with time to try it in practice, experiment with it, and implement it in matches. As soon as they feel more comfortable with the subjects, they will start to perform better in pressure situations and master the skill.

Corrections

There is a process that will increase the chances of making corrections and changes to any subject in development. This process can be more successful by following certain guidelines and directions. They are as follows:

- **Make corrections at the appropriate time.**
  When improper execution and strategies persist too long, they become ingrained as a bad habit. It takes far less time to train students correctly than to undo errors! This is definitely the case with more advanced players since they will have been using that specific method for a longer period of time. In making a change, it is important to find the proper time to make these corrections. You can wait for a break in the tournament schedule or make the changes during the off-season. Knowing how your player reacts to changes is also a factor. If a player is frustrated or agitated, they will be less receptive. During practice, find a moment when the player has calmed down with a break in the action before providing them

with advice. If players have already received corrections before, wait to see if they remember the information first before repeating the information. If they still don't remember, ask a question to make them think without providing the answer right away. When they are able to remember the correction, it will stick with them much longer than if you provide the information all the time. You, as a coach, should help them in training their own memory to better retain the information.

- **Correct one subject at a time.**
  Providing too much information is confusing to students. Try to break it down in parts. With just one or two things to think about, they will have a much easier time in the learning process. Ideally, you want this learning process to be as follows:

  1. Learn the correction.
  2. Give students plenty of time to practice.
  3. Provide feedback and encouragement during the execution.
  4. Try it out and point play and practice matches.
  5. Implement it in tournaments.
  6. After feedback, continue to make improvements.
  7. Master it before moving on to the next subject or progression.

Information

In coaching Alex Kuznetsov at a professional event, I was giving him information during the warm-up before his match. I was not only talking to him about tactical information, but also giving him technical pointers on subjects we had been trying to improve.

I could see he looked agitated while practicing, but put it off as nervousness before his match. Finally he stopped and said to me, "Too much, Martin." I looked at him perplexed and answered, "What's the matter?" He answered, "You are giving me too much information and I can't focus on the match this way." He was absolutely right!

In my efforts to provide him with all the information, I had actually increased the stress level before his match. I had chosen the wrong moment to talk to him about technical information. The night before was a good time to talk about the tactical game plan, and the technical information should be limited to practice sessions. After this point, we came to an agreement that he would simply warn me with a short sentence: "Too much." This seemed to work well from that point on.

As coaches, we need to find the appropriate time to deliver messages and reduce the length of time in communicating them without losing the essence of the message. Communication here is key in being as clear as possible with short instructions.

- **Correct the primary error first.**
  When making an analysis, it is important to find the origin of the problem. This takes experience and a keen eye. Detecting the root of the problem is critical before trying to solve all the side effects. Sometimes it can be very obvious, but it can also be hidden and not so visible to the "naked eye." It might require slow-motion video to detect any faults. Here is a method you can use for detecting errors in strokes:

  1. Look at contact point of the stroke. (The grip can be of influence.)
  2. Look at the key positions of the stroke. (See chapters on key positions.)
  3. Look at the balance of the body (before, during, and after the stroke).
  4. Find the primary error (the root of the problem).

- **Make a positive remark before making corrections.**
  Improve the student's state of mind and focus before making any corrections. Students can be very sensitive and may take instructions personally or feel you are insulting their performance. Female players can often be more emotional than male players; however, no matter what gender you are coaching, you should always maintain positive reinforcement. There are several methods to achieve positive communication with your student:

  1. The first method is to wait for the proper execution of the subject and immediately remark on how well that was performed.
  2. The second method is to remark on a positive improvement from another subject before introducing the correction.
  3. The third method is to start a conversation and ask a question on how to improve the subject. It is possible to lead the student to the answer by asking leading questions.

- **Don't move on till the skill is mastered.**
  Mastering the game of tennis takes time and patience. Most students are impatient and become frustrated when results are not achieved

at once. Be sure your players have conquered each step of the way to mastering each skill before moving on to the next level of skill or subject. Give players ample time to practice and implement your instructions in practice, during points, and in pressure situations.

- **When your corrections don't work, use another method.**
  Not everyone reacts to directions in the same way. Some players are visually inclined and like to see videos or an example shown to them. Others are auditory or sensory inclined, and you have to explain things or let them feel the sensation of the action. Knowing how your students absorb information can be very helpful in speeding up the learning process. And even then, you might have to try different methods if one particular approach does not seem to work.

> In becoming a good coach, you have to learn to be flexible and find what works for your students, not just what works for you.

- **Keep your voice and demeanor in check.**
  Your voice and body language sends a message to the player, just like the playing style and body language of a player sends a message to their opponent! The difference in coaching lies not only in what you say and do, but how you deliver the message. You want to be calm and determined in your delivery, just as you would expect your student to be in a match. Your voice and body language will often show your emotions, especially if you are coaching as a parent! So be aware and keep your emotions under control to improve those emotions of your students.

- **Indirect or subconscious corrections.**
  Students can become very nervous and uptight when they are overly aware of what subjects to improve. They can get so focused on the corrections that they tense up and become frustrated. To introduce the topics in an indirect or subconscious way can be

very helpful in this instance. For example, if players have trouble with their follow-through of the forehand, make them catch the racket above the other shoulder with the other hand. By focusing on catching the racket, they will loosen up the hitting arm automatically and follow through much more smoothly. There are many more indirect coaching methods like this that will have a positive impact on the teaching, improvement, and success of the subjects. Here are some examples:

1. *To improve the tempo of baseline strokes, students can practice hitting the balls on the rise by standing closer to the baseline. It improves footwork and timing under pressure situations and increases the racket head speed.*

2. *To improve the spin on the service action, have players hit over a heightened net. They will learn quickly to hit upward with the service stroke and therefore applying more spin and rotation to the ball. This indirect method takes all the explanation out of the corrections and speeds up the learning process for your students.*

3. *To improve the depth on ground strokes, draw a line in front of the baseline. The box formed in front of the baseline gives the students a target to aim for. This target area will automatically teach them to aim higher over the net to reach this target area. This indirect practice method makes them focus less on the technical aspects of the practice and more on the sensory and visual aspects.*

Different Approach

There are times when players are not paying attention to your instructions. This was also the case with a student while training at the National Training Center in Boca Raton, Florida. Don't get me wrong, this student was not lazy at all, nor did he have a bad attitude. He was just stubborn in changing his strategy that totally didn't fit with his size (5.2 feet). He was a talented player with great energy and flair for the game and was able to play with ease with the stronger players. Except for his stubborn nature, I really liked his game and felt I needed to do something to help him improve.

When making the court assignments, I placed him on purpose on a different court for the whole week. After this, he came to ask me if he could be on my court that week. I told him no. I knew he would not leave it at that, and I was not surprised when he came back some time later to ask, "Why not?" I explained to him that I thought he needed to be on a different court since he wasn't listening to my instructions and I did not want to waste my time. He looked surprised but immediately promised me he would listen better and try to execute the proper strategy.

From that moment on, he paid much better attention to what was said and was executing the strategies and tactics with great success. It is a good example of how to deal with stubborn students and to be creative in dealing with them. It won't work with every student, and you will have to know your student well to implement this method.

He went on to become a top junior and highly respected college player. I was happy to visit him four years later and was proud to see him do so well.

Methodology of Teaching Strokes

Teaching strokes is best performed when using a method of instruction with drills and exercises. This will create an organized progression of teaching that starts with the basics of the subject and slowly increases in difficulty. There is a certain order to the progression (learning process) that ensures a higher chance of success in each subject. Having a good methodology will make you look professional and knowledgeable as a coach while organizing the teaching material for your students. Here are some golden rules of methodology in teaching and coaching:

1. **Basic to more complex**
   Starting with the basic topics and working toward more complex subjects will assist players to learn at a faster pace and gain confidence in their accomplishments. Example: Learning the consistency first will create more opportunities to execute new subjects more easily.

2. **Logical order of progression**
   Having a logical order of progression ensures a buildup of the subjects through a connection of the content. Example: You would teach a normal forehand first with consistency, depth, and direction before trying to teach a topspin or a slice forehand.

3. **Excellence before progression**
   It is important to strive for a certain level of excellence before moving on to the next subject. Example: It is not uncommon to see players and coaches trying out advanced strokes before they master the most basic strokes. This could cause changes in the fundamentals with grips, footwork, and swing paths. This can hurt the progress and confidence of the learning process and should be avoided whenever possible. Don't go beyond the learning curve of the students.

4. **Master through repeated practice**

Only through repeated practice will players reach a high level of excellence. With repetition, the neural pathways are trained to a level of automation. These automated motions eventually become reflex actions that hold up well under pressure.

The Teaching Order

The development and progression of the strokes develop faster with a logical teaching order. This teaching order of each type of stroke should be as follows:

Consistency	Basic consistency and consistency under pressure
Depth	Consists of speed, height and spin
Direction	One direction or change of direction
Spin	Topspin, slice, sidespin or combinations
Power	The force or strength of the stroke
Tempo	The speed of the timing

Consistency

The basis of every stroke should be consistency in its conception and progression during practice and match play under pressure. The consistency increases in difficulty with the speed of the ball. To enhance the technical consistency, players and coaches need to pay attention to the following:

A. Early preparation of the racket and footwork
B. Good timing of the ball to create consistent contact points
C. Big targets with margin for errors with the lines and the net
D. Shot choice and rotation of the ball
E. Balance before, during, and after the stroke
F. Good recovery

1. **Early preparation of the racket and footwork**

   The early preparation starts with footwork through a "split step." The bounce on the toes while spreading the legs at the moment the opponent strikes the ball enables a player to move with speed and balance. The movement behind the ball and the preparation of the stroke with an early backswing ensures the readiness of the player and reduces errors. The timing of the split step is crucial to the reaction time.

   Practice: Have the student call out a number (1) when the opponent strikes the ball. This will indicate the timing of the split step and aid the player in early preparation.

2. **Good timing of the ball to create consistent contact points**

   Timing the stroke well will increase consistency of the contact points. Timing is a physical as well as a mental commitment to hit the ball with authority. A point of reference to good contact points is the position of the racket and shoulders at impact with the ball. Note: the grips will influence the position of shoulders and racket.

   Practice: Have the player call out number one when the ball bounces and number two when the ball is truck. This will assist the timing of the ball. Sometimes it can be instrumental to breathe out at the time of striking the ball or slightly grunting while exhaling. This method is used quite often with advanced and pro players and helps them to time the ball and to keeping their focus on the execution during long rallies. (Under pressure, the attention can shift to the fear of missing.)

3. **Big targets with margin for error with the lines and the net**

   Advanced players have to be even more disciplined with the target areas as the speed of the game increases. The margins are not just with the sidelines and baseline but also with the height over the net and the targets areas in the service box (service). This larger margin provides less anxiety when hitting the ball and fewer unforced errors. Competitors will play more freely with more commitment to the stroke. Teaching these skills is a difficult task to master. It takes a lot of patience to keep building the rally and to stay calm and committed under pressure.

Practice: Make a target area one yard from all the lines and have students practice points in this area. A target area box can also be used with the serve.

4. **Shot choice and rotation to the ball**

   Choosing the proper shot with the right amount of rotation takes a lot of experience. The factors that influence this decision are the speed, spin, trajectory, and angle from the opponent's ball in combination with the position of both players on court. There is very little time to make a decision on the target, the trajectory, and the rotation of the ball. The difficulty level of the approaching ball dictates the shot choice. The goal is to create high-percentage shots while pressuring or neutralizing the opponent. Experience will increase the decisions and consistency over time.

   Practice: Start the point with running forehands and backhands. The students learn to find solutions to difficult situations with high-percentage shots (targets, trajectory). Play out the points once the pattern has been completed.

5. **Balance before, during, and after the stroke**

   Organizing your balance before, during, and after the stroke is a key to better consistency. Good balance can be achieved by slightly leaning against the ball while keeping an athletic position (weight transfer) and recovering with the feet after the ball is struck. With corners shots under pressure, the balance becomes a tough task with the rotation of the body and arms. The balance has to shift from moving with the ball outside to slightly leaning back inside for the recovery and to apply pressure on the outside leg. Leaning too much inside will result in slipping of the outside foot with less downward pressure. Players should practice all three-balance points to enhance the strokes.

Practice: Balance can best be trained by making the player recover after each stroke. To make sure balance is maintained, step over once across the inside foot. This will ensure that the player does not fall over the top or lean too much inside.

6. **Good recovery**

The footwork becomes more important as tempo and speed of the game increases. There are six forms of recovery to keep in mind:

1. Stepping in forward (with balls closer to the middle or that fall short)
2. Open stance (on wide-ball situations)
3. Running around (while running around the backhand)
4. Running shots (on running forehands or backhands)
5. Moving backward (to use after deeper shots or overhead)
6. Approach shots (in going to the net)

All these need to be practiced until the balance is mastered. Repetition will cure most of the problems. Make sure the students fully understand the details of the recovery footwork since it is essential for advanced players.

Practice: Train recovery footwork for each situation separately with hand-feeding balls before going to live ball situations as the player improves, increase direction, spin, and tempo of the feed. Finally, try it out in points, practice matches, and get feedback from this footwork in tournaments.

Depth

The trajectory over the net with height, speed, and spin determines the depth of the ball in the court. Depth is important at all levels of play, but even more so with advanced and pro players. It not only neutralizes the opponent by backing them up, but also creates less angles for them to open the court. The factors that influence the trajectory are as follows:

- **The speed of the ball**

  The speed delivered to the ball is one of the major factors in hitting the ball with depth. The more speed is delivered to the ball, the less elevation and spin needs to be added in order to reach a deeper target. Using less speed results in playing the ball higher over the net to reach the same depth.

- **The height over the net**

  The angle of elevation over the net is the easiest way to create depth. By aiming the ball higher over the net, the ball will fly deeper in the court. The speed and elevation need to be coordinated to reach a deep target.

- **The rotation on the ball**

  The spin to the ball influences the trajectory and depth of the ball. With more spin added, the ball will want to drop sooner down in the court. With more slice added, the ball will stay elevated longer. The speed and height of the ball need to be coordinated with the rotation to reach a deep target.

Tactical Advantages of Depth

When hitting the ball closer to the baseline, the opponent is forced to move back. The depth of the stroke will force the opponent on the back foot and result in a less powerful stroke with a shorter return of the ball. With more depth, the opponent has less angle of attack. This makes it easier to defend the court with more reaction time to retrieve the ball and recover to a ready position. It also provides opportunities to move closer to the baseline and attack the net more easily. The tactical advantages of playing with more depth are summed up below:

1. It forces the opponent back behind the baseline.
2. There are more chances to receive short return.
3. There are less angles of attack for the opponent.
4. There is more time to react to the next ball.
5. There is more time to recover.
6. You can move closer to the baseline.
7. There are more chances to attack the net.

The improvements made in racket and string technology have improved power, spin, and ball control. Those added factors have revolutionized the game.

Practice: An easy way to train the depth with the trajectory is to use a net stick under the middle of the net to make players hit higher over the net. More height over the net will create more depth to the ball. After some practice, try it out in points and matches.

Direction

The direction or change of direction is the skill of moving the ball to one or different targets on the court. The objective is to move the opponent to force mistakes. The direction or change of direction of the ball is determined by the following:

1. **The angle of the oncoming ball**

   Physics demands that with a stationary racket, the incoming angle of the ball will be the same as the outgoing angle. However, this is not the same when striking the ball. In this case, the outgoing angle will be less, with the ball mainly following the direction of the racket strings. In order to direct the outgoing angle, it is important to adjust the angle of the racket.

2. **The racket and swing angle at contact with the ball**

   The angle of the racket at impact with the ball will affect the direction, spin, and elevation of the ball over the net. The swing angle and speed of the racket will influence the direction as well.

3. **The speed of the racket**

   Racket head speed will affect the outgoing angle of the ball as the mass and the strings of the racket become a dominating factor in direction. With increasing racket head speed, the outgoing direction angle will be forced ever closer to the direction of the racket angle through the mass of the racket.

4. **The follow-through**

   The strike zone will lengthen with an extended follow-through. This lengthened follow-through will have a dominating effect on the direction of the ball, as the ball is forced in that direction by the racket and the strings. The grips also play an important role in accommodating the length of the strike zone.

Changing directions with consistency and accuracy takes a lot of practice and patience at any level of play and needs to be practiced daily.

Practice: Learning to play to one specific target will practice the precision. Changing directions trains the angle and precision in timing of the contact points. It is possible to practice both by having one player stay on one side of the court and the other retrieve balls back to one side of the court.

Rotation

Brushing the strings past the ball during contact creates rotation to the ball. There are different types of rotation available in adding spin: topspin, underspin (or slice), sidespin, and combinations of topspin or slice with sidespin. The angle at which the strings brush past the cover of the ball determines the amount of spin and speed of the ball. The amount of rotation (spin) to the ball is determined by the following:

• **Racket head speed**

  The speed of the racket and strings at impact point determine the amount of spin generated to the ball. The higher the acceleration of the racket at impact, the more the rotation of the ball increases.

• **Angle of the racket (see picture)**

  The angle of the racket at impact with the ball will not only influence the trajectory but also the rotation of the ball. The amount of rotation is subject to the speed and swing angle of the strings against the ball.

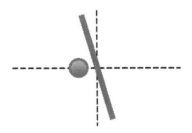

• **Swing angle**

  The swing angle, in approaching the ball at contact, is the trajectory of the racket through the strike zone of the ball. The swing angle, the angle of the racket, and the speed of the racket head determine the amount of friction of the strings with the cover of the ball in order to create rotation.

Ball control can be improved by rotation of the ball, but it takes much experience and experimentation. With the three variables available (see above), it is a challenging task to create the proper combinations for consistency in execution.

Martin van Daalen

Practice:

1. *Play over a higher net. It will automatically add spin through the trajectory.*
2. *Have the students hold the racket halfway on the grip. They will feel the use of the wrist much better and brush the ball more naturally. Start first at the net.*
3. *Play in the service box from the baseline. Practicing this from both sides creates a different perspective in the use of topspin.*
4. *Practice slice from the service line and work your way back to the baseline.*
5. *Hit volleys from the baseline and alternate with slice backhands. It will train both shots and stimulate the player to use the correct technique.*

Power

Power involves both strength and speed. In tennis strokes, it is generated by the mass and speed of the racket head in striking the ball. The racket head speed transfers the energy from the mass of the racket head through the strings to the ball. This energy can be generated by several factors: the length and shape of the backswing, the flexibility and strength of a player, the extension of the legs during impact, the rotational force of the body, and the weight transfer at impact with the ball.

Factors that Influence Power of the Strokes:

- **Basic strength of the player**

  Strength from a player can increase the speed of the racket head. Basic strength should be trained with advanced tennis players, but it is not the only factor to produce powerful strokes. It can have a great impact on the development of racket head speed if used correctly!

- **Length and shape of the swing path**

  With a longer swing path, the body is able to increase the speed of the racket head. Power is the force multiplied with the distance and divided by time. The shape can make a difference in lifting the racket in the backswing in a circular-oval shape. By using gravity through the mass of the racket and the arm, it is possible to increase the speed of the racket, resulting in more power.

- **Flexibility of the player**

  The flexibility in muscles, joints, and ligaments plays an important role in the power production of strokes with less friction in generating acceleration. In the loading and unloading of the body, the natural elasticity in the muscles and ligaments from the shoulder, elbow, and wrist will provide additional acceleration to the racket (whip action). Keeping the muscle pressure low during the preparation (shoulder, arm, grip pressure) increases the flexibility and elasticity in the forward swing.

- **Loading and unloading**

  The action of "loading" is created with the windup of the backswing, the backward rotation of the body, and the bending of the knees. The turning and bending creates an internal buildup of elasticity in the muscles and ligaments, waiting to be released. The release is called the "unloading" of the stroke in turning forward, extending the knees and releasing the arm through the impact with the ball. The amount of force of loading and unloading increases power.

- **Rotational force**

  This action is the power created by the speed of rotation around the body (centrifugal force). The outward rotational force creates acceleration to the most outer part of the swing. (Think about swinging a weight around you on a string.) The same effect happens when a player accelerates the racket around their body. The racket head will not only accelerate from the forward swing but also from the additional power from the centrifugal force.

- **Contact point**

  Hitting the ball at the proper impact point will provide much control and power transfer to the ball. A player will be able to feel a big difference in power if the ball is struck in front of the body. The stance needs to be coordinated to find the proper distance for good balance and weight transfer.

- **Weight transfer**

  Using the forward mass of the body against the ball during impact will produce additional power in striking the ball. Timing the forward motion of the body at impact with the ball is the key to more power production.

  Practice: Practice with foam balls to increase the racket head speed during impact with the ball. Practice in hitting balls at increasing speeds from half-court situations. Place the player increasingly farther back behind the baseline in order to increase the racket head speed in order to find the same pace. Have the players experience each of the points above separately. This will make them feel each factor independently.

Tempo

Tempo is the speed of the timing in making contact with the ball. This can be after or before the bounce of the ball. "Before the bounce" means a volley or hitting it in the air with a groundstroke (swinging volley). After the bounce, the ball will gradually lose speed and spin, hitting balls earlier after the bounce speeds up the ball with the higher energy still available from the speed and spin. With this in mind, the player can reduce the length of the backswing and add some spin for control. The top players will use this energy from the ball to redirect the power and use it to their advantage. It takes less power but requires great timing to control consistently.

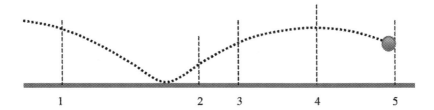

In the figure above, you can see the five different contact points and tempo of the ball. At the far left (1) is the volley in taking the ball before the bounce. The next (2) is right after the bounce with a half volley. The following is on the rise (3), at the highest point (4), and after the highest point when the ball is dropping (5).

Practice: Practice standing inside the baseline and control the rally. Practice to move in on high balls and hitting them out of the air (volley). Practice in moving into short balls and taking them on the rise with tempo. Playing against net players and taking balls at a faster pace is the most common way to practice tempo. There are drills shown (next page). Start with the drill on the left and progress to playing on the whole court.

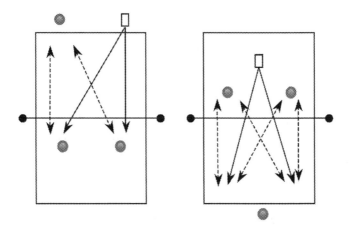

By practicing these drills, players will get used to the increased tempo in a playful way that simulates match situations with automated solutions. It forces players to take the balls on the rise with much faster exchanges in the rallies. They learn how to use the energy and redirect power in the pressure situations by shortening the backswing and making contact with a slightly closed racket face (spin).

Summary

In finding the correct methodology for teaching strokes, it is important to follow this list diligently. It will assist you in finding drills to perform with your student with a proper progression. By following this method, the students will very quickly understand the technical implications of how to improve their strokes.

With every new subject, you should start at the beginning and master each skill of the list, starting with consistency. It is not necessary to practice all aspects of the list before moving on to the next subject, but it does show the proper progression. Sometimes players need more time to practice and experiment before they can advance to the next progression. It can also be that the subject matter becomes too advanced for the student to master at that moment. This will require the coach to come back to the subject and continue the learning process at a later date.

It will also assist them in building their strategy and their tactical knowledge. Students will learn to make tactical priorities by following this list. It will make them understand how to go from easy strategies to more difficult ones and to make corrections when their game plan breaks down.

Teaching Process

There are times, as a coach, that you realize how important it can be to learn or improve a certain aspects of a student's game. You might realize that this subject will become one of the crucial aspects for them to master. This was also the case in teaching Rhyne Williams.

Rhyne was already a talented player at fifteen years of age and was making great strides at international ITF events. He was tall for his age and could hit the ball with great speed and spin. His upper body motions were loose and free-swinging, but the legs were tight and flexibility was a problem.

After trying to increase flexibility for several years, I never saw him improve in this area and realized it was holding him back in his movement. He could barely touch his knees, let alone his toes. He seemed to have trouble in crossing the barrier by himself, and I decided that bolder methods were needed to make a difference in his performance.

Michele Leigh was the trainer at the USTA facility in Key Biscayne at that time, and I convinced her that we needed a different and innovative approach to this problem. I suggested bringing Rhyne in for three separate weeks and focus on his physical training and specifically his flexibility. We only practiced tennis one hour in the morning and afternoon since the focus was the physical training. Michele would spend forty-five minutes on stretching him out before and after each tennis and physical practice. So in total, he was being stretched out four times a day. The objective here was to help him shift the boundaries of his flexibility by slowly pushing him farther with every stretching session. Besides this, he was taken through some tennis-specific movement exercises to increase his speed, balance, and flexibility in moving on the court. After doing this for three weeks, he was able to touch his toes quite comfortably. The results were evident in his mobility on court and with his results in tournaments.

Rhyne went on to become a valued member of the Tennessee College Team and has turned pro in 2011. I still see him regularly at events, and he has been progressing on the pro tour. I hope he has kept up with his stretching.

**Coaching Rhyne Williams at the Orange Bowl 14
(Miami), beating Grigor Dimitrov in the final**

Baseline Strokes

Baseline strokes are by far the most played strokes in tennis. They are the elemental strokes of each rally and have great impact on the outcome of each point. Even though the tactical purpose might be different, the return of the serve and the approach shots are basically baseline strokes with a specific technical execution. The offensive power of the serve can be dominating at times, but still only makes up one shot out of the whole rally. The baseline strokes carry most of the burden in the development of the game in being the technical backbone of each individual player.

There are many different shots and varieties possible in hitting baseline strokes. The technical execution plays a large role, but always keep in mind the tactical, physical, and mental aspects as well. You can use the baseline strokes to create offensive, neutralizing, or defensive situations. For advanced players to produce these types of shots effectively, there are some physical and mental requirements with an understanding of the tactical purpose of each shot. Baseline strokes can apply pressure to the opponent in different ways and can be effective in their own unique way:

- **Consistency** is the basic form of applying pressure with baseline strokes by hitting one more ball in the court than the opponent. This creates the impression that they are not going to miss, resulting in mental and physical pressure on the opponent. Most often this will result in errors by being too careful or too reckless.

- **Depth** pushes the opponent deeper behind the baseline and might generate errors or opportunities to take advantage of shorter returns. It creates a less angle of attack for the opponent and more opportunities to move in closer to the baseline to improve the tactical position of the player.

Martin van Daalen

- **Direction** of the ball can affect pressure on the opponent by moving the player to the outer parts of the court. This will pressure the physical ability and test their stamina in long rallies and matches. It will also pressure their mental capacity by giving them the feeling of being rushed or being pushed off balance.

- **Spin** to the strokes creates pressure on the opponent with the bounce of the ball in acceleration and in the height of the bounce. The amount of spin, in combination with the speed of the ball and the incoming bounce angle, are factors that can make it difficult to anticipate the timing and effect of the ball until after the bounce. With less time to react and make corrections, chances are it will result in more errors.

- **Power** to the strokes creates a faster ball flight and takes time away from the opponent. Less time will apply pressure to the speed and footwork of the opponent in setting up for the stroke or in making corrections to the timing of the ball.

- **Tempo** reduces the reaction time of the opponent by hitting the ball earlier. When taking the ball on the rise, power can easily be obtained by taking advantage of the higher energy available at that point of the trajectory. Taking time away from the opponent will increase their physical and mental pressure and most often push them in defensive positions.

- **Physical ability** can be of great importance in developing a player. It defines the possibilities of physical dominance with speed and endurance and applies pressure to the opponent on a physical, tactical, technical, and mental level. It can have a great influence on the development of power, spin, and tempo of the player and in executing the strategies.

- **Mental ability** will be of influence to the confidence and commitment of a player with the strokes and execution of the strategies. With a strong mental ability, it is possible to apply pressure on the opponent that shows in their demeanor. Almost all players will portray a certain level of anxiety in playing a rally. By appearing more calm, confident, and aggressive, a player is able to acquire a dominance that will carry over in every aspect of their game (attitude).

- **Overall strategy** plays an important role in the basic tactical concepts of the tennis game. The strengths and weaknesses of the opponent will determine how to apply these concepts in a match. Each player has to conclude the proper strategy that fits with their level of play in comparison with their opponent's game.

- **Patterns of play** in baseline rallies are the construction of points with reoccurring directions to outmaneuver your opponent. The objective of every pattern is to seek an advantage in strength with the proper sequence of shot choices. The key here is to understand what patterns bring out your strengths against the weaknesses of the opponent or that force the opponent in a pressured or defensive position.

There are many factors that play a role in developing the baseline game of advanced tennis players. As players mature with their game, they need to acquire a good sense of what shot to play in any given situation (shot choice). By laying the groundwork with good fundamentals, each individual player has the opportunity to make better choices with their style of play and develop their game for the future.

In the following chapters, I will show you the methodology in teaching the baseline game to advanced players with a progression of subjects. It is possible to use all the topics mentioned above with all the strokes in the tennis game, but I will focus on the specifics of the baseline strokes from consistency to tempo. The other topics will be discussed in the physical, mental, and strategy chapters. I will show you the most common mistakes made in teaching the topics and some examples on how to correct them. The practice drills will be organized from easy to difficult and can be used as a guideline for your lessons.

The Bribe

Sometimes you have to use some unusual methods in convincing young players how to play certain strokes. This was also the case I was taking some of the top junior boys to an ITF event in Panama (Central America). Chase Buchanan was fifteen at the time and was one of the team members playing the event. He had this bad habit of slicing his forehand whenever he was pressured or pushed out wide to the forehand.

Now don't get me wrong, I don't think there is anything wrong in slicing the forehand in extreme situations, but Chase would use this shot too frequently when he didn't need to. The type of ball actually required a much more offensive stroke from that position, but he obviously had grown accustomed to just slicing it back. I had talked to him in previous matches how to change this, but without much success. His next opponent was a tall and crafty player from Mexico that competed quite aggressively. I knew Chase would not win the next match this way and decided I needed a totally different approach to change his mind.

In discussing the strategy with him before the match, I made it clear to him how important it was to hit his forehand offensively with topspin rather than slicing it. Knowing how much he liked ice cream, I offered him a bribe by promising him an ice cream cone if was able to play his match without using more than three slice forehands in the whole match. He looked at me for a while, smiled, and accepted the challenge.

Right from the start of the match, he played much more aggressively out of the wide forehand position and soon saw the value of this method and strategy. He ended up winning the match and played his best match of the tournament. As promised, I immediately bought him the ice cream cone. I knew he had been eyeing it for the past few days.

Sometimes it takes a different approach to teach a student a valuable lesson. One year later, Chase would win an event at the age of sixteen and, at eighteen, reach the finals of the junior US Open event in New York. He went on to be a valuable player on the Ohio State College team and is playing on tour today.

I wonder if he still remembers this match......

Chase Buchanan (14)

Martin van Daalen

Key Position and Analysis

The key positions are recognizable technical aspects of a stroke that indicate a certain "key" part of the stroke that are common in most players. They all have an important impact on how the stroke is performed. Grips have a very high impact on the execution and swing path of the stroke. The key positions, together with grips, make up the fundamentals of the stroke. Below are the key positions as they are performed in sequence:

1. Ready position
2. Backswing
3. Loading
4. Forward swing
5. Contact point
6. Follow-through
7. Recovery

The key positions are not exactly the same for every player. The variations of one key position will lead to differences in other key positions of the stroke. The grips and shot choice of the player will lead to changes in the backswing, contact points, and follow-through. They all work together within the mechanics and the style of the player, to be consistent and reliable. Key positions are elemental in looking for errors in the stroke production! Make sure you are aware of the particular shot choice and grips before making judgment on a correction or instruction. In fact, it would be wise to first make a thorough analysis. To study the key positions properly, you need to videotape the stroke production. Make sure to take several shots from the same stroke to see if they vary. Also, take the shots from different angles (side, back, and front) to make sure the player's body does not block your view of the stroke.

Analysis

The key positions will provide the information and details to make the analysis of the stroke. By isolating each key position in turn, it is possible to identify any possible problems, hitches, changes, or abnormalities in the stroke. Keep in mind that each key position change can lead to alterations of the key positions following later in the stroke production. Knowing this makes it important to look at several regular strokes from start to finish. That way, you can see if this is the player's own style of play or if it happens to be an irregular stroke from the norm.

Key Positions of the Topspin Forehand

Ready position

- Athletic posture
- Hands relaxed
- Knees slightly bent
- Split step
- Alert disposition

Backswing

- Rotate shoulder with racket
- Rotate hips outside
- Turn toes outside
- Swing racket back

Ready Position

Loading

- Bend knees farther
- Turn hips back
- Turn shoulders back
- Extend both arms
- Balance arm to side

Forward swing

- Unload legs
- Unload hips
- Unload shoulders forward
- Track oncoming ball
- Line up racket path

Loading

Contact point

- Hand in front
- Stability in wrist
- Weight transfer
- Hitting zone

Follow-through

- Arm forward and around
- Skip foot around
- Full turn of the hips
- Full turn of the shoulders

Recovery

- Recovery footwork
- Overstep outside foot
- Position body to cover
- the court

Contact point

Teaching the Forehand with the Key Positions

In teaching the forehand to intermediate or advanced players, the key positions are an excellent guideline in building the stroke. The progression from ready position to recovery makes you go from start to finish of the stroke without skipping any steps. Individually, you can analyze the stroke and focus more on the problem areas. Introduce the whole stroke first and show what it is supposed to look like before getting into specifics. If the student has had some coaching elsewhere, analyze the stroke first and find out what they have covered so far.

Follow through

Martin van Daalen

Closed Stance (Del Potro)

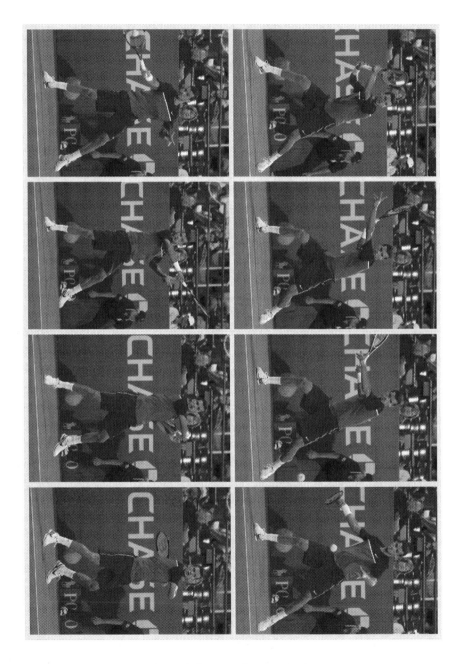

Open Stance (Dimitrov)

Key Positions of the One-Handed Backhand

Ready position

- Athletic posture
- Hands relaxed
- Knees slightly bent
- Split step
- Alert disposition

Backswing

- Rotate shoulder with racket
- Rotate hips outside
- Turn toes outside
- Swing racket back

Backswing

Loading

- Bend knees further
- Turn hips
- Turn shoulders
- Extend both arms
- Balance arm to side

Forward swing

- Unload legs
- Unload hips
- Unload shoulders
- Trace oncoming ball
- Line up racket path

Forward swing

Contact point

- Hand in front
- Stability in wrist
- Weight transfer
- Hitting zone

Follow-through

- Arm forward and around
- Skip foot around
- Full turn of the hips
- Full turn of the shoulders

Recovery

- Recovery footwork
- Overstep outside foot
- Position body to cover the court

Contact point

Teaching the Backhand with Key Positions

Using the key positions to learn the one-handed backhand will simplify the progression of teaching and organization of your lessons. There are some differences with one- and two-handed backhands in grips, backswings, contact points, and follow-through. And when you are organized as a coach, your students will be organized as well. For beginning players, you want to make sure they are fully aware how to perform the stroke. These are excellent topics for group lessons as they can learn from each other's errors. In a group, you don't feel singled out or that you are the only one having trouble with the stroke. But you can also learn from the good examples from other students and try to copy

Recovery

them. In a group, the students always will try to compete with each other in performance. The backhand has very simple mechanics in comparison to other strokes, and you should convey that message to your students.

One-handed Backhand (Wawrinka)

Key Positions of the Two-Handed Backhand

Ready position

- Athletic posture
- Hands relaxed
- Knees slightly bent
- Split step
- Alert disposition

Backswing

- Rotate shoulder with racket
- Rotate hips outside
- Turn toes outside
- Swing racket back

Backswing

Loading

- Bend knees further
- Turn hips
- Turn shoulders
- Extend both arms
- Balance arm to side

Forward swing

- Unload legs
- Unload hips
- Unload shoulders
- Trace oncoming ball
- Line up racket path

Forward Swing

Contact point

- Hand in front
- Stability in wrist
- Weight transfer
- Hitting zone

Follow-through

- Arms forward and around
- Skip foot around
- Full turn of the hips
- Full turn of the shoulders

Contact Point

Recovery

- Recovery footwork
- Overstep outside foot
- Position the body to cover the court

Teaching the Backhand with Key Positions

Using the key positions to teach the two-handed backhand will simplify the progression of teaching and organize the structure of your lessons. The are some differences with the one-handed backhand in teaching the key position. You can start teaching the stroke in the backswing position to simplify the execution. By "freezing" the follow-through position you can make it clear where to finish the swing. In a group the students always will try to compete with each other in performance. The two-handed backhand has very simple mechanics in comparison to other strokes.

Recovery

Closed Stance (Djokovic)

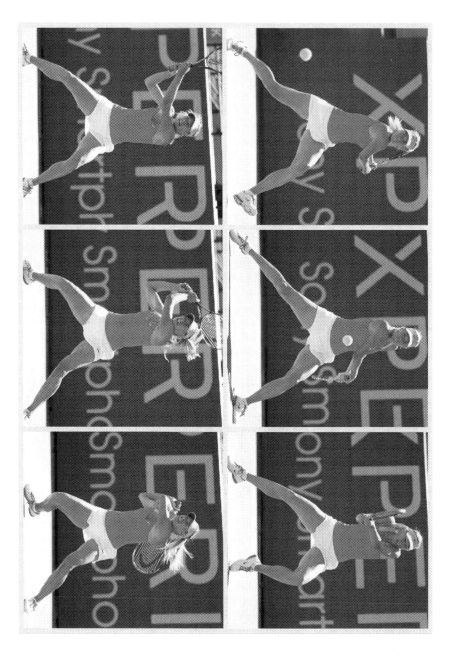

Open Stance (Sharapova)

Progressions from Intermediate to Advanced Baseline Play

After the students show proficiency with their consistency and footwork, it is possible to introduce some specialty strokes for advanced players. The topspin and slice strokes become more prevalent in controlling the ball with more pace and tempo. In order to do this well, it is necessary to follow a methodology or learning sequence. This will ensure a higher level of success to more difficult subjects and learning at a faster rate. Teaching these strokes too early can hinder the development of the players when they are physically and mentally not ready for this change. Their footwork and strength has to be sufficient before you decide to introduce the specialty strokes. Mentally, the players also have to be ready to try some of these strokes themselves and show a passion for the game. In teaching specialty strokes, it is important to follow some guidelines:

Teach for success. Players will succeed when they are properly challenged but not overwhelmed. When a coach is able to keep players motivated and victorious, they will feel accomplished. It will increase confidence and improvements, and success will quickly follow. Having the proper timing to introduce the new topics is the art of coaching. The introduction of specialty strokes for development of advanced players is totally dependent on the skill level of the players and the experience level of the coach. (For example, don't teach a kick serve to a junior that is not physically ready to execute this stroke.) As a coach or parent, we have to be patient not to rush the development. Choosing the proper time to introduce new subject is the key to success and development.

Make it skill based. The level of learning is different for each player with students learning at their own pace. Some players develop early but slow down in their development, whereas others start slowly but accelerate at a later stage. Keep the students with the same skill level together to stimulate each other. Also, don't be afraid to mix it up; move students up or down in skill level so they can learn to play against other levels. Make sure that the new topics are skill based to their technical, tactical, physical, and mental development. The players will be much more confident and successful when the new topics are in their competence level and tactical understanding. Moving too fast through the progressions or jumping over important topics in the sequence of learning will often cause frustration and setbacks.

Follow a progression. Having a proper progression is the most important factor in teaching advanced tennis techniques. Making sure you start easy, practice the skill extensively and master it before you move on to the next progression of the stroke. This method will provide the player sufficient time to explore the different problems with this skill and give them time to experiment and automate the stroke before introducing the next progression or skill. A good progression would be the topics listed in the following pages from consistency to tempo. Be patient and keep in mind that it takes many years to master the specialty strokes from intermediate to advanced level of play.

How to Dominate with Your Forehand

The forehand is one of the strokes you can use to dominate your opponent. It can be developed as a very strong weapon to attack or hit winners from any corner of the court. There are some very good examples of dominant forehands on the pro tour, with Rafael Nadal (see picture) being the most prominent. He has not only speed and spin in the stroke production but also possesses the quickness in the legs to run around his backhand and set up on time to hit the ball with purpose. Without this forehand, it would be very

Nadal

difficult for him to dominate his opponents like he does. Running around the backhand gives you many advantages in opening the court, applying pressure, hitting winners, and camouflaging the strokes to wrong-foot your opponent.

Six Steps to Develop a Dominant Forehand:

1. **Consistency**
   Before you can develop any weapon, you have to obtain consistency in this particular stroke. No stroke can be called a weapon if you cannot rely on the execution. You have to train the forehand by practicing longer rallies and testing your skills under pressure in point play. You can start by improving the accuracy of your forehand in cross-court, long-line, and inside-out drills. Try to only use your forehand even though the ball goes in the direction of the backhand. This will train your ability to read the trajectory and react accordingly. After you are satisfied that the consistency has improved, you can introduce drills to change direction to better your footwork.

2. **Footwork**
   In order to cover both sides of the court with your forehand, you have to be quick and agile. It takes great footwork to run around your backhand and set up your feet to step in and strike the ball on time and still cover the open court with a running forehand when necessary. You can do this with on-court drills and off-court footwork training. The on-court drills can include feeding drills and life-ball situations. By feeding the ball to both corners, players can get adjusted to running around the backhand and hitting running forehands and developing a rhythm with the footwork. Life-ball situations are best executed with two-on-one drills using only your forehand. By playing to different targets (two players), you can practice your footwork speed and setup in combination with the accuracy of your strokes. Off-court physical training should be a

combination of weight training, speed training, movement training, and plyometrics to enhance your footwork and agility.

3. **Train runaround shots and running forehands**

   You should only run around your backhand to use your forehand when you are able to hit a running forehand. By running around the backhand, it will leave the forehand side wide open for the opponent to strike, and most likely they will take advantage of this. The more confidence you acquire in covering the court with your running forehand, the easier it becomes to use your runaround forehand. Once you master both shots comfortably, you will have less fear of running around the backhand and leaving the court open. You might even choose to position yourself slightly on the backhand side to use your forehand more often.

4. **Power and spin**

   The speed and spin of the ball play a large role in developing your forehand. The racket head speed creates both speed and spin of the ball. The racket angle at impact with the ball and the swing angle through impact determine the speed, spin, and the trajectory of the ball. These can all be applied to outmaneuver the opponent. The speed of a ball can beat the opponent's running speed in many situations whereas the spin can create a "heavy ball" or an angle shot to pull your opponent out of position. The trajectory of the ball is important to speed up or slow down the pace and/or play outside the strike zone and comfort level of the opponent.

5. **Strategy**

   By running around the backhand, you are able to use the power of your forehand to the weaker side of the opponent, to open up the angles of the court, and to keep the opponent off balance and on the run at all times. Keeping your opponent off balance and on the run makes them hit shots with very little or no time to set up with their feet. This will cause them to play defensive and make more unforced errors. Knowing the strengths and weaknesses of your opponent will assist you in your strategy and the timing of your attack. It will make you the dominant player on the court.

6. **Camouflage**

   As you become more proficient in the execution of your strokes, footwork, and strategy, it is possible to camouflage your intent. By setting up the same way, as if you are hitting the ball inside out, it is still very easy to change direction and hit the ball down the line (inside in). Your opponent will have a hard time "reading" your intent. The longer you are able to hold your position, just before the strike, the more you can hide your intent and camouflage your shots. It will increase your effectiveness of your forehand even more.

Following these six steps in progression will develop your forehand into a powerful and dominant weapon for your future game. Best of luck!

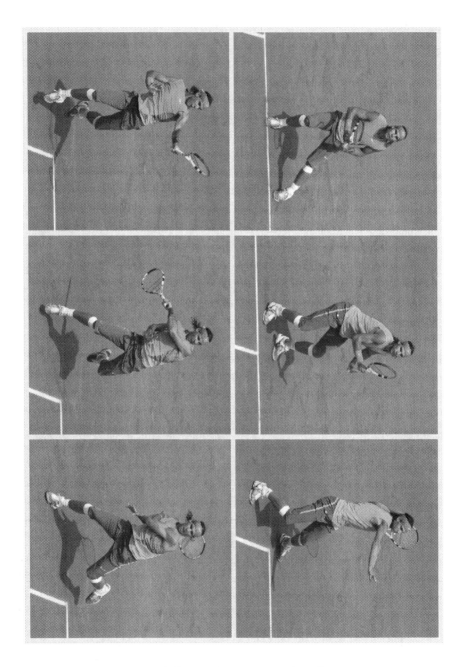

Nadal (Inside-Out Forehand)

Martin van Daalen

Consistency of Baseline Strokes

The reliability and consistency of tennis strokes is one of the basic requirements to becoming a better tennis player. Without consistency, a player will not be able to construct many rallies and will often be on the losing end in matches. Reliability of the strokes will give players more possibilities to play the game with enjoyment and confidence. Therefore, it makes perfect sense to master the strokes with consistency before trying to hit the ball with too much power and spin. To become a consistent tennis player, you have to practice and master certain components of the technique in combination with the tactical, physical, and mental skills. All four components have to work together in order to make improvements. In the past years, it shows clearly how endurance, focus, and strategy have improved to enhance consistency. Think of the match between Djokovic and Nadal in Australia that lasted almost five hours. Or the match at Wimbledon with Isner and Mahut that was played over three days. As players progress, they will experience a positive feedback from enhancements they make in the individual components. This positive feedback leads to what we generally know as confidence and is extremely important for improvements of any stroke. Especially when playing under pressure, the confidence drives the player to hit the stroke with commitment and determination with less chances of technical breakdown during execution. Let's have a look at all the components that influence the consistency of the strokes.

**Djokovic beats Nadal in a five hour match
Australian Open Final 2011**

Martin van Daalen

Technical Components

The technical components will help you execute each stroke with uniformity that promotes muscle memory. This becomes important, after much practice, in order to hit the ball with an automated motion. Automated motions are more consistent and break down less under pressure. To practice the technical components, you have to pay attention to the following points:

1. *Early preparation of footwork and racket*
2. *Correct and consistent contact points of the stroke*
3. *Good timing of the stroke with different speeds, spin, and trajectories*
4. *Proper and complete follow-through*
5. *Good balance before, during, and after the stroke (recovery)*

The best way to practice these technical aspects is to train them first individually. As soon as they are mastered separately, you can try to put them all together in a combined drill or pattern.

Physical Components

The physical skills of a player can greatly enhance the performance with consistency. To play longer rallies, you need endurance, improved coordination and timing, balance, and more power to track down the balls in the corner and to perform with efficiency. The technology of rackets and strings has been much improved and makes it possible to hit harder and still keep the ball in the court.

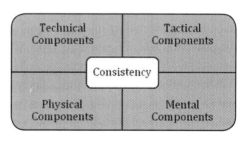

Consistency is not just a technical issue, but is also constructed by all four components. See the influence and relationship of all aspects

So players need to move much quicker to reach these balls for better consistency. You have to practice the physical components of consistency by spending time in training the following aspects:

1. *Practice coordination by hitting with less power and producing smooth strokes*
2. *Improve the balance before, during, and after the stroke with recovery footwork and returning to a tactical positioning on the court*
3. *Improve efficiency of the strokes with a weight-training program*
4. *Improve endurance of consistency by practicing long rallies and a running program*

Tactical Components

Making the proper shot choices and choosing the proper strategy can improve the consistency as well. The shot choice will depend on the positions of each player on the court and the possible shots available to each player. It will determine if a player is able to play a defensive, neutral, or offensive shot. The basic strategy of each player can assist in improving the consistency when the strengths and weaknesses of the opponent are exploited to your advantage. To improve consistency in a tactical way, target choices have to be chosen wisely with a larger margin for error. Good shot choices improve the possibilities of reaching the next ball by understanding the shot choices of the opponent and the angles available to them. To practice the tactical aspects of consistency, use these methods:

1. *Place targets areas on the court to practice a larger margin for error*
2. *Play with a higher net to improve consistency with spin and trajectory*
3. *Practice offensive and defensive patterns and improve consistency in both*
4. *Practice the use of different shot choices to enhance ball control*
5. *Practice different styles of play to enhance skill levels*
6. *Practice different strategies and tactics to improve focus and discipline*

Martin van Daalen

Mental Components

The mental aspects are of great influence to the consistency and quality of the execution. It takes excellent focus and composure to make continuous adjustments to footwork, strokes, and strategy. The footwork and setup of the stance needs to be very accurate to perform the strokes with control. Once the strokes begin to improve in quality, there is a mental feedback that we call confidence. It is this feeling of accomplishment that instills passion and pushes players to excel even further. To practice the mental aspects of consistency, try the following:

1. *Improve focus and concentration by playing different games and scores.*
2. *Improve mental toughness by playing up or down in score.*
3. *Practice the mental endurance by playing more sets and matches in one day.*
4. *Get positive feedback for your confidence by keeping track of your improvements.*

As you can see, becoming a consistent tennis player entails a lot more than just hitting the ball more often over the net. Playing under different circumstances and pressure is the key to mental improvements. Practice components separately for optimum results in consistency. When mastering this skill, you will experience the joy of accomplishment every time you win long rallies.

Directional Consistency

In order to control the ball and the rally, it is necessary to direct the ball in every instance to a chosen target. This can be in the same direction as the oncoming ball, but it can also be a change of direction. Changes of direction require more skills due to the different angles and corrections needed. There are four different types of rallies to consider in training consistency of direction:

1. Consistency in the middle of the court
2. Consistency in hitting cross-court
3. Consistency in hitting down the line
4. Consistency in changing directions to different targets

All four options have their own individual purpose during match play. Coaches and players need to be aware to train as many different situations possible. This will make it very clear what direction poses the most trouble in executing.

1. **Consistency in the Middle of the Court**
   This is usually the method players use to warm up for practice and for singles matches. However, for doubles competition, it makes more sense to warm up in cross-court. The amount of times the ball goes back and forth indicates the skill level of the player. Advanced players should have no problem performing this task with each rally lasting twenty hits or more. Coaches need to explain the value of consistency through the middle in neutralizing the opponent when in trouble. We call this "the Center Tactic." Returning the ball deep through the middle (preferably to the weaker side of the opponent) is a high-percentage shot and the largest possible target with the smallest angle of attack for the opponent. (See also "Direction.")

Most Common Mistakes

   a. Not moving the body out of the way of the path of the oncoming ball
   b. Not stepping forward toward the ball and using the weight transfer

Corrections and practice

a. This is often the case when the ball is coming straight at a player. This vision angle limits the depth perception of any player and makes it more complicated to judge the speed, spin, and trajectory of the oncoming ball to coordinate all the movements and timing of the ball. This can be corrected by stepping out of the line of the oncoming ball to enhance the depth perception and timing. You can practice this by alternating forehand and backhand strokes up the middle of the court. This drill is great for footwork and movement in general and will enhance the consistency in rallies in point and match play with shots through the middle of the court.

b. When stepping out of the line of the oncoming ball, players often step backward or refrain from stepping into the ball. They lose control of the ball due to a loss of balance and weight transfer. You can correct this error by making sure students step slightly forward with one foot, just before making contact with the ball. By using cones in a V shape behind the student, you can limit any backward movement and stimulate the balance, weight transfer, and commitment to the strokes.

2. **Consistency in Hitting Cross-Court**

These strokes are the most used in rally exchanges. When practicing these strokes, it is imperative for players to recover after each shot, close to the middle of the court. Without this movement, there is little difference with practicing through the middle of the court. Cross-court strokes provide high-percentage shots in point play and can be used as a safe selection under pressure. They provide a large margin for errors as long as players don't play too close to the sidelines. That way they will not open the court with angles or create unforced errors. Players should practice these often to improve consistency and comfort levels of movement.

Most Common Mistakes in Practicing Cross-Court

a.   Not cutting off the angle of the oncoming ball
b.   Improper setup of the feet and backswing
c.   Hitting too much cross-court with ever-increasing angles
d.   Not using all cross-court targets available

Corrections and practice

a.   The basic cross-court drill is to
have two targets 1–2 yards from
the sidelines and have both
players recover back close to the
middle of the court. You can also
set up cones behind the player in
a V shape. This forces the player
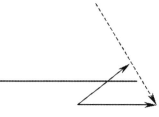
to cut off the angle and move forward diagonally in order to
square off the shoulders in the hitting direction of the ball. (See
pictures.)

b.   Hitting cross-court from the
middle of the court requires a
different setup than in the corners
of the court. In the middle of the
court, players will often use a
neutral or semiopen stance, and
the backswing is easy to adjust
for the directions. For the corner

shots, the players often use open stances or slide up to the ball
(clay). This is to rotate open more easily around the outside of
the ball. The backswing should be adjusted to the cross-court
direction. Practicing cross-court and recovering to the middle
will train this type of footwork and backswing.

c. Another drill involves hitting two target areas in the cross-court, two feet from the sideline, and the middle of the court. The player alternates both targets, and you can follow their accuracy closely. Both players will have lots of movement and recovery footwork. This drill can be executed for the forehand and backhand side, as well as for the inside-out forehands.

d. One of the best drills for cross-court practice is alternating shots from forehand and backhand. This enhances the movement and preparation in anticipation of the next shot from the opponent. With the target area being relatively small, the players have to hit the ball very accurately. With all the types of shots and movement involved, it makes for an all-inclusive drill and competition in point play.

3. **Consistency in Hitting Down the Line**

This stroke is usually hit as a change of direction from a cross-court shot. It is also used by advanced players to "wrong-foot" the opponent by hitting the ball behind them back up the line. In practicing the down-the-line strokes, most players are not aware of the importance of 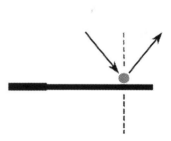 accuracy. With the target area being much smaller, unforced errors are common. The problem of execution lies mostly in nonspecific practices without the use of movement. Players will practice down the line by hitting balls to each other on one side of the court. This will not be realistic with the oncoming ball angle being straight in the racket versus from an angle. Make sure to practice these strokes specifically in a pattern and sequence of shots to mimic the life-point situation.

Common Mistakes with Consistency down the Line

a. Aiming too close to the sideline
b. Improper shot choices and positioning
c. Height over the net
d. Not adjusting the spin
e. Recovering too soon before finishing the stroke

Corrections and practice

a. In changing direction down the line, players often will aim too close to the sideline. Set up targets at least one yard from the sideline. It is also possible to use two balls to show the target area (balls at one and two yards from the sideline). Another possibility is to use tape on a hard court at one yard from the sideline. Players have to practice to play inside these lines.

b. The court positions, ball trajectory, and depth are important factors to consider when hitting down the line. A good rule of thumb is to only go "long line" when players are still within the sideline and close to the baseline. Make sure to use this direction change with easier bouncing balls. You can practice this by playing a cross-court rally and having one's side choose when to go down the line and play out the point.

c. Playing too close to the net will create unforced errors with the net being higher at the sides. Shaping the shot with height and spin is important to increase consistency.

d. The distance down the line is a shorter trajectory than cross-court shots. This should be taken into consideration when playing long line. Using topspin will bring the ball up, over the net, and down again within the baseline. You can practice this with one player hitting the ball cross-court and down the line. The other stays on one side for control. This will force them to adjust the height over the net and add topspin.

Martin van Daalen

e. When recovering to the middle of the court, it is imperative to maintain the balance after the stroke for control and consistency. In covering the court, students will often start leaning to the inside of the court before the stroke is fully completed. This will cause the arm and racket to pull away from the trajectory of the ball. On clay courts, this can also result in less pressure on the sole of the shoe with the outer foot slipping away. You can teach players to apply pressure on this foot by skipping on the outer foot and then stopping to maintain balance.

4. **Consistency in Changing Direction to Different Targets**
    This is the most difficult skill to master and requires great footwork, experience, and good timing. The angle difference between the targets is quite small and demands great accuracy. Advanced players need to practice this skill on a daily basis to keep up the timing and coordination in order to play with control and consistency.

Common Mistakes

a. Bad or late preparation
b. Inconsistent or lazy footwork.
c. Anxiety buildup in long rallies
d. Squeezing the grip or muscling the stroke

Corrections and practice

a. The early preparation of backswing and footwork provides a player rhythm and calmness in their stroke production. With bad or late preparation, a player feels rushed, and shot choices will be affected. The strokes also have a tendency to be forced and less smooth in motion and release and affect control and consistency.
b. It requires constant energy and focus to make footwork adjustments to movement and stances to find the proper contact points and

stroke production. You can practice this by having three or four targets on the court and calling them off by number for execution. By providing increasingly less time before the strike, it is possible to increase the movement, focus, and flexibility of the player to make quicker adjustments to targets and increase consistency in point play. (You can practice this by feeding the ball or with live ball situations.)

c. With longer rallies, there is more the anxiety buildup to win the point. This effect will be magnified in hitting to several different targets. The anxiety can be reduced by increasing the consistency in general and by practicing certain patterns of play. Students will often dislike working on their consistency, especially if they are not good at it! Practicing long exchanges with targets, patterns, and point play will only increase the enjoyment level and confidence of the student in the long run.

d. Playing to various targets demands a high-skill level of the player. The confidence and experience of each player will determine the level of anxiety during play. With less confidence, players usually grip the racket tighter, resulting in a loss of "feel for the ball" through coordination, timing, and release of the racket head. This buildup of anxiety can be controlled through practice and increasing the pressure in point play. After a while, students will become less affected by the stress of the situation and perform better with consistency to multiple targets.

Depth of Baseline Strokes

After consistency, depth is the next subject in the technical progression of learning. Playing deeper in the court has several advantages:

1. The player has more time to get ready for the next ball, as the distance increases between both players.

2. The opponent has less angle of attack, as the angles become smaller with more depth in pushing the opponent farther behind the baseline.
3. The possibilities of shorter returns of the opponent become an opportunity to apply pressure.

The depth of the ball is determined by three factors:

1. **The speed of the ball**
2. **The elevation of the ball**
3. **The spin of the ball**

The speed of the ball is determined by how hard the ball is struck with the force of the racket. The length of the backswing, the power applied to the stroke, the amount of spin applied, and the speed of the follow-through are some of the main factors to increase or decrease the speed of the ball.

The elevation of the ball has two different factors that play a role to direct the initial angle of the ball flight: (1) the first is the racket angle at contact and (2) the second is the swing angle of the racket through

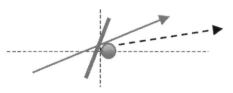

contact with the ball. As you can see in the next picture, the swing angle and racket angle (side view) can be different from the ball angle.

With a topspin forehand, the swing angle (see solid arrow) starts from below the ball and finishes higher over the ball. With the racket angle slightly closed, the ball flight will be directed somewhat lower (see dotted arrow) than the swing angle.

The spin of the ball is created by the force and friction of the stroke and strings as they make contact with the cover of the ball. The factors involved in rotation of the ball are as follows:

- The speed of the racket head
- The racket angle at contact
- The swing angle through contact

Depth and Angles

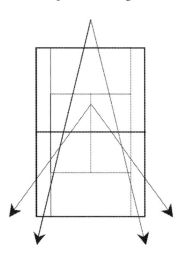

As the racket head speed increases, so will the amount of spin through the friction of the strings with the ball. The angle of the racket head at contact and the swing angle have to be coordinated to create the most optimal friction with the ball. There is a tipping point where racket angle and swing angle become too extreme and where the friction to the ball is not efficient anymore. The same will happen when players cover the ball too much on the follow-through of the stroke with the ball losing its "heavy" bounce and becoming less effective with spin. Here are some examples of adjustments that can be made by players when using the different speeds, elevation, and rotations of the ball.

Examples:

- A harder struck ball has less elevation with less spin added.
- A higher elevation over the net has more spin and less speed.
- With more spin, the elevation and speed is increased to reach the target.

Advanced players need to experiment and learn to mix these three factors to reach the same target area. It takes a lot of repetition and practice to gain experience in order to execute these strokes in pressure situations.

There are two types of depth to consider:

A – Average depth in the court

B – Change of depth (short-long)

This "average depth" is the general depth the player uses to apply pressure on the opponent. The opponent will be pushed farther back behind the baseline or forced to hit lower-percentage shots by taking the ball on the rise.

D. The "change of depth" is adjustment of the depth with a tactical purpose. Playing the ball shorter in the court creates angles to play behind the opponent and make them reach for the ball. This strategy requires more advanced technical skills.

Common Mistakes with Depth

a. Don't use speed alone to hit the ball deeper.
b. Not being able to vary the depth of the strokes.

Corrections and practice

a. The most simple way for players to comprehend this topic is to raise the net higher. This can be done with several devices available at tennis supply shops online or by simply using the single stick under the middle of the net. It also teaches the player to hit the ball slightly higher over the net when playing cross-court with the net now being higher at that point. Have the players also play points with the net height raised. It is also possible hitting through two lines over the net, as if hitting through a window (see picture A below). The same can be practiced with the use of target fields or target areas (see picture B below).

Picture A

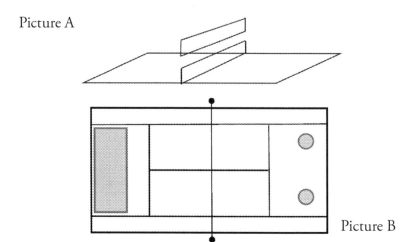

Picture B

b. The change of depth is one of the more difficult subjects to learn, even for advanced players. Not necessarily for practice, but more so in match play, with the proper and timely shot choices and execution. It is easy for students to get carried away with this concept in trying continually to outangle the opponent instead of trying to use it to draw the opponent inside the court and hit behind them to force a defensive position. This can best be practiced by first alternating the depth in the cross-court strokes. You can start off with trajectories in the service box and behind the service box. After observing a good execution, it is possible to try this on the whole court. (See picture.)

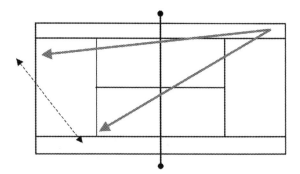

Martin van Daalen

Direction or Change of Direction

It takes great accuracy to hit the targets in a certain directions and subsequently apply pressure on the opponent. It takes even more skill as the speed and tempo increases. With less time available to make corrections, the swing speed, swing angle, racket angle, and the timing of the ball become more critical. Here are some factors that can play a role in the direction of the ball:

1. Footwork and racket preparation
2. Contact points and hitting zone
3. Weight transfer
4. Balance of the body before, during, and after the stroke
5. Follow-through and recovery

The footwork and racket preparation influence the stance and setup to hit the ball in a balanced position to control the ball. The footwork needs to be well organized to prepare and position behind the ball, to transfer the weight in the hitting direction. The racket preparation needs to be timely and simple, with the setup in the direction of the target. Unnecessary or elaborate motions in the backswings lead to inconsistent swing paths and, consequently, inaccurate directions.

The contact points and hitting zone have the most influence on direction. The timing of the contact points and the swing path and angle of the strings through the hitting zone will determine the direction of the ball. The hitting zone is the area just before and after the contact point where the racket angle stabilizes in one direction. This hitting zone can be lengthened by footwork setup, hip and shoulder rotation toward the ball, and the lengthening of the follow-through. The more you are able to lengthen this hitting zone area, the better the results of direction will be.

The **weight transfer** applies pressure of the body by stepping in or by leaning forward. This pressure helps to steer the ball and increase the speed and spin. It can also enhance the balance of the body before, during, and after contact, to increase ball control. In some cases, there is very little or no weight transfer possible when players are put in extreme positions in moving sideways or even backward. These are defensive positions that limit weight transfer and require great footwork and balance for stroke production.

The **balance of the body before, during, and after the stroke** has an impact on the stability of the stroke during impact with the ball. With off-balance strokes, the body will involuntarily try to correct this falling or pulling effect that change the swing path and the ball flight. You will be able to notice this in sudden movements during the stroke and/or pulling of the shot. Most often they will have a much different follow-through and recovery motion than usual. This inconsistency in motion and footwork will cause inconsistent directions of the ball and unforced errors.

The **follow-through and recovery** assists the steering of the ball in the proper direction. The follow-through can lengthen the hitting zone and increase the control of the ball. The recovery footwork facilitates the rotating of the hips and shoulders to lengthen the follow-through. In unexpected circumstances (like a bad bounce of the ball), the follow-through and the recovery footwork become factors to rescue a stroke: (1) the follow-through in making directional adjustments and adding spin and (2) the footwork in making quick directional adjustments to restore the balance and assist the follow-through.

Common Mistakes with Direction

    a. Inconsistent contact points with the ball
    b. Not squaring of the shoulders at contact
    c. Not following through consistently

Corrections and practice

a. *The correct impact point* is imperative to hit a straight shot in the chosen direction. Contacting the ball too early or too late will make the strings of the racket steer the ball in a different direction. Finding the proper contact point is an ongoing quest every time you are playing tennis. A good method is to have the player count "1" when the ball hits the ground in front of them and "2" when they are striking the ball. This rhythm method will assist players in creating consistent contact points. There are several technical aspects to help students find the correct contact points:

- *Proper foot stance and timely stroke preparation* help the player with rotating the hips and shoulders to square off the racket in the hitting zone.
- *The shoulder position at impact* with the ball is a physical memory point for the player and will assist in extending the racket through the hitting zone.
- *The impact point in relation to the body* is a reference point for the player with the timing of the contact point and the coordination of the swing.
- *The timing and rhythm* assist the player to hit the ball at a consistent point that is learned by experience and memory.
- *The follow-through* is instrumental in assisting the player to steer the ball by extending the hitting zone. It also is helpful in making adjustments in direction.

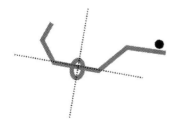 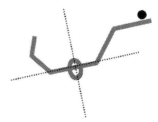

b. *The hitting zone* is the area, from the stroke, just before the contact point till just after the contact point. The length of this area can be manipulated by the turn of the shoulders through impact. Many players have trouble with lengthening this area due to the angle of the shoulders at impact with the ball. Look at the difference of the two pictures below. In the picture on the left, you can see how the player is able to lengthen the contact zone by squaring off the shoulders at contact. On the right, you can observe how the contact zone is shortened by not squaring off the shoulders at contact with the ball. The follow-through will come around the body much sooner. The grip can also be a factor in squaring the shoulders at impact with the ball. (See figures below.)

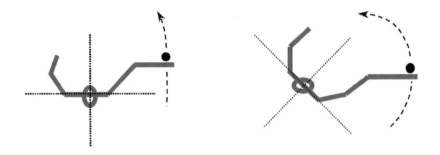

Note: The hitting zone is much more circular with a different angle of the shoulders. The arm will wrap around the body after impact with the ball.

c. The finish of the stroke, or follow-through, can be a very valuable tool in correcting many errors. Even though the direction is mainly constructed with the contact point, the follow-through can assist with further corrections. Each player will learn by experience to make minor corrections with adjustments of the racket head speed and angel, to correct the trajectory of the ball.

Note: Sudden corrections to contact and swing path are more easily made with a higher racket-head speed!

Change of Direction

Returning the ball back in the same direction is the high-percentage shot choice. There is no angle deviation from the oncoming ball and the returning ball direction. With change of direction, the angle of the oncoming ball deviates from the outgoing angle. With slower speeds of the ball, the incoming and outgoing angle will be almost the same. As the player increases the racket-head speed, the outgoing ball angle will take over the direction of the racket angle. This change of direction takes some experience in learning the skill of adjusting the direction of the racket head. This skill is even more important when hitting shots down the line. (See consistency of hitting down the line.)

Common Mistakes with Change of Direction

a. Not setting up the feet behind the direction of the ball
b. Shot choice and timing when to go down the line
c. Correcting too much with the hands and follow-through

Corrections

a. The proper foot stance before the strike of the ball will enhance the balance and weight transfer during contact and therefore influence the accuracy of the stroke. If the players are hitting shots on the run instead of setting up the feet before contact, they will be less accurate with the direction since less weight transfer and follow-through is possible in the direction of the ball. Teaching players to move quicker off the mark with good split steps, covering the distance to the ball with greater speed and setting up faster behind the ball with the correct stance for maximum weight transfer, will increase the accuracy in fast rallies and change of direction.
b. Accuracy and consistency in direction will improve greatly if players know when to change direction with the appropriate shot

choice. They should learn to only change direction when they are in balance and control versus being under severe pressure and feeling off balance. The shot choice (target, trajectory, speed, and spin) will enhance the consistency and accuracy of the strokes and point play when players stay within their own technical and physical capabilities. The targets don't need to be so close to the line. This seems to be one of the more difficult things to learn, and you could see many players making this mistake. Learning to play to big targets (1–2 yards from the sideline) is an indication that players understand the strategy and margins for errors to play consistently.

c. If the proper foot stance has been achieved, it is possible to swing more freely with fewer corrections of the hands and swing path of the follow-through. In learning to change direction, players tend to use their hands and follow-through more instead of relying on the contact point and racket angle. This often leads to squeezing the grip and forcing the ball. The racket head does not release naturally and can have an effect on the timing of the ball. It also stiffens the arm that can cause under and overcorrections, with less accuracy when changing direction.

Practice

- The direction of the ball can be practiced in several different ways. Start by using big targets and then moving to smaller targets as the skill levels improve. By using one-half of the court, you can hit to half sections of the court. Most often it helps the player to use a target or target area on the court (cone or small mat). It stimulates the focus and creates a goal to hit the targets as many times as possible. This is also a good time to make technical corrections and to show how they influence the outcome and results.

- Playing inside a line setup down the line makes the players aware of the margin of error they need to keep with the lines.

- In changing directions, there are some very useful drills for advanced players in combination with training the footwork recovery. The drill on the right (see picture) illustrates the change of direction in a two-on-one drill. This drill is also very suitable with one-on-one practice. The coach can take position next to the player and feed the balls in play if they miss. This way, the rally is extended and they learn to refocus quickly on the 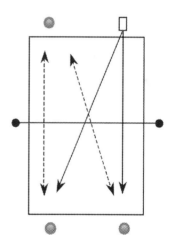 next ball. Recovery to the middle of the court helps with timing of the strokes and training of the footwork. Stimulating to aim at "big targets" helps consistency in executing the drill and promotes the players to hit freely instead of playing tight and squeezing too much.

- There are many different patterns possible here: (1) two balls cross-court and two balls down the line, (2) two balls cross and one down the line, (3) one ball cross and two balls down the line, and (4) one ball to each target. You only have to think of match situations to make up your own patterns of drills with either two or three players.

- Another excellent drill is to have one side of the court play on one-half of the court and the other player play across the whole court. The player on one half uses only the forehand stroke and alternates directions left and right. The other player has to direct the ball to the outside of the court and to the middle of the court. The player on the one-half has to run around and position in time to play the other shot. This drill takes a lot of fine control in directing the ball. (See picture above.)

- Playing the down-the-line pattern with points is important to control the strokes and footwork under pressure. After exchanging two shots cross-court, players have to find the correct situation to go down the line and play out the point from there. This open-ended method teaches players to get comfortable with their strokes, footwork, targets, shot choices, and anticipation of the next shot.

Spin Baseline Strokes

Applying rotation to the ball requires more racket-head acceleration to create friction from the strings to the ball. Advanced players are able to adjust the amount of rotation to control the trajectory or ball flight. There are many types of rotation possible. The main types of spin are as follows:

1. Topspin
2. Slice
3. Sidespin
4. Combinations of rotations

Rotation of the ball should be introduced when player starts hitting too many balls over the baseline due to increased racket-head speed and power.

The Effects of Rotation to the Ball

The rotation of the ball builds up air pressure through the hairs on the cover. The pressure builds up on the side of the ball that is rotating forward and increases with the amount of rotation. With more forward speed, the spin will have less eaffect on the ball flight. As the ball speed diminishes, the oscillating eaffect (deforming of the ball from the spin and the strike) diminishes, and the spin will take more eaffect. Advanced players not only use the spin to control the ball flight, but also use it to apply pressure on the opponent with acceleration and bounce of the ball (think topspin or slice).

Topspin Shots

These shots have a forward rotation to the ball. The air pressure builds up on the top and front side of the ball and pushes the ball downward. Players learn through trial and error to combine the proper amount of topspin and elevation to the ball to reach a target. The topspin can be used in various shots: offensive and defensive baseline strokes, topspin lob, service, short- angle shots, and returns. When the ball bounces on the ground, the forward rotation accelerates the ball forward and up-wards ("hHeavy ball"). Topspin can be used for different strategic purposes:

1. Offensive (acceleration, angle shots, approach shots, aggressive topspin)
2. Defensive (height, depth, slowing bouncing balls)
3. Neutralizing (aggressive bouncing balls through the middle of the court)

Slice Shots

These shots have a reverse rotation of the ball. The air pressure builds up on the bottom and front side of the ball to push the ball upward. The ball seems to have a "floating" eaffect in the air as it moves to the other side. As the speed on the ball decreases, the ball will start descending, but still maintains a more linear trajectory due to the rotation. As the ball makes contact with the ground, the slice rotation causes the ball to stay lower after the bounce. Low-speed slice shots will slow down after the bounce and "sit up.". High-speed slice shots will skid off the surface and actually speed up after the bounce. The impact angle of the ball will determine if the ball skids or bounces up. With a lower-impact angle (low over the net), the ball will skid and stay low after the bounce.

Slice shots can be used for different strategic purposes:

1. Offensive (approach shot, drop shot)
2. Defensive (defensive lob, slower deep slice)
3. Neutralizing (slice through middle)

Sidespin

These shots are not common with ground strokes and are mostly executed with the service action. With ground strokes, the sidespin can be used with running forehand and backhand strokes, short-angle passing shots, and with low-bouncing balls with the approach to the net. When applying sidespin, the ball is struck out in front of the body, from inward to outward, past the outside cover of the ball. The follow-through can vary according to how much sidespin is added and how low the ball is struck. When struck in front, the follow-through can still finish around the body. When struck at the side of the body, the follow-through will often have a reverse finish on the same side of the body where the ball was struck. The running ground strokes and passing shots need some sidespin to redirect the ball flight back into the court.

Rotations Combinations

These combinations of rotations are topspin and sidespin and slice with sidespin. Most low-bouncing balls will have a combination of sidespin rotations with either topspin or slice. When the ball bounces really low, it makes it virtually impossible to fully get the racket behind and under the ball. Adjustments can be made by either using topspin and sidespin or slice and sidespin to control the ball flight. Whenever attempting this combination of rotations, the player has to adjust the direction of the ball more away from the lines to adjust for the curve of the ball.

Common Mistakes with Adding Rotation (Spin)

a. Grips are not adjusted well for the rotation needed
b. Dropping the racket too early in the backswing before the start of the swing
c. Hitting the ball late (timing and/or contact point)
d. Aiming too low with topspin and/or too high with slice
e. Decelerating the racket head after contact (follow-through)

Corrections

a. Sometimes the grips need to be corrected or adjusted to hit better topspin. Due to high-bouncing balls and reaching above the shoulders, juniors have a tendency to slide too far under the grip on the forehand side and not far over enough in the backhand grip on the backhand side. With adults, the effects can be reverse in not adjusting the grip enough on the forehand side. Both don't promote forceful topspin due to the racket angle and the grip position. The most suitable grips for topspin are semiwestern and western grips for the forehand and an eastern to semiwestern backhand grip for the backhand. These grips keep the wrist more relaxed.

b. Dropping the racket head and initiating the swing under the ball requires much more power to accelerate the racket head. The energy of the racket head needs to be stored as long as possible with the racket weight above the wrist. The forward swing is accelerated by the downward swing and the use of gravity of the arm and racket. The downward swing path changes direction with the racket swinging forward and upward as it makes contact with the ball. The change of swing path provides acceleration and elasticity from the wrist to whip the racket head through the ball to create spin. Not only is the swing much more efficient (with the use of gravity), but it also provides the acceleration needed without squeezing the racket too tightly. A relaxed, stress-free stroke creates much more ball control on the spin shots, and the "touch" or feel will be increased.

c. Late-hit shots are not uncommon in any level of players, but with a higher level of play, the speed of the ball increases. Therefore, reaction time decreases and becomes much more critical to the timing of contact points. Playing against a heavy topspin ball makes it difficult to judge the amount of spin and the bounce of the ball. The player has to make very quick adjustments to the bounce and spin to time the contact point well. In general, you have to reach more in front of the body (time the ball earlier) to compensate for the spin, bounce, and acceleration. The same effect can occur with slice shots that have a tendency to skid and accelerate after the bounce. Elevating the ball higher over the net creates a larger margin for errors.

d. Aiming too low over the net is a common mistake with any stroke. Topspin creates more downward movement of the ball. The ball falls too short in the court if no adjustments are made in elevation over the net. With slice rotation, the ball has a lifting effect. Players almost have to aim at the net strap in order to hit this stroke properly. The lift on the ball will raise the flight path over the net and have a better angle of approach at contact with the surface.

e. Decelerating the racket head causes many problems. This can often be observed with less-experienced players. The racket-head speed needs to increase during contact with the ball and in the follow-through.

Power and acceleration need to be developed over time when players are physically ready and able to perform the strokes correctly. In the meantime, young players can achieve acceleration with a high backswing and releasing a looser arm through the follow-through. Slowing the racket head down after contact will not provide the consistent directional control at higher ball speeds.

Practice

- Holding the racket higher on the grip is an excellent method to teach the racket head and arm acceleration. With a shorter racket handle, more acceleration is demanded from the legs, hips, shoulders, wrist, and elbow.

- Creating topspin, slice, or a combination thereof are easily trained by using shorter distances, practicing first in the service box then from service line to baseline or the reversed. The shorter distances force the player to use a more extreme form of rotation to the ball. This helps the process to accelerate not only the wrist and elbow but also bringing in the power and acceleration sources from the legs (loading and extending), hips and shoulders (loading by rotation and unloading).

- By using movement on the baseline or at the net, this exercise becomes much more difficult. Especially when returning all balls to one side of the court or to a section of the court.

- The next progression would be to use a line over the net to make a barrier to hit the ball over for topspin and to hit under for slice. This, combined with drills of consistency, depth, and direction, make for great practice. The topspin can also be trained by hitting in between two lines hung above each other over the net.

The European Slice

The first time I met Pete Sampras was during a practice session in Tampa at the Saddlebrook resort in 1992. I was coaching Jeff Tarango that summer, and he had asked me if he could invite another player to come and join us that afternoon for practice. Pete had been making great strides over the past years and was looking to take the number 1 spot on the ATP ranking.

He came over that afternoon, and we started our practice session in the afternoon on the clay courts with some two-on-one drills. Pete started on one side against Jeff and me on the other side. We would play some baseline rallies, and Pete would eventually come into the net on a short ball. On one of the exchanges, there was a short ball in the court, and Pete stepped up to the ball and ripped a cross-court approach to my backhand. I reacted automatically and ran over there to slide out wide on the clay to hit a slice backhand down the line. It ended up passing Pete for a winner. He paused for a while, glanced at me, but then went back to the baseline to continue the practice. After this happened one more time, he stopped at the net and said, "You are not from the US." I was perplexed at that and asked him, "Why do you say that?" His answer was "Nobody slices their backhand like that in the US."

I had obviously never thought about it quite like that, but was amazed to hear him say that. I was impressed he would pick that up just from looking at my backhand slice two times. Pete ended up using Saddlebrook as his base for the next six years, and almost every time we practiced together, he would ask to spend some time on the slice backhand.

Key Positions of the Slice Backhand

Ready position

- Athletic posture
- Hands relaxed
- Knees slightly bent
- Split step
- Alert disposition

Backswing

- Rotate shoulders with racket
- Rotate hips outside
- Turn toes outside
- Swing racket back

Loading

- Bend knees farther
- Turn hips
- Turn shoulders
- Extend both arms
- Balance arm to side

Forward swing

- Unload legs
- Unload hips
- Unload shoulders
- Trace oncoming ball
- Line up racket path

Backswing

Forward swing

Contact point

- Hand in front
- Stability in wrist
- Weight transfer
- Hitting zone

Follow-through

- Arm forward and around
- Skip foot around
- Full turn of the hips
- Full turn of the shoulders

Contact Point

Recovery

- Recovery footwork
- Overstep outside foot
- Position body to cover the court

Teaching the Slice Backhand with Key Positions

Using the key positions to teach the backhand will simplify the progression of teaching and organizing the structure of your lessons. Teaching the stroke from start to finish without missing a step helps you with your year plan. And when you are organized as a coach, your students will be organized as well. For beginning players, you want to make sure they are fully aware of how to perform the stroke. The details of the stroke do become important to the player as they improve

Follow-Through

and want to excel. These are excellent topics for group lessons as they can learn from each other's errors. In a group, you don't feel singled out or that you are the only one having trouble with the stroke. But you can also learn from the good examples of other students and try to copy them. In a group, the students always will try to compete with each other in performance. The backhand has very simple mechanics in comparison to other strokes, and you should convey that message to your students.

Andy Murray (Slice Bachand)

Power

Power in the strokes is generated by the speed of the racket head and the strings in striking the ball. The racket-head speed transforms the energy from the mass of the racket head and the flexibility of the strings to the ball. Strength can be an important factor in hitting the ball harder, but is not the only factor in gaining power in the strokes. The factors influencing power in ground strokes are the following:

1. Strength in the muscles
2. Flexibility of the muscles and ligaments
3. Loading and unloading
4. The rotation
5. The length of the swing
6. Coordination
7. Weight transfer
8. Contact points
9. Acceleration of the stroke
10. Recovery and balance

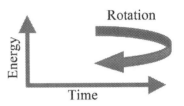

Basic power (energy × time) in combination with the centrifugal force (rotation) of the body will accelerate the speed of the ball.

Strength for tennis players is not only measured by maximum power, but also the ability to use the energy in the muscles for short bursts of action in order to accelerate the motions. The strength lies also in the endurance of these muscles to repeat these short bursts of action over an extended period of time. Weight training can also be beneficial for tennis players, as long as it is combined with specific strength training to improve endurance and speed for movement and strokes.

Flexibility and elasticity of the muscles and ligaments play an important role in using the stored energy to accelerate the motions. General flexibility in the joints in combination with elasticity in muscles and ligaments will propel the motion of the strokes like a trampoline effect once they are accelerated. The relaxation of the muscles just after contact with the ball will cause less resistance to the follow-through of the stroke and further stimulate the acceleration of the motion.

"Loading" creates a buildup of energy by bending the knees and rotating the hips and shoulders in the backswing. This buildup of the stored energy (elasticity) can be felt in the resistance and pressure to the flexing, rotating, and extending of the muscles and ligaments. Lifting the racket head and arm in the backswing in a circular-oval shape is also a storage of energy (read: loading with the use of gravity). This storage of energy needs to be contained until the point of release in the forward swing in order to gain full momentum. Slowing down the backswing or holding it in position at the top of the backswing is the key to storing energy.

The unloading of the stored energy in the muscles and ligaments occurs with the extending of the knees in coordination with the uncoiling of the hips and shoulders. The effects of gravity will stimulate the acceleration of the forward swing and ultimately the momentum to the mass of the racket in striking the ball with efficient power.

The rotation of the body and arms is one of the most important aspects in providing power and acceleration. The energy exerted from the body and arms within a certain time span defines the amount of basic power of the motion. The rotation of the body creates a centrifugal force through the arms and wrist to the racket head. The basic power and the speed of rotation will accelerate the racket head even more.

The length of the swing path provides more opportunity for the racket head to pick up speed and momentum to produce power. Think of a short backswing versus a long backswing or a long follow-through versus an abbreviated swing.

Coordination is the synchronization of the body parts to time the contact point of the stroke with the speed of the oncoming ball. This can be accomplished by loading and unloading the muscle groups in the proper sequence. Proper coordination leads to proper contact points out in front of the body that produce the most efficient power and control.

Weight transfer of the body against the ball enhances the power and control of the ball. Leaning against the ball, during the strike, will not only use the body mass to provide more energy behind the ball, but also improve the direction. Power in a tennis stroke is initiated from the ground up. As the legs extend and push forward in the direction of the ball and the body starts to uncoil toward the contact point, these movements follow each other in coordinated sequence ("the Kinetic Chain"). Teaching players how to use the power from the opponent with the use of weight transfer, and timing is a very useful tool for advanced and pro-level players.

Contact points determine the striking point of the ball. The most efficient contact points are the ones where the ball is struck in front of the body just before the arm reaches an extended position (arm at an approximately forty-five-degree angle). The distance of the body to the ball becomes important to create the proper contact point with the arm position. If the ball is struck too late or too early, it will not receive the best power transfer from the body mass and becomes harder to control in direction, elevation, and rotation.

Acceleration of the stroke promotes power and needs to be fluid in motion by starting slow and accelerating through the contact point with a faster follow-through. The grip pressure needs to be low and the arms relaxed. This will accelerate the arm and wrist and prevent squeezing the racket and "muscling" the ball. *Note: A good way to train this low-grip pressure is to let go of the fingers in the follow-through by showing the fingers off the grip and by holding the racket solely with the thumb and palm of the hand. This can be accomplished by supporting the racket with the other hand.*

Recovery and balance are essential to accelerate the stroke with power. Recovery after the stroke keeps the body in balance. Whenever the body is off balance, it will prevent the acceleration of the stroke by an automated response to restore the balance. With an off-balance action, energy will dissipate, and power transfer to the ball will be decreased. The placement of the foot in the opposite direction of the movement plays an important role in the recovery of the stroke in keeping a good balance after contact with the ball.

Martin van Daalen

Common Mistakes With the Use of Power

a. Not leaning against the ball just before making contact
b. Using too much power at the start of the swing
c. The player might squeeze the racket too much
d. Hitting the ball too hard

Corrections and practice

a. It is important to maintain forward-weight transfer pressure against the ball. Not leaning forward will often result in the body falling backward away from the ball. This form the reactionary force of the forward swing (action-reaction). To compensate for the reaction, the player needs to keep the weight slightly forward against the ball without losing balance and falling over the front foot.
b. Most junior players will jerk on the stroke to accelerate it instantly rather than throughout the motion. This particular method can cause several errors. The player might start dragging the shoulder and arm in front of the body. The shoulders will not square off properly with the direction, and the follow-through will be hard to finish. The player might end up having trouble rotating the body this way and hit with solely an arm action. Coaches should pay special attention with young juniors since these two possibilities often occur with them due to a lack of strength.
c. Squeezing too hard will stiffen the joints and adversely affect the coordination (60 percent max). It will also affect the timing and accuracy of the shot. *Note: think of when players get nervous under pressure.* The correction should be to attempt the reverse by releasing the fingers during the follow-through. As players become comfortable with this method, they will notice an increase of control and power of the strokes. (Grip-pressure measure: Scale from 1 to 10, with 10 being the most power. Grip pressure during the swing needs to be 2 to 3 in the backswing, 4 to 6 during contact, and 2 to 3 during the follow-through).

d. Most advancing players like to hit the ball slightly faster than they can control. This is also the case with most juniors. They relate power with the level of play. They don't realize that top players use the energy from the opposing ball to generate power through the reaction force of weight transfer of the body and the timing of the racket mass against the ball. Injuries usually follow with persistently trying to overhit and with misuse of the strokes (technique).

Tempo

The speed of play in timing the contact point after the bounce of the ball is what we call "tempo." The timing of the ball after the bounce varies on the height and spin of the ball. The easiest contact points to hit the ball are between hip and shoulder height, but speed, spin, and the height of the bounce of the ball could dictate to hit the ball on the rise or to let the ball drop below the top of the bounce. With the change of quality and materials from rackets and strings, players are able to hit the ball harder and still maintain ball control. Tempo can be used to attack, neutralize, or defend against the opponent. Tempo changes require great footwork and timing. To execute tempo shots properly, players and coaches need to pay attention to the following:

1. **Reading the trajectory in combination with the speed and spin of the ball** is important in making the proper shot choice. It takes talent and experience to read all these situations in a fraction of a second and make the appropriate shot choice. Coaches and players need to train as many situations as possible to hone their skills in timing the different strokes necessary at a higher and advanced level of play.
2. **Make proper adjustments with the preparation** of the backswing and footwork. After reading the shot, a choice needs to be made with the preparation of the backswing in length and height. The length and height of the backswing are determined by the speed and trajectory of the ball and the time available to set up for the

shot. The timely positioning of the feet makes it possible to hit the ball balanced, more in front, with the weight of the body against the ball.

3. **Weight transfer against the ball** assists in controlling the ball flight. This becomes an important component with taking balls on the rise or backing up. To maintain balance during contact and follow-through (recovery), the body weight needs to stay slightly forward against the ball as a reactionary force. Otherwise, you will lose balance during or after contact, which will affect control of the ball. In taking balls on the rise, it is often necessary to keep the ball lower over the net. This depends on where the ball is struck. (Think about being caught on the baseline and with a shorter distance available.)

4. **Adjustments of the contact points** become a factor in taking balls early on the rise or backing up. With low-bouncing balls under the knees and high-bouncing balls at shoulder height or above, the contact points are farther in front of the body. The distance to the ball will always relate to the contact point in front of the body and the height of the ball. *(Note: forward contact points result in closer distance to body.)*

5. **Recovery** of the stroke maintains balance and control of the ball flight. In taking balls early on the rise or backing up behind the baseline, fast recovery is needed to maintain the best position on the court. In either situation, it is possible for the opponent to take advantage if you don't get back in position fast enough. Recovery footwork needs to speed up in taking balls on the rise to maintain balance and to recover on time. This is the same in adding extra power to shots in backing up and more power and spin is required.

How to Use Tempo in Different Ways

- **Hitting the ball on the rise when it is too late to back up** is an efficient way to counter a fast-hit ball deep to the baseline. If you don't have time to back up, you might lose your balance and fall on your back foot while hitting the ball. This is where you can use a tempo change instead by taking the ball earlier after the bounce. Taking the ball on the rise might not be a high-percentage shot, but falling back while hitting the ball will be an even riskier shot choice.

- **Taking the ball early after the bounce to apply pressure to the opponent** has been a development in the game over the past twenty years. Advanced and pro players are now constantly attacking the ball whenever possible. It takes time away in reacting and running down the next shot. The opponent is eventually forced in off-balance shots to draw mistakes, short returns, or to open the court.
- **Attacking a shorter ball and approaching the net** could be the follow-up shot from the bullet point above. Moving the opponent around the court will eventually result in a shorter response. Taking advantage of these shorter balls means closing in on the ball fast with the feet and taking the ball early to the open court or hitting the ball behind the opponent to wrong-foot them. There is no need to hit the ball any harder since the forward speed of the body adds additional power.
- **Cutting off a high-bouncing topspin ball** prevents the player from moving deep behind the baseline in a defensive position. The choice here to be made by the player is the risk between the deep defensive position and the difficulty of the ball control. The factors that could determine this decision are the surface, speed, and spin of the ball, combined with the skills of the player and the opponent. In some instances, it is also possible to take the ball in the air (if it is high enough) without letting the ball bounce on the ground (drive volley).
- **Taking the approach from the opponent early** can create a surprise in catching them off balance or passing them before they can close the angle with the net. Playing a higher tempo on the passing shot takes time away and can disrupt the timing of the opponents' split step, leaving less time to set up properly for the volley.
- **Changing the tempo** is advanced tactical and technical method in disrupting the timing of the opponent. Tempo change can be used to draw mistakes from the opponent by slowing them down,

mixing up their timing, or "holding" the shot in hitting the ball a little later than expected, to hit behind the running direction. It is also possible to change the tempo here with topspin, slice, trajectory, and speed of the ball. Change of tempo is the most difficult form of tempo. It requires great timing of the players themselves before they are capable of applying this strategy.

Common Mistakes Made with the Use of Tempo

a. Falling off the shot or backing up while trying to hit the ball on the rise.
b. Squeezing the racket too hard will result in a loss of control.
c. Not bending the knees.
d. Not shortening the backswing.
e. Not adjusting the height of the backswing.

Corrections:

a. This method will result in errors with no forward pressure of the body against the ball. It is also more difficult to line the racket head up with the trajectory of the ball. It will become easier to control the racket head with better balance when stepping in and/or leaning slightly forward.
b. The racket head will decrease in speed, provide less spin, and the feel in the shots will diminish. It will also negatively affect the coordination and lead to poor ball control (see graphic on page 93). The key is to stay loose in the fingers to relax the shoulders, arm, and wrist to keep acceleration during impact and improve feel and control with the ball.
c. Not flexing the knees will result in less control during contact. As the ball is struck, the player will smoothly extend the knees to accelerate the arms and wrist in the follow-through. In order to do this, the player has to get used to flexing the knees first. The

extension of the knees will also assist the repositioning of the feet with the recovery footwork.

d. A long backswing makes it more difficult to make adjustments in swing speed and acceleration. This becomes important to time the ball well with faster ball speeds and tempo shots. Making adjustments to the length of the backswing is a necessity to compensate for speed, spin, and trajectory of the ball.

e. Having the same height of backswing will make it increasingly more difficult to line up the ball with the trajectory of the ball. For low-bouncing balls, keep the backswing slightly lower. For high-bouncing balls, lift the racket higher in the backswing and swing slightly up, not down.

Practice:

•   Start off by tossing some balls with the students taking the ball on the rise on every shot. This can be made much more difficult by switching the direction and depth of the toss and moving the player around to practice the contact point and footwork adjustments. The players will soon learn to find the bounce point on every shot.

•   Feeding the ball with increasing speeds will enhance the timing and footwork in taking balls early after the bounce. Same drill with changing depth and spins.

•   Practice a higher tempo by standing on or inside the baseline. This drill can be trained by just one player, but later on also trained by both players.

•   The next progression could be taking one ball on the rise, inside the baseline, and one ball deeper behind the baseline. This can be performed either by feeding balls or by having the players hit against each other in a rally.

•   Train to take the approaches early by hitting up the middle or cross-court, and on a short return, attack the ball on the rise to transition to the net position.

- Practice to hit passing shots on the rise by stepping in closer to the approaches of the other player. The tempo changes occur when players step forward to hit the approach shots when the opponent is not expecting it. The key here is to pass the opponent before they can properly cover the net. Adjust speed and spin.
- High topspin ball exchanges can be changed with a tempo change by taking the ball out of the air. The most important factor is to recognize the appropriate situation and then being decisive in moving forward. This can either be a drive volley (spin) or with a regular volley (slight slice).
- It is possible to pressure the opponent by attacking the return and taking the ball early. This can be practiced with slice or topspin strokes. Practice also with points.

Service

The service motion is the most complex and difficult stroke to learn in the tennis game. There are many motions and actions that need to be coordinated together to perform this stroke. The arms move simultaneously, with the toss of the ball and the backswing of the racket. The trunk and shoulders rotate in position to accelerate the racket upward and forward toward the contact point. The knees bend to load the body for the upward thrust. The hips shift forward into the court to maintain the balance of the body and to create an improved upward extension of the body and hip flexion in combination with the shoulder-over-shoulder rotation during the forward swing. During all these motions, the feet and the balance arm (after the toss) take on an important role in the balance and recovery of the stroke.

Motions of the serve:

1. The preparation and stance of service motion

2. The toss of the ball and the backswing
3. The knee and hip action
4. The foot action
5. The forward swing with the trunk and shoulder rotation
6. The elbow and wrist action
7. The follow-through and balance action
8. The recovery and preparation

The coordination of these motions in sequence with each other requires a lot of training and experimentation to become consistent in controlling the ball with target direction, spin, and power. They can all be practiced separately or in combination with each other. The sequence of the motions is important for the transfer of power and should be executed from the ground up. The force of each segment will flow over from one segment to the next and so on. We call this **"the Kinetic Chain"** of the service motion.

When students practice technique and are correcting certain segments of the serve, coaches and players should pay attention to the flow of energy in the kinetic chain. In analyzing the service action, start observing the segments from the ground up. This will help with detecting any flaws in the segments themselves or any problems 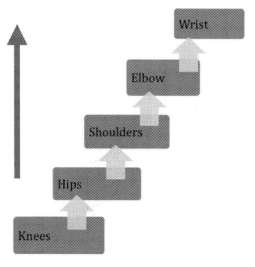 with the transfer of energy from one segment to the next segment. This systematic approach of correcting the service action will assist in analyzing the stroke without skipping over any possible errors during execution.

Key Positions of the Serve

Ready position

- Bouncing of the ball (rhythm)
- Arms relaxed down
- Transfer weight to back foot
- Bend back knee
- Come up arms slightly

Backswing

- Toss ball and separate racket
- Transfer weight to front
- Turn shoulder
- Turn hips
- Forward hips for balance

Backswing

Loading

- Bend knees farther
- Turn hips
- Turn shoulders
- Hips out in front for power and balance
- Drop racket behind shoulder

Forward swing

- Straighten (unload) legs
- Unload hips
- Unload shoulders
- Extend arm up and forward
- Straighten hips
- Drop to stomach balanced arm

Loading

Contact point

- Hand in front
- Swing upward
- Toss arm in stomach
- Stability in wrist

Follow-through

- Outward turn of the wrist
- Extend arm first
- Upward kick back foot
- Land on left foot
- Posture upper body

Recovery

Contact Point

- Back foot recovery in front
- Recovery footwork
- Position body for next shot

Teaching the Serve with Key Positions

The serve is a complicated and coordinated effort from the whole body. Both arms move separately in opposite directions with a different purpose. In teaching beginning tennis players, keep in mind that they are not able to perform the same actions that advanced players can perform. The knee, hip, and shoulder actions will also not be as prominent as with more experienced students. Therefore, it is advisable to take it slow with the development of the service action. Most often, the students themselves will show when they are ready to take the next step. They will show signs of fluidity in the stroke and hitting action and become proficient in consistency and direction. That will be the time to further develop the serve with specifics. Until that time, teaching the service action with the key positions will be very instrumental.

Roger Federer (The Serve)

Progressions from Intermediate to Advanced Service Motions

As players progress from intermediate to advanced players, it is important to gradually introduce the new techniques to advanced players. Young players don't have the strength in the knees, trunk, or shoulders to perform advanced techniques. You can make a start in teaching them as long as you don't expect the same results as when they are more physically mature. A good method of teaching advanced techniques for the serve is to start with the toss and backswing and to continue with the knees from the ground up and work toward the end of the stroke. (See "Motions of the Serve" above.)

The preparation and stance for the serve is different for many players in where they find their balance point. Some players start with their weight on the front foot and move slightly back but immediately into the service motion (Federer). Others might start, after bouncing the ball, with the weight on the back and then move slightly forward into the toss (Sampras). It is crucial, as a coach, to see how a player respond to different methods of preparation and to choose the one they are most physically and technically comfortable with instead of forcing a certain method on them. Students also need to be physically ready to make technical changes. The time to introduce this is when they start showing signs of physical strength in the knees, trunk, and shoulders to support the technical changes. Doing these changes too early will cause players to make more errors with the serve and lose confidence in their own ability. The arms have to start in a relaxed straight fashion without overextending the arms. The racket head has to be supported by the toss arm with the use of the fingers. The loose arms in the backswing will create more racket-head acceleration in the forward swing. Making players aware of this acceleration effect by relaxing the shoulders, arms, and fingers is one of the most underestimated factors in producing spin, power, and control with the service action.

Practice: *Try out different stances and preparation phases. Discuss with them which one suits them the best. This all has to be performed with the whole motion with the toss. Actively practice the relaxation of the shoulders, arms, and fingers in the preparation phase in practice and match play by letting students call out their grip pressure (1–10).*

The toss will determine the accuracy and possible service motions. When students are learning the service motion, the toss is out in front, just in front of the right shoulder. As players advance, the toss moves slightly more to the side of the body rather than in front (kick serve above the head). This toss motion is also due to the extended shoulder rotation in the backswing. By tossing the ball more to the side, it becomes easier to rotate the shoulders and to apply spin to the ball. The extended shoulder rotation and longer backswing will generate more racket-head speed, speed, and power to the service action. Tossing the ball more at the side of the body can cause some problems with the accuracy of the toss. The ball will have a tendency to drift over the head of the player. This can be corrected by turning the wrist angle of the toss downward and/or releasing the toss earlier in the motion. The time to introduce the different toss is when they are ready to execute the spin serves. Teaching the spin serves (slice, top slice, kick) should be functional to the progress in their game rather than teaching it for the sake of teaching something new. It can seriously hamper their progress in the service motion when introduced too early.

Practice: *The best ways to practice the toss is to lay down a racket in line with the front foot. The blade of the racket is positioned just in front of the baseline. First, practice the toss alone, followed with the use of the backswing to check the balance. The toss can also be practiced close and along the back fence to control the height and direction.*

The **backswing** of the service action is important for tempo, balance, spin, and power of the swing. It is the first "loading" action of the service action to store energy for release. The backswing starts straight back, but as the toss is finalized, it will start to swing more around the body as the shoulder rotation is extended. The knuckles of the hitting hand stay on top throughout the first half of the backswing until the racket head drops behind the shoulders. As the toss arm is extended, the elbow of the backswing starts to bend. The shoulders will, in some cases, line up close to parallel with the baseline (Sampras). This rotation will create a lag of the racket head for spin and power. The tempo of the backswing is important for the timing and acceleration of the forward swing. If

the backswing is too fast, the player will swing up toward the ball too early and usually end up hitting down in the net. It is better to slow down the backswing as it reaches the top. Most good servers have a slowdown at the top of the backswing or even a slight pause. The backswing will position the hand in a throwing pose above the elbow. This slowdown will relax the wrist and ensure an upward motion of the racket toward the ball. The relaxed-wrist action accelerates the ball effortlessly with more accuracy.

Practice: It is very valuable to practice these motions of the backswing in front of a mirror. Players are able to view themselves and have instant feedback on the technique and the tempo of the swing. The toss, backswing, and shoulder rotation will be much more visible, and changes can be introduced immediately. (See picture, M Roanic.)

The knee and hip action follows the toss and the start of the backswing in loading the body with energy for the forward swing. The hips move slightly forward with the finish of the toss and the rotation of the shoulders in the backswing. This weight transfer of the hips has several advantages. It enables players to use their knees better and still maintain a good balance during the toss. This enables them to unload the knees and body more powerfully upward and forward, not unlike the way a bow releases an arrow. The forward-hip action creates a slight upward shoulder angle that keeps the shoulders under the ball to release the racket upward. It also loads the trunk muscles for the unloading of the shoulder rotation and activates the shoulder-over-shoulder action in the follow-through. The key to watch with this knee-and-hip action is that the line from shoulders to the knees stays straight. Students bending too far back in the lower back could develop back or stomach muscle problems. Having an angle in the hips will provide less power by locking out the trunk muscles.

Practice: This knee-and-hip action is best trained in front of a mirror. Players are able to view the angle along knees, hips, and shoulders. Turning ninety degrees will enable you to see the forward-hip action. The coach can show the line by using a net stick along the line from knees to shoulders. By holding this position for a while in the knees (with the toss and the backswing), players can train the balance and power in the knees.

The foot action can be twofold with a turn of the front foot as the backswing is completed and with some players making a shift of the back foot closer to the front foot. The turn of the front foot is quite common for players to accommodate the turn of the hips and shoulders. The back-foot shift is a style from the player that enhances their balance and weight transfer. Some players prefer having the feet stay in the same wider position (Sampras, Federer). With this particular serve, the weight is transferred from the back foot into the court by pushing off the back foot. It is a very stable serve and assists the balance greatly during the motion. Others might start with the feet much closer together (Roddick, Monfils). In this case, the weight is distributed over both feet. The push upward and forward is performed by both feet equally. But there also have been some great servers that like shifting the back foot forward as they complete the toss and the backswing (Tsonga, Murray, Berdych, Isner, Del Potro, Serena Williams, Sam Stosur). The weight is transferred from the back foot to the front foot. Both feet push off upward and forward, with the front foot being the dominant factor with this method. Not every player is comfortable with this shift, but in some cases, it can help the upward motion and rotation of the body. Trying several techniques will show you which method the player likes the most. Make sure it is their preference and not yours as a coach.

Practice: To practice the isolated motion of the toss and the backswing in combination with the foot action can be very helpful for the whole motion of the service action. The repetition of the action will assist the tempo and rhythm of the motion. Try to hold the position at the top of the toss and backswing for a few seconds each time. This will stimulate the balance and power of the swing once it is practiced as a whole motion.

The forward swing with the trunk and shoulders is initiated with the push from the feet and the knees, followed by an uncoiling of the hips and the shoulders. The feet and the knees are the starter engine of the service motion. Most players will struggle finding the rhythm of the swing when swinging with the arms first rather than starting the service motion from the ground up (see "kinetic chain"). The knee action should set into motion all the other parts in sequence (hips, shoulders, elbow, wrist). The jump forward over the baseline is important to add the weight transfer into the ball. This jump forward might be less with a second serve, but much more when playing serve and volley. By starting the knees first, the other body parts are accelerated in sequence with increasing speed and with less power usage (efficiency). This will result in a higher racket-head speed that can be maintained for a longer period of time, with less stress to the joints and muscle structures (think of five set matches). Students that try to use too much power or use the body parts out of sequence will have less racket-head speed. It can also cause many different injuries (stomach muscles, back, and shoulders). The swing path of the forward swing depends mainly on the type of serve. A good method to use is the clock method in showing players how to swing around the ball. Example: a right-handed kick serve is struck from eight to two o'clock.

Practice: Make players aware of starting the service motion from the ground up by jumping over an object on the baseline (racket handle). The knee action has to start before the hip, shoulder, and arm action. By landing on the front foot and keeping your balance, the hip and shoulders have to fully rotate forward in the direction of the ball. The swing path can be trained by using the clock method (see above) and by practicing different types of spin shots with the service motion. This can be practiced to one target at first, but can be extended to using multiple targets. The ultimate test would be to have the coach call out the type of serve with a specific target and mix them around.

The elbow and wrist action is the final acceleration of the body parts before the racket strikes the ball. When all the motions are executed in the proper sequence, the elbow and wrist will follow with an increasingly higher speed, not unlike the end of a whip. The players that are able to coordinate these motions well are able to have a higher skill level in consistency, spin, and speed of the serve. The elbow and wrist action of the service motion is very similar to the throwing action used in football and baseball. You will find that the top servers in tennis also possess great skills in throwing a football or baseball. Therefore, it is advisable for coaches to spend some time in training advanced players in throwing a football or a baseball. Using heavier objects will be especially helpful since a tennis player has to use a tennis racket. It is important to note here that it is helpful to throw upward with a high arc to simulate the upward motion needed with the service motion. The release of the elbow and wrist is maybe the largest contributor in generating the acceleration in the throwing and service motion. By using the larger muscle groups in sequence (kinetic chain), it is possible to release the shoulder, elbow, and finally the wrist and racket head for optimum acceleration.

Practice: The practice of the throwing motion will have the largest effect on the elbow and wrist action. The use of a (small) football or baseball is highly recommended for this exercise. If the students are still young, try to use a smaller-size football (Nerf ball).

The follow-through and balance action is the finish of the service action coordinated with the balance of the body throughout the swing. There are a few factors that will have a positive effect on the development of the service motion for advanced players, and one of them is the method of the follow-through. The follow-through shows more than any other factor how the service was performed. If the player is able to stay in balance at the end of the follow-through and not fall over, it will indicate a good toss, swing path, and good use of the balance arm. The acceleration of the racket head decreases with the balance arm moving to a bent position in the stomach area before catching the racket in the follow-through. The back foot has to swing upward in the opposite direction of the ball to help maintain the balance and to act as a counterbalance in keeping the upper body more erect. Most players have a tendency to fall too far forward with the upper body. This motion will decrease the height (arc) of the ball over the net and decrease the consistency and spin of the serve. Keeping the upper body tall in the follow-through also assists in the recovery of the service action in getting ready for the next stroke. After jumping into the court and landing on the front foot, the balance can be maintained by stepping through on the back foot to recover for the next stroke.

Martin van Daalen

Practice: *The best practice for these actions is to execute the service action and to land in a balanced position on the front foot. By keeping the balance for a few seconds, it will train several different aspects of the serve all at once. Besides training an accurate toss-and-service motion, it will also practice the follow-through and balance of the swing. Check to see if the students are landing inside the court, in the direction of the ball, the upper body slightly forward, with the back foot in an upward and opposite direction.*

Recovery of the service action can be twofold in moving forward for a serve and volley or by moving backward to take position behind the baseline. The recovery of the serve and volley action is mostly executed by landing on the front foot and accelerating the movement forward in the direction of the ball. The recovery of the service action to stay at the baseline is mostly executed by landing on the front foot inside the baseline and stepping through on the other foot. This foot is also responsible for the recovery action by pushing the body back behind the baseline. Sometimes the player is able to anticipate the return and recover in the direction and depth of the ball.

Practice. There is a progression in learning and practicing the recovery of the service motion:

1. *Try the recovery motion, right after the service motion, by explaining the specific footwork needed for the recovery.*
2. *Feed the ball with hand tosses to practice consistency with the recovery.*
3. *Feed the ball with hand tosses in different directions to increase the footwork and adjustments of the recovery.*
4. *Feed the ball from the other side, after the serve, to specific targets to teach the patterns needed for match play and practice consistency in each pattern.*
5. *Feed the ball to different targets to test the skill level of the player and for them to recognize the directions and shot choice.*
6. *Feed the ball from the other baseline with different speeds, trajectory, and spin. This will increase the skill level of the player for optimum recovery.*

Consistency

The reliability of the serve can be measured in the uniformity and stability of the motion and its impact on the accuracy of the target areas with the amount of spin and power. With this particular stroke, we need to keep in mind that the consistency with the service motion is individually determined between first and second serves.

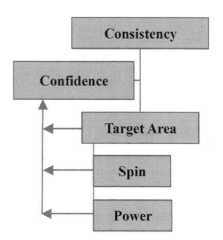

The diagram on the right portrays how the stability and uniformity of the service motion influences the consistency and confidence of hitting the target areas by gradually adding spin and power. The progression of learning consistency with the service action should be taught in the same manner. Start by teaching the uniformity and stability of the technical execution of the stroke before teaching target areas and adding spins and power. With increased results in consistency, the feedback to confidence is optimized.

Common Mistakes with Consistency of the Serve

a. The technical execution of the service stroke is unstable.
b. The toss of the ball is inconsistent.
c. Hitting the serve too hard.
d. Balance problems during the service motion.
e. Target choices and consistency of the serve.

Corrections

a. Increase the consistency with uniformity and stability of the service motion by making improvements to the technical execution of the stroke. The target area is not the focus point yet and can include the whole service box area. Consistency and confidence will follow. The approach should be to focus on the feet first and work your way upward, one segment at a time, finishing with the snap of the wrist.

b. Players can practice the toss by practicing the whole motion without striking the ball. Place a spare racket on the inside of the front foot. Students can let the ball drop down after the toss to check where the ball bounces on the ground.

c. The practice of consistency with the service action should be performed at a much slower pace than students realize. The less power is used with the motion, the better the performance eventually will be. Students should feel as if only the large muscle groups (legs and trunk area) generate the acceleration. Go from a deliberate slow motion to a faster motion.

d. Using target areas can help with consistency of the service action when the target areas are big enough to stimulate confidence. The target areas assist the focus of the player with direction and balance to promote a better control of the ball.

e. The consistency is tested by how many times a player can hit the serve in a specific target area. By counting the amount of times, it will increase the consistency of the serve. As the amount is increased, it also gradually increases consistency under pressure that players might feel in point and match play. Coaches can influence this even more by calling out "match point" (or a certain score) to test if the player can handle the consistency with a score in mind. Once each target area is practiced sufficiently, it is possible to change the target areas. At this point, the coach can call out the specific target areas to enhance the control of the ball and eventually improve the consistency of the service action.

Practice:

• To increase consistency, hit many serves at a medium pace. The slower pace will help you with the coordination, will not tire the muscles as much, and will increase the confidence with more balls in the court.

- Break up the practice time by hitting serves for ten minutes and then switching to another topic before returning to the serve later. The serve has a tendency to break down when serving too long a time in a row and injuries can occur. By breaking up the practice, the focus will be maintained with consistency and confidence.

- Spend time focusing on the toss to increase consistency on the serve. The toss is one of the foremost important aspects to influence the consistency. Practice the direction and height of the toss for accuracy. Use targets on the ground in front of your front foot to check the direction of the ball where the ball would bounce if it were not struck. Use the back fence to check the consistency of the height of the toss.

- Always use targets to increase the consistency of the serve. The focus on the target area will assist the player to visualize the trajectory. This will help later on during competition when there are no targets and players have to visualize the target.

- After mastering the different targets individually, start practicing the direction by switching the targets with each shot. This will increase the direction and control of the service motion and increase consistency.

- Practice using targets with a margin for error to increase consistency in matches. If the targets are placed too close to the lines of the service box, players will choose the same targets in matches with a larger chance of mistake.

- Use a slightly higher net (line) to increase the height, spin, and therefore the consistency of the serve. By increasing the height of the net, players will automatically practice spin on the serve and are able to control the trajectory more easily.

Mental Notes on Consistency of the Serve

Whenever you are practicing consistency, it is important to understand the methodology and development from a mental point of view:

- Learning
- Practice
- Practice with points
- Practice in a match
- Mastering the skill further

Besides the technical development, there are other factors that can influence the confidence of a player in executing the serve. The mind plays an important role in becoming proficient and mastering the serve with consistency, even when players are under stressful situations. As coaches, we can assist players by having a good method and progression that stimulates confidence. After the basic techniques are mastered, it is important to give players sufficient time to practice and experiment. Be very encouraging when they are performing new serve motions well (think slice and kick serve). A player is very capable of seeing how he or she is performing. Making too many remarks and comments can often be very distracting to improvements. Since this is a very technical and coordinated motion, it takes more time to develop. If coaches increase the stress level on the technical aspects and consistency too much, it is possible that players will improve less or slower than necessary. In trying to improve consistency, it can be helpful to give players a visual picture of the trajectory of the ball. Setting reasonable goals to increase the consistency over a period of time is also a good tool to use. A tactical tool can be used to explain the trajectory necessary to cause the opponent trouble with returning the serve and/or opening the court. Becoming stronger, more flexible, and conditioning the muscle groups you need for the serve can also be helpful to improvements to this stroke. Automated stroke production will help the consistency under pressure. Whenever players have goals for themselves, it will increase the level of performance higher than adding additional pressure from others. All these tips and methods of improving consistency are in some way connected to the mental side of the tennis game (focus, willpower, execution under pressure).

Depth of the Serve

The depth of the service stroke is determined by several different factors. Some of these factors are due to the speed, elevation, and spin of the ball. One of the largest factors to determine the depth in the service box is the toss of the ball. With the toss too far forward, the serve will usually go into the net. The reverse is also true; with the toss being too far back, the serve will go outside the service box. (See picture below.)

The racket angle needs to be in the right position in order to create the correct angle for the ball to land in the service box. With beginning tennis players, the grip can sometimes be a factor when using a forehand grip. This grip will favor the toss being more in front than usual. This method will also cause a lower toss with many errors.

The basic strategy of the serve is to generate an error or to impose a defensive position from the opponent. The depth of the ball plays an important role in this strategy in applying pressure. Whenever the ball falls short, the opponent can step inside the court to attack the ball and can turn the tables on this basic strategy.

Common Mistakes with Depth of the Serve

a. Tossing the ball too far in front or too far back
b. Using the incorrect grip
c. The balance of the service action
d. Not jumping high enough or using the wrong timing of the jump
e. The upward swing of the arm and wrist

Corrections

a. The height and position of the toss will influence the quality and depth of the serve. See some of the corrections for the toss in "consistency." By stringing a line across the net, it is possible to improve the depth of the serve with a higher trajectory over the net. If a line is not available, you can also use a net stick under the middle of the net. This is an easy way to making the net higher when traveling to tournaments.

b. An incorrect grip can limit the consistency, depth, direction, spin, and power of the serve. A continental or eastern backhand grip will increase the possibility to swing up against the ball to improve the trajectory and depth of the serve. It will improve the racket angle at contact and increases the wrist action in the follow-through.

c. By using the hips forward in the loading position of the service action, players are able to control the balance of the body much better before striking the serve. This hip action keeps the body's center of gravity above the feet in order to push up. This particular method not only provides more upward thrust of the body, but also prevents the body from falling on top of the ball for a lower trajectory with less depth to the serve.

d. The height and timing of the jump are important for the trajectory and power of the serve. The height of the jump will affect the upward motion and the speed of the racket head of the serve. By placing a racket on the ground in front of the feet, players are able to jump over the racket and create a higher jump. It is also possible to use a thick flat board to jump on top to create the same effect. The timing of the knee action needs to be just before the unloading of the hips, shoulders, and arms. The timing of the knees makes it possible to relax the arm, elbow, and wrist in order to create a whip action for maximum acceleration to the racket head.

e. The upward swing of the arm and wrist creates the acceleration, spin, and depth of the service action. By placing a high obstacle a few yards in front of the player, they will automatically swing up instead of down toward the net. By standing outside the fence of the court and serving balls to the inside of the court, it is possible to train this upward swing in an extreme fashion. A shoulder-high obstacle (box) in front of the player will be more realistic on the court to improve the upward swing and trajectory of the service action.

Practice:

• By mixing up the distance to the service box, the students will get a much better idea how to adjust the angle, speed, and spin to control the depth of the ball. You can have the students start at the service line and work their way back to the baseline. As they become more proficient, the students can move even farther back from the baseline to increase the speed. Make use of targets or target areas.

• Mix up speed and spin by alternating the first serve and second serve. This will make players aware how to adjust the speed and spin to create to proper depth.

• It is possible to use lines across the net to manipulate the depth of the ball. Players can hit either over a line or between two lines. By raising the height of the line over the net, the students will be able to practice the different types of spin and depth at the same time. The spin on the second serve is of importance to create more height or jump on the ball to push the opponent farther back.

• The depth on the service can be practiced with targets or target areas, not only the targets in the service box, but also target areas on the back fence. With this method, it is possible to check the depth of the serve by the penetration of the ball with the amount of speed and spin. After the bounce in the service box, the amount of speed and spin will determine how high the ball will bounce on the back fence.

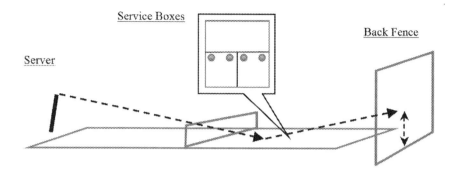

(As depicted in the picture above, you can see how the server aims for the targets in the service box and also for the height of the target on the back fence. By adding speed and spin to the ball, the height of the target on the back can be increased. The combination of using targets in the service box and targets on the back fence will not only increase the speed and spin, but also the accuracy of the service action.)

Direction of the serve

The service motion is one of the most accurate strokes in the tennis game. In trying to hit the small target areas in the service box with speed and spin, it takes great effort and patience for players to practice their timing with accuracy while executing this stroke with consistency. The direction of the serve is derived from a sequence of motions that need to be accurately timed in order to find the desired flight path. Unlike with the ground strokes, there are many more moving segments that play a part in steering the ball. The racket is also used above the head with the racket head moving around the ball with a different axis of rotation in directing the ball.

The factors that determine the direction of the serve should be observed and taught from the ground up. Here are some points for you to consider in order of moving sequences and teaching progression:

1. **Starting position and grips**

   The starting position of the body can be of great influence on the direction of the serve. The placement of the feet and the sideways body angle and with the court will create the swing path of the racket through the strike zone of the ball. The grip is of great importance to position the racket in the correct angle at the point of contact with the ball. The continental grip is the most comfortable in providing the wrist with stability at contact without being restrictive in flexibility.

2. **The toss**

   Throwing the ball up in the correct position to strike the ball is not only difficult, but also the least practiced part of the service motion. The toss needs to be directed with the correct height and point in order for the racket to strike with the arm in an extended position. Whenever there is inconsistency in the toss with the height, forward and backward, or sideways deviation, it will be difficult to direct the ball on the chosen flight path. It is possible to make corrections with the timing of the shoulders and arms, but these corrections will not be accurate and consistent. The toss needs to be in the area straight up over the hitting shoulder at contact.

3. **The hip and shoulder action**

   The rotation of the hip and shoulders are largely responsible for the proper timing and swing path of the racket head. The timing of the hip and shoulders is set into motion by pushing off with the feet and the extending of the knees. The timing of the forward rotation of the hips and shoulders needs to be coordinated with the height of the toss and the anticipated contact point in order to create the direction of the ball.

Martin van Daalen

4. **The swing path**

   The trajectory of the racket head is dictated by the backswing and the resulting forward rotation of the shoulders and hitting arm. The backward rotation of the shoulders in the backswing creates the angle of the forward swing path of the racket past the ball. The wrist angle at contact with the ball needs to be coordinated with the swing angle in order to hit the ball in the desired direction. The direction becomes more difficult by adding spin to the ball and adjustments are made to the swing path.

5. **The elbow and wrist action**

   The flexion of the elbow and the wrist in the backswing will prepare the swing path and extension of the upward and forward part of the stroke in directing the ball. Following the impact with the ball, the elbow will flex again with the wrist pronating to facilitate maximum racket acceleration through the strike zone. (See picture, Milos Roanic.) This particular technique of wrist and elbow action should be reserved for advanced players. This motion requires physically mature bodies to avoid any injuries to shoulder, elbow, or wrist.

Common Mistakes with Direction of the Serve

a. The use of incorrect grips
b. The accuracy of the toss
c. Hitting too hard
d. The balance of the stroke
e. The timing and speed of the shoulder rotation
f. The swing path of the racket
g. Small target areas

Corrections

a. Using incorrect grips will cause more difficulty in finding the direction with the correct angle of the wrist at impact with the ball. A continental grip will allow the player more flexibility without compromising the stability and control of the wrist.

b. An incorrect toss will have a direct influence on the direction of the ball. The three-dimensional position of impact with the ball is determined by the height of the toss and the distance in front and at the side of the body in relation to the ball. Most often the toss will be too far forward or above the head or other shoulder. Students need extensive practice in tossing the ball the correct way on the tops of the fingers with the wrist flexed downward. Practice the toss separately and with the stroke.

c. Serving too hard will negatively affect the coordination and timing of the stroke. This will result in less consistency in directing the ball and its trajectory.

d. One aspect that is often neglected during the serve is the balance. It will affect the power, consistency, and control of the direction. This can either be caused by the toss of the ball or by the dynamic balance of the motion. Players and coaches need to be aware of the cause before trying to correct the problem.

e. The timing and speed of the shoulder rotation creates the impact point and direction for the service motion. Common mistakes are not squaring off the shoulders or turning too late with the back shoulder. The arm, elbow, and wrist cannot accelerate properly without the shoulders accelerating first. When the shoulders rotate first, the arm is able to relax during the motion and direct the ball more accurately.

f. The swing path of the racket needs to be across the ball, from inside to out, instead of straight forward through the ball. Most beginning players will swing straight through and have many difficulties in directing the ball consistently on target.

g. Use large targets instead of placing them too close to the line. As coaches and players, we often train to hit aces instead of hitting more consistently to the weaker side of the opponent. This will set up the serve to take advantage of the weaker return and to keep the initiative in the point.

Practice:

- The direction can best be practiced with the use of targets. To maintain confidence, the progression should be from large target areas to small targets. Students will be able to count how many times they can hit the same target. Start off by using one-third of the service box by dividing the service box into three equal parts.
- The next progression can be to alternate the three target areas by playing one serve in each target area. Continue by increasing the amount in each target area. Increase the amount of target areas to five equal parts in the service box. This will increase the accuracy and control of the player to a higher level. (See picture below.)

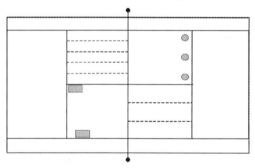

- Practice as before with consistency and direction to the different service boxes and while adding different types of spin to the service motion.
- Explain the different types of strategies and tactics of each target and run through the scenarios of how the point is played out. The basic three targets in the service box (wide, body, middle) all have patterns of play that suit the situations.
- When the students show an increase in the consistency and control of direction, the target areas can be made smaller with cones,

balls, or mats. It is also possible to use tape to mark an area when practicing indoors or on a hard court.

- Take time to practice the different serves to the body of the opponent. This serve is one of the most undertrained in direction and spin. Players should learn how to use this shot properly to surprise the opponent and take advantage of the situation.

- To increase the pressure, you as a coach can call out the direction of the serve to the player before each next ball. The same drill can be performed with direction and variations in spin from slice, top slice, topspin, kick serve to reverse serve.

- Players can add camouflage to their serve by making the shoulder turn and toss as identically as possible. The coach can call out the spin before the toss and the direction during the toss of the ball. Players will adjust the grip and swing path rather than show the opponent the direction of the ball.

- Use the serve direction and spin to construct a point. The player can tell the coach before each point what his intentions are and why. This method instills strategy as a goal instead of the speed and spin of the serve alone. Players will be more aware to use the serve to gain initiative in the point by setting up the serve for a weak return.

Spin of the Serve

With the advancements in racket and string technology, it is possible to hit the ball much harder and still produce the amount of spin necessary to keep the ball inside the lines. The new types of strings are very flexible and responsive and make it possible for the strings to slide more easily without losing contact with the ball. There are many different rotations of the ball, all with a different tactical purpose. Rotation of the ball is created by the frictional force of the strings brushing past the cover of the ball. The amount of spin depends on how much the racket is brushed past the ball and how much the racket swings forward through the ball.

Martin van Daalen

As you can see in the graph on the right, there are two different shots displayed, shot A and shot B. Both are executed with a certain amount of spin and speed that makes them very distinguishable from each other.

Shot A will have a lot of spin with less forward speed while shot B has more speed than spin. For example, if you wanted maximum spin, you would swing upward in the direction of the word "spin." With acquiring maximum speed, you would swing horizontally in the direction of the word "speed." Of course, there are many combinations possible with multiple variations of spin and speed. The two shots **A** and **B** in the graph are just two examples of them.

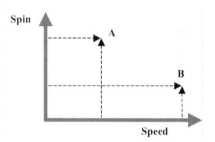

The different types of serve:

- **Flat serve**
  The serve motion is hit with very little spin and is used as a first strike weapon. These flat serves are best hit over the lowest part of the net just over the net strap.

- **Top-spin serve**
  This serve is hit with spin from slightly under the ball and over the ball. It is used to make the ball bounce up high, out of the strike zone, to force a weak return.

- **Slice Serve**
  This particular swing is hit from around the side of the ball to make it curve. Players use this serve to play the ball out wide, off the court, or to play it through the middle. It is also used to curve the ball at the body of the opponent.

- **Top-slice serve**

  The combination of topspin and slice can be used on a first serve but is mostly reserved for the second serves. It provides forward speed as well as control to the ball with depth and direction to enhance consistency and a high-percentage serve. It is the most common spin serve of competitive tennis players.

- **Kick serve**

  The rotation of the ball is the most aggressive in this service action than any other. The ball is struck from around the ball and over the ball to make the ball curve as much as possible and jump away in the opposite direction after the bounce. This service action is very effective to pull the opponent out of position and to play the ball out of their strike zone with the sideways high bounce of the ball.

- **Reverse serve**

  This spin is the least known and more complicated in execution. The ball is struck around the inside of the ball to make the ball curve with a slice to the opposite direction. The toss of the ball is more in front of the player and should be struck with a continental forehand grip to accommodate the direction and reverse slice.

Common Mistakes with Spin of the Serve

a. Not adjusting the grip with the use of spin serves
b. Not adjusting the toss
c. Not rotating the shoulders enough
d. Not adjusting the swing path

a. The grip is responsible for the racket angle with the ball to create the necessary friction for rotation of the ball. As the grip moves over from a continental grip to the eastern backhand grip, more rotation will be created. Players and coaches need to be aware that the additional spin will cause less forward speed to the ball. Finding the right combination of grip, spin, and speed is important to the shot choice and strategic situation.

b. The toss has great influence on the execution possibilities of the various spin serves. As the serve is tossed more to the outside, away from the body, it is easier to add the slice to the ball by swinging around the ball on a horizontal axis. When the ball is tossed more above the head of the player, the swing path of the racket allows for more topspin and kick to the serve. The forward and backward motion to the toss will affect the amount of speed and spin applied to the ball.

c. The shoulder rotation will lengthen the swing by turning the shoulders away from toss to load for the forward and upward swing. Lengthening the backswing will add more speed to the racket head for power and spin.

d. The swing path is important to determine the type of rotation you want to use. The swing path will determine the direction of the racket head and strings past the ball to add the rotation to the ball. This will result in a certain trajectory and reactionary direction of the ball after the bounce of the ball.

Corrections and practice:

• Students should first experiment with the different grips and the various rotations on the ball to get a feel for the combinations of grips, toss, and swing path.

• The change of the toss should be practiced for the different types of serve and the various rotations of the ball. Consistency in each individual type of serve needs to be mastered before trying to mix up the type of spins.

• Consistency of the spin serve can be improved by using big target areas followed by smaller target areas. The object of the exercise is to hit a certain number of spin serves of each type of rotation in each target area and then to increase that number. You can start with half the service box then splitting it into four or five equal boxes.

- The direction of the spin serve can be improved by using target areas in the service box. The best target areas are mats placed on the outside of the service box and one in the middle to practice body shots. (When practicing indoors, you can use newspapers as target areas.)

- Practicing body serves should be a separate practice in explaining and showing the importance of the body serve and the different spins you can use: the slice serve to curve it from right to left into the body and the kick serve to curve it to the forehand and make it kick back into the body.

- The power of the spin serve is accomplished through the gradual increase of the racket head speed by accelerating the knees and the rotations of the body. You can stimulate this further by placing a target on the back fence and by the increasing height of the ground or by moving the player farther back behind the baseline.

- Video is an excellent feedback for the player to recognize the various techniques and effects of the ball after the bounce. Videotaping the serve from an elevated position behind the player will show the different toss, swing path, and the trajectories of the balls.

- Camouflage of the serve becomes important for advanced players to conceal the direction of the intended serve. The opponent can deduct the direction from the toss of the serve. With the toss more to the outside, the server will most likely intend to hit a slice serve out wide. With the toss more over the head, the server will most likely try the kick serve through the middle or out wide to the backhand. As players advance, you can practice the various spin serves using one specific toss position. This can be practiced by having the player toss the ball and the coach calling out the direction of the target or the spin of the serve.

Power of the Serve

The serve has always been a dominating factor in the game, and with the development of new types of string and rackets, this has only

Martin van Daalen

added to the strength of the serve. Nevertheless, the quality of the serve is not just rated by power alone. Accuracy, spin, and the ability to camouflage the direction are valuable assets to the quality of the serve. As you might have noticed from watching top players, not every big server has overdeveloped muscles in the arms and shoulders, so there is obviously more to it than just hitting the gym. The technique of the serve is the largest contributor to the speed of the ball. The kinetic chain from the ground up, with the uncoiling of the hips and shoulders, generates the speed and acceleration to the arm and racket head. The coordination of movements with the timing of the ball not only assists with the acceleration, but also is responsible for the accuracy of the direction, spin, and depth of the ball. Flexibility and elasticity of the muscles, ligaments, and joints will play a factor in the maximum acceleration.

Common Mistakes with Power of the Serve

a. Not having a proper serve grip
b. Using too much power and "muscling the ball"
c. Having the wrong position on the toss
d. Improper coordination and timing of the serve
e. Improper timing of the knee action
f. A lack of forward hip action
g. Improper use of the shoulder action
h. Improper arm and wrist action

a. The grip can have a great influence on the power of the serve. The grip creates the angle of the racket as it impacts the ball. A flat serve will create more pace to the ball than a ball struck with more spin although almost every ball has a little spin as it moves through the air. A flat serve is usually struck with a continental forehand grip whereas a kick serve will be best executed with an eastern backhand grip. Most advanced players slide the grip farther down in the palm of their hand to increase the flexibility and elasticity of the wrist joint. Having improper grips for the type of serve you intend to hit will adversely affect the power of the service action.

b. Muscling the ball is common to every player trying to use more power on the serve. Not only will the coordination deteriorate, but the speed and acceleration will also be less with restricted joint movements due to the continuous pressure throughout the motion instead of the release of the muscles on the noncontracting side of the joints. Flexibility and elasticity of the joints, ligaments, and muscles will also be restricted by the muscling of the stroke and adversely affect the power. Learning to be relaxed in the backswing and accelerating the service action from the ground up with a coordinated transition of power in sequence from one section to another will create a lag of the racket head that will be accelerated with the elasticity of the muscles and ligaments for maximum speed at impact with the ball.

c. The toss plays an important part to the impact position of the stroke and the possible power transfer of the kinetic chain to the ball. With the ball too much over the head of the player, the shoulders will be restricted in the rotation around the body and the shoulder-over-shoulder forward rotation. The length of the arm will be less due to a bent elbow to make proper 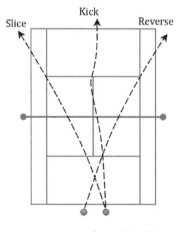 contact above the head (power = energy × arm length). These restrictions are alleviated as soon as the toss position is slightly more to the side of the body. The position to look for is straight above the hitting shoulder. The position of the toss in front of the body is also crucial to power development. Too much in front will restrict the upward motion of the body and restrict the elbow and wrist action on the follow-through. Too far back will restrict the weight transfer and release of the arm, elbow, and wrist action with the follow-through. The position of the toss plays an important part to

Martin van Daalen

the contact angle at impact with the ball and the swing path of the racket for the intended rotation of the ball.

d. The improper coordination of the movements usually is contributed to the initiating movement of the service action. Most players start by applying pressure with the arms instead of initiating the movement from the ground up. By starting with the arms, it is very difficult to stay loose with the muscles and take advantage of the flexibility and elasticity of the muscles and ligaments. Initiating the movement from the feet up will release the muscles in the proper sequence with a transfer of acceleration through each segment from the feet to the racket head. It will greatly improve the coordination and the timing of the service action and add to the speed and power of the stroke.

e. The feet and knee action are the initiating force to the start of the forward swing of the service action. They help maintain the balance during the backswing and assist with the rotation of the shoulders and the loading of the serve. The position of the feet needs to be wide enough to maintain proper balance and to provide maximum power for the knee action. Less knee action causes less loading to the serve, resulting in less speed (power) to the serve. The timing of the serve is created by the start of the feet and knee action. Make sure the shoulder and arm action is generated from the feet and not the other way round.

f. The forward hip action is usually not performed at all or not enough to maintain the balance during the backswing and to provide the loading of the knees, trunk, and shoulders for the forward swing. By bending the hips forward in the backswing, the player can create a balance point before pushing up and swinging forward. The hip action also allows the body to load properly to extend upward more from the knee action. The forward action of the hips creates a forward reaction of the shoulder-over-shoulder rotation. This provides more power and control to the service motion.

g. The shoulder action consists of the rotation of the shoulders around the body and the shoulder-over-shoulder action from back to front. The lack of loading (rotation) or insufficient loading of the shoulders in the backswing can lead to many errors or problems in the forward swing. With proper rotation, the shoulders turn back away from the net to where the shoulders are at least facing the net pole. Some well-known pro players turn the shoulders even farther till they are almost parallel with the baseline. This will assist the racket head to swing around the body and pick up additional acceleration from the rotational force. The forward rotation of the shoulders should be initiated from the feet upward to fully create the accelerated service action. Most players try to create power with the arm or hand instead. This will result in "muscling" of the ball with less racket-head speed. Once the hip forward and rotational hip action is set into motion, the shoulders will accelerate and create a lag motion of the racket head. The shoulders accelerate fast until there is an almost square position of the shoulders. At this time, the arm, elbow, and hand action catch up and accelerate past the point of impact with the ball. This results in a release of the racket head after impact for better ball-flight control. The shoulder-over-shoulder action is set into motion by the hip action and the shoulder rotation. They both create a loading of the trunk muscles to facilitate the shoulder-over-shoulder action (action-reaction). The coordination of the hip action, the shoulder rotation, and the shoulder-over-shoulder action need to be trained to optimally benefit the speed, spin, and control of the service action. The shoulder actions are crucial to the development the service action of advanced players. The coordination of the movements is the most important factor for timing and consistency.

h. The arm and wrist action form the last link of the kinetic chain before the racket head makes contact with the ball. The elbow action of the arm is often not loose enough, resulting in less flexibility to produce acceleration to the wrist and racket head. On the forward motion, most players do not bend the elbow again after impact with the ball. The flexing of the elbow should not be a forced action, but a release of the elbow with the timing and release of the wrist combined with a pronation (inward and downward flexing) of wrist. The release of the wrist can only be accomplished when players swing upward with the elbow and wrist toward impact with the ball and properly time the release of the wrist right after contact with the ball. Proper use of the knee, hip, and shoulder-over-shoulder action will assist in performing this action.

Corrections and practice:

- To practice staying loose on the service action, students can practice the swing of the arm and racket by holding the grip with just three fingers. The thumb, index finger, and ring finger should fit loosely around the grip as the player feels the racket head swing through the imaginary impact point of the ball. The player should get a good feel of how loose the racket should be held and the importance of generating the momentum and timing of the racket head to produce the power to the service action.
- The loading of the body, shoulder, and arm and the unloading with the throwing action can be trained with the use of a football or training ball. These training balls come in different forms and shapes. I personally like the "Wuffle ball." It is smaller in size, has a softer nose, and has tail fins for stabilization. Some create a whistling noise when thrown in the air. The correct throwing action should be upward around forty-five degrees to simulate the upward motion of the service action.
- To coordinate all the segments together, coaches should practice with the focus on each segment separately from the ground up. This will ensure a power transfer for the kinetic chain from one segment to the next (feet to the wrist action).
- The loading of the knees and hips are an important segment in producing power with the serve. By starting the forward swing, in sequence from the knees and then the hips, it generates the acceleration in the shoulders that creates the lag and acceleration in the hitting arm. Contrary to what you might think, this can only be obtained by relaxing the hitting arm and keeping the grip pressure low.

- By backward rotation of the hips and shoulders, the power of the serve can increase quite dramatically. Some of the big servers of the game turn the feet slightly more sideways to accommodate this motion. The shoulders can be rotated backward to an almost parallel position with the baseline.
- The forward rotation of the serve can produce added power by timing the forward motion slightly later. This will automatically accelerate the shoulder rotation and create more power to the serve. The toss arm folds in the stomach area and assists in the shoulder rotation and balance with the recovery of the service motion.
- The elbow and wrist action through contact with the ball create added power to the service motion. The timing of these two motions is important not only for power, but also for depth, direction, and spin to the ball. It is crucial that these motions are created by the timing of the motion rather than being forced with power in the elbow or wrist. This will maintain control and consistency in the service motion.
- The power of the serve can be measured with a radar gun. It will give a pretty accurate reading on the speed and power of the serve. Another easy method is to measure the height of the impact point of the ball on the back fence. (See depth of the serve.) To practice this, it is possible to move farther back behind the baseline for a while to stimulate the action. Make sure the students keep the arm relaxed and don't squeeze the grip too hard during the execution of the service motion.

Tempo of the Serve

The tempo of the serve is largely determined by the coordination and the timing of the toss with the service motion. The height of the toss plays an important role in regulating the timing of service motion. With a higher toss, the tempo of the serve will be slower. The backswing of the service motion will need to slow down to coordinate the forward swing with the longer airtime of the toss. The reverse will be the case with a lower toss, where the service motion follows the toss much quicker. The key is to find the correct rhythm and tempo of the service motion with the speed of the backswing and the timing and height of the toss. The tempo of the serve can be used in several different ways:

- **Technically**

  The tempo of the service motion is technically determined by the coordination and timing of the toss with the service motion. The tempo has a great influence on the rhythm and consistency of the motion. By coordinating the tempo and rhythm of the service motion with the physical capabilities of the player, a higher consistency and confidence will be achieved and result in a high-percentage first and second serves.

- **Tactically**

  It is possible to change the tempo and timing of the service motion to throw off the timing of the return player. By slowing down or speeding up the tempo, it makes it much more difficult for the returner to get accustomed to the timing of the speed and spin. When the returner already is especially experiencing problems with the timing of the return or to surprise the opponent, this can be a valuable tactic to use. However, since it is very difficult to change the rhythm and tempo of the serve, it is not advisable to use this at any time, and players are better served with a consistent and reliable service action that has one rhythm and tempo.

- **Physically**

  Another application in using the tempo of the serve is to speed up the time in between points to affect the recovery time of the opponent. By providing them with less time to recover, it is possible to wear them out physically, resulting in unforced errors from the opponent. Since the returner has to play at the tempo of the server, they have no chance but to keep up with the tempo of play. This strategy does require good physical conditioning in order to be successful.

- **Mentally**

  By changing the tempo or rushing the opponent, you can affect the opponent mentally. The opponent will start thinking of the change of tempo and what the server is doing instead of thinking about how to play. The focus and attention to details will be interrupted and distract the opponent from thinking of strategy and tactics, which will result in unforced errors.

Common Mistakes with Tempo of the Serve

a. Rushing the service motion
b. Improper loading of the serve
c. Improper timing of the serve
d. Lesser knee action

a. Rushing the service motion can be a result of the tempo changes. The coordination of the toss and the service motion need to be in sync with each other to be effective. In an effort to hit the ball harder, it is not uncommon to see the server rush the motion and start the forward swing too early. The timing of the unloading of the forward swing is important to the speed, depth, direction, and spin of the serve.

b. The loading of the serve can be compromised when trying to speed up the tempo of the service motion. Players will have a tendency to not complete the backswing and start the forward swing too early with less power from the loading. This can lead to less consistency in the motion and a low-percentage serves in service box.

c. The timing of the serve becomes more complicated with a higher tempo of the service action. Slowing down the tempo will alleviate this problem. The slower the player makes the windup of the toss and service action, the easier it becomes to time the ball and accelerate the motion. With a faster motion, the coordination of the toss with the hitting arm becomes less consistent and reliable.

d. With a faster tempo of the serve, the knee action will become less distinct. Players tend to rush the motion and the knee action, resulting in less upward push from the knees. This causes the trajectory of the serve to be much flatter and contain less spin. This can result in a lower-percentage serve with more serves hitting the net or flying long.

Corrections and practice:

*   In many cases, players rush the motion of the serve and need to practice to slow down the backswing and toss to acquire the proper timing and acceleration. This can be achieved by having the player count from one to four in a predetermined tempo. The backswing will be timed during the count from one to three while the forward swing is performed during the fourth count. This method will slow down the backswing and accelerate the forward swing.
*   The height of the toss determines the timing and tempo of the serve. Most players make contact with the ball as the ball is descending after the ball toss has reached its highest point. There are some players that speed up the tempo as the ball reaches the highest point of the toss. And in some rare cases, the player actually hits the ball as the toss is still rising. Try to find the tempo of the serve with the height of the toss. Tossing the ball too high will cause the player to suspend the forward swing too long with a loss of momentum of the body motions and racket head. To practice these different tempos through one another is very difficult and not recommended as a tactical application. It will adversely affect the consistency of the player. But you can try out different heights of the toss to see what suits the timing and rhythm of each specific player. You will find that many players are very individual and specific due to their personal style.

- Most players have a tendency to rush into playing the next point too quickly and speed up the tempo of play unnecessarily. It causes players to make hasty and irrational decisions that lead to unforced errors. The higher tempo of play will also put more strain on the player's stamina. It is important to learn the proper tempo of play by obtaining a routine during play. This needs to be taught in the beginning by going to the towel after every point and walking back to the back fence. A good tempo of play will stimulate focus and concentration in long matches.

The Return

The return of the serve has been the most improved stroke in the last twenty years. With the improvement of racket technology and strings, it is possible to play the return much more aggressively with spin. This has changed the speed and strategies of the game in a large way. Players are attacking the return and taking more risk with the shot choices and targets. This has greatly reduced the amount of serve and volley players with this game style becoming almost obsolete in singles play. Doubles players still benefit from this particular style of play since two people cover the court space.

Technical Differences with Ground Strokes

In general, the technique of the forehand and backhand is suitable for the return of the serve. However, due to the speed of the serve, players will have far less time to react to the ball, and the bounce might propel the ball above the shoulder level. These two factors dictate a technical adjustment:

- **The backswing needs to be higher** to adjust for the higher bounce of the ball. With a normal backswing, the swing path would be too steep upward to the impact with the ball. It would become very difficult to swing up and over to bring the ball down in the court. Players would have to add too much spin to control the trajectory and lose a lot of pressure and speed on the ball.
- **The backswing needs to be shorter** to accommodate the timing of the ball. With a longer backswing and increased speeds of the serve, it becomes very difficult to time the ball consistently and make solid contact. By turning the shoulders, it creates enough backswing to generate plenty of power on the return and increases control and consistency.
- **Creativity is a necessity** in order to become consistent on the return. Most often the returns are hit when reaching for the shot or trying to get out of the way of a body shot. It takes good reflexes to quickly make a decision and execute the stroke while maintaining balance. The wide returns are on the run and should be trained as such. As the speed of the serves increase, the backswing will shorten even more, and spin or slice is added for control.

Consistency

It is no coincidence that the better players also have great consistency with the return of serve. The first objective in winning points in return games is consistency. It creates rhythm at the beginning of the rally that leads to confidence of the player to push on. The percentage and consistency of first- and second-serve returns usually varies due to the speed, spin, and accuracy of the opponent's service action. As players become more accomplished and hit serves with greater speeds and accuracy, there will be more direct winning shots (aces). It takes a lot of mental perseverance to stay the course and not let this affect your game. The surface of the playing field will influence the consistency as well. (Think of grass courts and indoor surfaces, where players hit many more aces in matches.)

Djokovic (Forehand Return)

Martin van Daalen

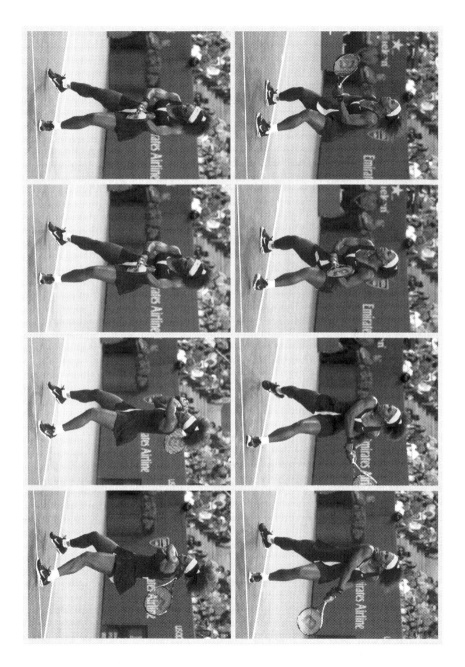

Serena Williams (Backhand, Open Stance Return)

Common Mistakes with Consistency of the Return

a. Improper starting positions
b. Improper timing of the split step
c. Improper backswing
d. Improper target choices

a. Positioning the body in the proper place for returning the serve can increase the consistency of the return. Most often players are standing too close to the baseline or to one side of the service box to guard against their weaker return. Standing too close or inside the baseline will decrease the reaction time to the serve and create more unforced errors. Players need to adjust the distance behind the baseline to the reaction time of the return. Positioning to one side of the service box to protect the weaker return will send a message to the opponent where to aim. It also will leave one side less protected and vulnerable to outright winners of the serve. Playing against lefty players also requires some positioning adjustments. With the serve curving more easily to the left, a good rule of thumb is to change from your normal positioning and take one step over to the left. This will solve many problems in returning against lefty players. With the speed being less on second serves, it can be beneficial to move one or two steps forward on second-serve returns to find good contact points. However, this can change on clay courts with heavy spin balls. In this situation, it can be beneficial to move a couple of steps backward to let the ball drop down to a more comfortable hitting zone below the shoulder level.

b. The timing of the split step and unit turn are important aspects to improve the return and the consistency in particular. Whenever the timing of the split step is too late or too early, it will affect the timing and rhythm of the return. This can lead to many unforced errors. The unit turn of the arms, hips, and shoulders immediately follows the split step and needs to be in coordination with the speed and spin of the ball in order to time the contact point correctly with the ball.

c. The height of the backswing will influence the quality of the return of the serve. It needs to be high enough to swing the racket head through the ball rather than swinging too much up or down on the swing. Most players start too low with the take back of the backswing and end up having to swing upward too much or pull it down on the follow-through. Learning to hit slightly upward but through the ball is the key to a consistent contact and trajectory of the return of serve. The length of the backswing needs to be kept shorter to improve the timing and contact point with the ball to positively influence the consistency of the return. Many players make the mistake of having the same length of backswing with different speeds of the ball. Even with ground strokes, players should adjust the length of the backswing to improve the timing of the ball. In a rally, players can rely on the rhythm of the rally to maintain the timing of the ball. When returning serves, the rhythm is not established yet. By keeping the backswing shorter, it is easier to make adjustments to the swing path and timing of the forward swing of the return.

d. The target choices need to be kept simple with a large margin for error with the net and well inside the lines. This will avoid unforced errors, cut down on the angles of attack, and improve confidence and consistency of the rallies and returns. Players often do not realize the importance of large targets and avoiding angles on the return. Unless it is possible to hit a winner on the return, players should learn to find the weaker side of the opponent and hit deep through the court. By using this method, players can improve consistency and prevent the opponent from attacking on the first ball after the serve (neutralize). This might create opportunities to apply pressure on the opponent and draw unforced errors from them.

Corrections and practice:

- Try out the different positions when returning serves. Standing farther back behind the baseline can provide more time to return the ball and dramatically increase the consistency of the return. Note: be aware that it opens the court when standing farther back behind the baseline with more angles available to the server.

- As the server hits the ball, have the players call out a number or the word "split" at the time of contact with the ball. This will increase the timing and reaction time of the return and make players much more aware of the importance of the split step and how it relates to consistency of the return.

- To make players aware of how short the backswing needs to be, you can have them stand close to the back fence and restrict their backswing by not touching the fence. Videos can also be a helpful tool here to show how short the backswing needs to be.

- Setting up targets for the return can be very useful to show the target area, but also to practice the accuracy of the return. The target deep in the middle on the backhand side should be the most practiced target area.

- Playing higher over the net increases the consistency of the return. Attaching a line over the length of the net can improve this. The server will be able to play under the line while the returner can play over the line. Players will automatically adjust the trajectory and have far less mistakes with balls in the net.

- To increase consistency under pressure, you can stand inside the court and serve balls from that position. Always have designated target areas for the return. Serving first to one target can improve the technical aspects of the return. As the proficiency improves, different targets can be used to improve anticipation and reaction.

- This same exercise as above can be intensified by adding serve and volley. Not only will this train the reflexes and adaptability of the player, but they will also have to react and recover for the next ball, an important next step for competitive players.

Depth of the Return

Playing the return with depth can have a profound effect on the outcome of a point. The opponent has two choices in this case. Take much more risk by hitting the ball on the rise or move back from the baseline and play a defensive or neutralizing shot to continue the rally. Either way, it is a great advantage to return the ball with depth. The opponent will have much less angles to attack on the next shot and could be forced in a defensive position on the court. The determining factor of depth on the return is the trajectory of the ball. The proper elevation, speed, and rotation of the ball have to be coordinated together to find the correct trajectory.

Elevation. The height and angle of the ball over the net will have the largest influence on the depth of the return. By playing the ball higher over the net, with the same speed and spin, the ball will fly deeper in the court.

Speed. The speed of the ball will influence the depth of the return. By playing the ball with more speed, with the same height over the net and the same spin, the return will land deeper in the court.

Rotation of the ball. The rotation on the ball (spin) will influence the trajectory of the return. By using rotation on the ball, it creates friction with the air and can dramatically change the trajectory of the ball. This can be accomplished with slice, topspin, and sidespin to the ball.

Common Mistakes with the Depth of the Return

a.   Improper starting position
b.   Moving backward during the return
c.   Playing too low over the net
d.   No use of spin or slice to control the trajectory

a. The positioning of the body can be of great influence in creating the proper depth on the return stroke. Most often players take position close to the baseline and then end up stepping back. This will cause them to lose balance and control of the ball flight. By starting three to four feet behind the baseline and stepping forward to make a split step, the body weight will keep its forward momentum against the ball, and it will be easier to cut off the angles to reach the ball. This forward momentum will generate energy against the ball and will facilitate the player to make a shorter backswing. Standing too far back will open the court only further and make the player reach even more. On second serves, the returner can move closer to the baseline, or even slightly inside, with less pace of the serve. It also accommodates the return by taking the ball early and making contact with the ball before it rises above the shoulder. On clay, it can be advantageous to actually move farther back and let the ball drop into the strike zone. Most often juniors will not make the adjustment in hitting it higher over the net. This may result in unforced errors in the net. This moving back on the return is only possible if the server does not immediately move in forward to volley the ball.

b. Moving forward against the ball is important to create depth to the return. When a player moves back just before or during the return, it is much more difficult to judge the speed, spin, and trajectory of the return. Movement will also be hindered with the wider angles to cover the court and in not being able to cut off the corners.

c. The height over the net determines for a great part the trajectory and depth of the ball. With the speed of the serve, it is usually not necessary to add more speed. Finding the proper trajectory and height over the net is a matter of experience and practice. The height of the backswing can assist in creating the correct circular-oval swing so that the racket head approaches the ball with the proper elevation in the swing.

d. The spin or slice to the ball can change the trajectory and the depth of the ball. Adding topspin to the return will make the ball curve downward sooner in the trajectory. Adding slice will keep the ball up longer in the air, but the ball will move slower through the air and lose speed over time.

Practice

- Using a higher net will correct the height and the depth of the return. By serving inside the court, it is possible to gauge the speed and spin of the ball for better practice. It reduces the reaction time and increases the focus of the player.
- Practice the return as above, but hit every return with the intent to approach the net. This will train players to attack the return and automatically hit deep returns.
- Practicing depth can also be in reverse by having to play the ball short in the court. In playing serve and volley plays and doubles play, it is useful to hit the return at the feet of the net player or with an angle for a passing shot. This requires topspin or slice returns that dip down after passing the net. Set up three targets on the service line to practice the return. One target on the T and two others three feet from the single line. Have the players return to different targets to increase accuracy.

Direction of the Return

The direction of the serve is an important tactical aspect to establish an initiative from the first ball on. A well-placed return to the weaker side or directly at the body of the opponent will most often dictate the rally or create a weak response. (Note: sometimes placing a forceful return to the stronger side can open up the weaker side). This opens many opportunities to take charge of the rally to force opponents to make errors or to open up the court for a winning shot. Advanced players always have a plan before returning the ball to where and how they are going to hit the return. This plan mostly depends on the quality of the serve, the capabilities of the returner, if it is a first or second serve, and the score and flow of the game. Having a target for the return makes you more committed to the return and will help you focus on the pattern you want to establish in the rally. It is best to have a primary and secondary target for your return. A primary target is the one you use when the serve is executed the way you expected. A secondary target becomes necessary when the serve turns out to be more difficult to return than expected. It is basically a backup return that you keep as a standard solution for difficult serves and to neutralize the opponent. This backup return should be deep, just out of the middle of the court, on the weaker side of the opponent. By using this method, you can decrease the chances of outright winners by closing the angles, and it is a relatively easy target to execute and accomplish. In general, the hard first-serve returns should be dealt with in the same manner as a secondary or back-p return since the target area is larger and the reaction time of the server is shorter with the ball returning that much faster at their feet.

Factors of Direction of Return

There are several factors that determine the direction of the return, and most of these are actually dependent on the preparation and setup of the stroke. With the higher speeds of the serve, it leaves the returner with less time to react, set up, and execute the stroke than with any other stroke in the game. Playing against a top-level server leaves you with less than half a second to react and execute the motion. This time constraint dictates a different approach in adjusting the technique to the circumstances and will heavily play a role in the direction of the serve. Some of the factors of the direction of the return are the following:

a. **Early and fast preparation**

An early setup of the stroke will give a better opportunity to execute the stroke in a timely fashion to control the direction of the ball. Footwork and backswing have to work together by making a split step when the opponent serves and moving the feet to position the body behind the line of the serve. The backswing starts after the split step with a unit turn by turning the shoulders and arms together as one. The unit turn provides a short and compact backswing in order to react faster and to maintain the balance before and during the return to improve control and direction.

b. **Short and compact backswing**

With less reaction time on the return strokes, it is necessary to shorten the length of the backswing. By making a unit turn with the shoulders and the arms together, it is possible to combine both movements into one and speed up the preparation phase. At the beginning of the backswing, the arms spread apart on the forehand side to maintain balance. The front arm stays at a forty-five-degree angle in front of the body to keep the body weight forward against the ball. With the backhand, the other hand supports the backswing to maintain balance with the swing and the body. By lifting the arms and racket in a circular motion, it is possible to swing more freely in the forward motion using less power. This increases the accuracy in direction.

c. **Stepping and leaning forward into the return**

Making a split step forward at the time of the serve, it is possible to keep the weight forward against the ball to maintain a better balance during the return. By leaning against the ball just before contact, the force of the body weight counteracts the pace of the ball and the backward reaction force of the forward swing. This does not only assist in the power of the return but also helps maintain balance during and after the return to improve direction and control.

d. **Correct timing of the contact points**

A better timing of the ball ensures better contact points to maintain the technique of the return. Whenever the contact points are compromised, there will be a breakdown or correction of the racket head to keep control of the trajectory of the ball. In most cases, the return is struck late with the contact points being more at the side of the body instead of in front. This will often cause players to block the return or to pull the racket down and over the top of the ball in an effort to correct the stroke. These corrections will heavily affect the direction and depth of the return. With the correct timing of the return, the strokes should look very similar on the follow-through as regular forehands and backhands in order to control direction.

e. **Good recovery for optimal balance**

Whenever a player loses balance during the follow-through, it will often affect the quality and control of the stroke. This will usually exhibit itself with a sudden falling motion of the body and a shorter follow-through. A good recovery of the stroke with the use of the feet can maintain or restore the balance of the stroke when judgment errors are made with the timing or contact points. It is also very helpful to recover sudden, bad bounces of the ball that could not be foreseen. A good recovery of the stroke improves the balance of the body to direct the ball with accuracy.

Most Common Mistakes with Direction of the Return

a. Improper timing of the split step
b. Improper backswing
c. Late contact points
d. Abbreviated or incorrect follow-through

Corrections

a. In order to reach the balls from the serve and return them in a chosen direction, it is necessary to get off the mark on time and maintain balance during the return stroke. This is only possible if the split step is timed correctly to the contact of the server with the ball. The split step needs to be timed just so that the returner is in the air on the way down to the ground as the serve is struck. The jump of the split step is close to the ground to create less "hang time" in the air. After reading the direction of the serve, players will be able to move quickly to the ball as soon as the feet hit the ground. Having the proper timing of the split step provides players with a quicker reaction time to reach wide serves and maintain a better balance for direction.

b. The backswing of the return is one of the most important preparations in striking a return in the correct direction. The backswing needs to be a compact short unit turn with the hips, shoulders, and arms. The backswing of the return also is slightly higher in the backswing to compensate for a higher-impact angle of the serve and the higher bounce of the ball. Without these adjustments to the technique of the return, it is very difficult to maintain a proper forward swing to direct the ball.

c. Timing the return is a crucial aspect of the return to direct the ball to a target. Without proper contact points, it is almost impossible to direct the ball in a chosen direction. Most returns are struck slightly late and rarely struck too early. This is mostly caused by the lack of established rhythm with it being the first ball in the rally and the different speeds and spins of the ball. Players also have a tendency to be conservative on returns in an effort not to miss. Not committing to the serve with the footwork and forward swing causes the timing to be slightly delayed. As players settle into the match, the rhythm and timing usually improves the contact points and direction of the ball, especially if confidence increases in connection with some good returns.

d. By extending the follow-through, you can increase the accuracy of the return. The follow-through acts as a steering mechanism in directing the ball. An abbreviated follow-through can be quite common with very vast first serves. You can witness this with pro players when they have very little time to react, let alone to make a backswing. If they would try to make too long of a swing, they would either be too late and/or have more trouble timing the contact point. They are only able to block the ball in front and keep the racket angle in the direction of the target. When time permits, it is important to do just the opposite and follow-through all the way to increase the direction of the ball. This is especially important with hitting second-serve returns to counteract the spin of the serve and direct the ball.

Practice

- Set up three targets on the court and serve balls from inside the baseline. Serve first to forehand or backside and call out the target direction. After this exercise, you can alternate and/or mix up the directions of the serve to one or different targets to improve reaction time and direction of the return. Watch for the timing of the split step and the abbreviated backswing, coordinated with the strike of the serve.
- Use the same drill with the players trying to hit the return as an approach shot. This will train them to commit to the return by stepping forward, leaning in, and reaching in front for the contact point. This will greatly improve the direction of the return.
- The return is trained very well in a serve-and-volley exercise by choosing a target for the return and playing out the point. Players learn very quickly the importance of attacking the return and recovering for the next stroke in the rally. The targets will improve the direction of the return and teach players the different possibilities of these rallies as they develop. Start by hitting the return through the middle.

The Volley

A volley is a stroke that is struck in the air. It is a stroke that is mostly used at the net and is a very useful tool in finishing the point or rushing the opponent to return the ball. Formerly, tennis was played on grass and indoor courts, and the volley was a very important stroke that was used in almost every rally. The courts' surfaces have since been slowed down for viewer purposes, and the new racket and string technology has increased the speed and spin of the ball. These changes have led to less serve-and-volley-style players and more aggressive baseline play. Players have less opportunity to attack the net in singles play. Obviously, it is still used quite a lot in doubles play, but even then some teams are choosing to stay back and hit attack from the baseline. At this moment in time, the serve-and-volley player has almost disappeared. The volley is still used in singles play as a finishing stroke after a buildup from the baseline. Occasionally, the serve and volley is visible as a changeup in strategy, but it has basically become a lost art that once was a key part of the game.

Teaching Progressions of the Volley

Most players and coaches have a tendency to make the execution of the volley much more complicated than necessary. The execution can be fairly simple if you stick to a few simple concepts. Essentially, the volley is a shot where the ball is blocked back in the opposite direction by the flexibility of the string and the forward motion of the body with the step forward toward the ball. The key is to get the racket in the correct position, in front of the body with the racket angle facing the target. Once this is established, it is possible to progress from there to more advanced techniques. See the full progressions under "Practice and Progressions."

Common Mistakes of the Volley

a. Improper timing and execution of the split step
b. Improper backswing
c. The position of the wrist and racket angle
d. Not stepping in and timing of the step in
e. The follow-through

Corrections

a. The timing of the split step needs to be executed at the time the ball makes impact with the opponent's racket. This will provide time to step in toward the ball and make contact out in front. The weight of the body stays forward on top of the toes with the knees bent for a proper split step. Most often players only make split steps on the first few shots, but it imperative to do this every time.
b. The backswing is often too big with too much shoulder use. The backswing should be short and executed mainly with the underarm and the wrist. The racket head comes back first in order to get the racket head in position as soon as possible.
c. With the forehand, the wrist is bent back so the arm is in a forty-five-degree angle in front of the body. The racket head is pointing in a forty-five-degree angle of the wrist, at the side and in front of the body, in the direction of the target. With the backhand, the racket is in the same position but with a straight wrist position and the knuckles forward.
d. Stepping forward into the volley provides the majority of the power. Whenever the players are not stepping in, they usually end up swinging more with the arm. This will negatively affect the accuracy of direction and depth of the volley. The forward step into the volley needs to be timed at the same time you make contact. This will create balance, power, and control to the volley.
e. The follow-through of the volley is to be kept short with the strings facing in the same direction as the target. Most juniors swing through

the contact point and end up with the top of the racket facing forward. The bottom edge of the racket head needs to lead in the short punch as the racket moves through the ball. A good rule of thumb is to lead the bottom edge of the racket to the top of the net band.

Practice and Progressions

- Block the ball back from the feeds with no movement of the racket or arm. With this particular method, the students learn to find the proper racket position and contact point in front of the body. The feet move behind the trajectory of the ball with the racket head above the wrist in a forty-five-degree angle and the arm in front of the body in a forty-five-degree angle. At first, the grips are adjusted to the volley with a continental forehand grip and a continental backhand grip for comfort and learning. The knees are bent to the extent to keep the eyes close to the level of the ball.
- Step into the ball at the moment of contact with a short punch of the underarm. Start by feeding the ball and progress to life-ball rallies. The step forward against the ball needs to be timed simultaneously with the punch of the underarm against the ball. The racket angle stays stable in the target direction. Both actions will create more pace to the ball.
- Same drill as above but add slice to the volley for control. Slant the racket angle to create slice and improve speed and depth control of the volley. By turning the bottom edge of the racket toward the net, the short, forward, and downward punch toward the top of the net will create a natural slice for optimal control of the ball.
- Learn the differences of high and low volleys. Feed two different balls with high and low trajectory. Once the players get the technique down, you can try life-ball rallies. The racket angle and contact points need to be adjusted to the trajectory, spin, and height of the ball. The contact points are farther in front of the body in both situations to compensate for low and high trajectories of the ball. The bottom edge of the racket always moves to the direction of the net strap.

- Add wide volleys by playing all the balls back to one corner with a target. Make adjustments to wide-volley situations by changing the racket angle. Opening the racket angle and closing it slightly around the outside of the ball will ensure that the wide balls can be redirected in the proper direction.

- Learning to produce winning volleys with swinging volleys. By setting up high and easy volley situations, players can learn to finish off points with winning strokes. It is important to close the net and create less distance to the net. This will eliminate the chances of making mistakes in the net, with the opportunity to hit more downward in the court.

- In learning deep and short volley situations, it is not always possible to play the deep volley since players are able to run these down. Playing short or angle volley adds another dimension to the tactical situations. The angle or short volley can be executed by adding more slice to the ball by opening the racket angle or cutting around the side of the ball with the strings.

- The serve and volley situations develop many different types of shots that develop the volley. The split step and various volley strokes need to be coordinated to the timing and stroke of the opponent. The volley after the serve will require time and experience to learn since there are so many different possibilities and options.

- In closing the net for doubles play, this type of volley play requires players to move constantly closer to the net in order to close the angles for the opponent to play into and to open up the angles for the rushing net player. By closing the net, you take time away from the opponent to react to the following ball. The key actions of these types of volleys are split steps, stepping in to the volley, and short punches with the underarm to produce short, quick, and aggressive shots.

- Poaching the ball in doubles play. Players need to learn to anticipate the return of the server to cut across the net and volley the ball in the open court, in between the two opponents. The timing of when to move, at the time of contact with the return, is the key factor to successfully execute these poach volleys.

Martin van Daalen

Key Positions for the Volley

Ready position

- Athletic posture
- Relaxed hands
- Slightly bend knees
- Split step forward
- Alert disposition

Backswing

- Flex wrist backward
- Rotate hips outside
- Turn toes outside
- Racket swing back

Backswing

Loading

- Bend knees farther
- Turn hips
- Turn shoulders
- Extend both arms
- Balance arm to side

Forward swing

- Unload legs
- Unload hips
- Unload shoulders
- Trace oncoming ball
- Line up racket path

Forward swing

Contact point

- Hand in front
- Stability in wrist
- Weight transfer
- Hitting zone

Follow-through

Contact point

- Arm forward and around
- Foot skips around
- Full turn of the hips
- Full turn of the shoulders

Recovery

- Recovery footwork
- Overstep outside foot
- Position body to cover the court

Teaching the Volley with Key Positions

The forehand volley is generally a simple action, but is often made more complicated than needed. Teaching the volley can be simplified by starting beginning players to catch the ball with their hand instead of using the racket. They will lose some of the fear at being closer to the net, and it teaches them to the automated movement in bending the knees and catching the ball out in front of the body. The coach can throw the ball or feed balls left and right from the player or even straight at them to make them aware how to move out of the way. Creating the same position of the arm at impact with the ball is the key to solid and consistent volleys.

Forehand and Backhand Volley

The Overhead

The overhead or smash is a stroke that is imperative for advanced players to finish off a high ball or lob with a winning shot. The opponent is usually in a defensive position when this stroke is utilized by hitting the ball high up in the air to drive the player back from the net position. The stroke itself resembles the service action; but with the trajectory of the ball, the movement of the feet, and the timing of the contact point, it is one of the most coordinated shots in the game. Without the skills, practice, and experience, this stroke is difficult to execute, especially moving backward as a jump shot. Most juniors forget to warm up the stroke when preparing for match play and end up missing the overhead in crucial situations. The overhead can also be a useful tool to enhance the serve over time in power and speed. It will automatically train the muscle groups of the service motion and increase the racket-head speed. There are three types of overheads to consider in training:

- **The overhead after the bounce of the ball**
  The stroke is hit after the ball has bounced. There are several tactical situations that dictate to let the ball bounce before attempting to strike the ball. If the ball is retrieved from a high lob, it can be advisable to let the ball bounce in order to time the ball better. Sometimes a short lob is easier to execute when letting the ball bounce first. The same method can be used when looking straight into the sun.

- **The overhead in the air**
  It is not always possible to let the ball bounce to take an overhead. In most cases, the ball is traveling too fast in the direction of the net player or is too low in trajectory. In these cases, players need to take the overhead in the air without bouncing the ball first. The timing of the contact point takes some practice but is similar to the impact point of the service action. Players would do well to keep this motion and coordination in mind when hitting the overhead in the air.

Martin van Daalen

- **The overhead as a jump shot**

  When the lob is executed well and the ball flies over the head of the net player, there is only one option: the jump shot overhead. The net player has to quickly move back and jump off the back in order to reach the lob. It takes great skill and coordination to pull this shot off and shows the athleticism of a player. In order to maintain balance during and after the stroke, the back leg has to swing up as a counteraction. The body is balanced on the other leg in the follow-through.

Teaching Progressions of the Overhead

The progressions of teaching the overhead can be similar to the list above, with some additions of net play to practice the setup, movement, and recovery of the overhead. The easiest and best way to teach intermediate and advanced players is to start with the three types of overhead separately, starting with the bounce of the ball first. You can see a full progression of the overhead under "Practice and Progressions."

Key Positions of the Overhead

Ready position

- Arms relaxed in front
- Racket in the ready position
- Weight on the balls of the feet
- Knees bent
- Athletic position

Backswing

- Turn to a sideways position
- Raise both arms in a strike position
- Aim front hand at the ball
- Move behind the ball
- Spread the feet

Loading

Loading

- Bend the knees
- Weight on back foot
- Turn shoulders
- Hips out in front for power
- and balance
- Drop racket behind shoulder

Forward swing

- Straighten (unload) legs
- Unload hips and shoulders
- Add top slice for control
- Extend arm up and forward
- Shift weight to front foot
- Balance arm drops to stomach

Contact point

- Swing upward
- Add top slice for control
- Extend elbow upward
- Balance arm in stomach
- Pronate the wrist

Follow-through

- Outward turn of the wrist
- Maintain posture
- Swing around to other side
- Finish with knuckles outside
- Catch racket

Recovery

- Back foot recovery to front
- Recovery footwork
- Position body for next shot

**Jump and "scissor kick"
Contact Point and
Follow Through**

Teaching the Overhead with Key Positions

The overhead is a complicated and coordinated effort from the whole body. Both arms are raised in the opposite directions. In teaching advanced tennis players, keep in mind to seek a progression from the start of the action to the completion of the stroke. The footwork and contact point of the overhead become crucial to the execution. Most often the students themselves will show when they are ready to take the next step in teaching more difficult overheads like the jump shot. They first have to show signs of fluidity in the stroke and hitting action and become proficient in consistency and direction. That will be the time to further develop the overhead with specifics. Until that time, teaching the overhead with the key positions will be a very valuable exercise.

Common Mistakes of the Overhead

a. Improper setup with grip, feet, and arms
b. Incorrect contact points
c. Improper weight transfer
d. Posture and balance
e. Target choices

Corrections

a. Look at the grip first to make sure players are using the correct grip on the overhead. It is advisable to use the same grip as the service action (continental). The feet and arms have to work together to hit proper overheads. Most of the mistakes are made in the preparation phase of the overhead with bad positioning behind the ball and with a bad setup of the arms. The movement of the feet has to be coordinated correctly with the oncoming trajectory of the lob in order to make impact with the ball at the correct contact point. The feet make quick adjustments to position the body behind the line of the ball with bent knees and the feet spread to transfer the weight forward. Spreading the feet provides more balance. The setup of the arms is organized by raising the arms, the front arm as a targeting device and the hitting arm in the ready position for the strike. This position creates balance before the swing and to the total setup of the overhead.

b. When overheads are difficult to control in direction and depth, most often the contact points are incorrect. The contact point of the overhead needs to be over, and just in front of, the hitting shoulder in order to hit the ball with control. From this contact point, it is easier to time the swing and the flexion of the wrist and elbow.

c. When hitting overheads, players often get stuck with the weight on the back foot. In some cases, this is due to the contact point, but it can also be the improper use of the weight transfer. In transferring the weight from the back foot to the front foot, just before contact with the ball, it will ease the timing of the stroke but also produce an increase in power and control of direction and depth of the ball. Unloading and flexing the knees will help the stroke by swinging up toward the impact point.

d. Increasing the posture of the body will enhance the performance of the overhead. In many cases, the players will bend from the hips forward in the follow-through. This will cause the racket to come down from the contact point instead of swinging up and over the ball at impact with the ball. Maintaining body posture, in staying "tall" during the forward swing, will enhance the contact and control of the ball.

e. It is always a devastating sight to see a buildup of a rally be diminished by hitting an overhead outside the lines. By choosing big targets against the running direction of the opponent, this can be avoided. The shot choice needs to be clear and decisive to avoid confusion. Changing your mind on a target is usually a bad idea and leads to many mistakes in overheads.

Practice and Progressions

- Serve balls from inside the service line in order to create the same motion and contact point of the serve. This will remind players of the similarities with the serve.
- Hit the overhead after the bounce. Start with the same high ball to different targets. After consistency has been established, try feeding high balls all over the court.
- Hit the overhead in the air. Start with easy short lobs from inside the baseline before moving back behind the baseline.

Martin van Daalen

- Vary the depth and direction of the lobs to practice the footwork and setup of the overhead.
- Start at the net and play lobs behind the player to practice jump shots. After every lob, the player touches the net again.
- Alternate standing overheads and jump overheads by playing shorter and longer lobs to make players feel the difference of footwork and setup of both strokes
- Play a short ball in the service box followed by a deep lob to practice the jump overhead. By alternating both feeds, it is possible to simulate a point situation.

Jada Robinson (Jump Overhead)

Martin van Daalen

Transition to the Net

The transition to the net is a multifaceted action in moving forward from a baseline position to the net position. There are many ways to approach the net, but they all have one thing in common, and that is to pressure the opponent. This action and movement should have a preparation phase in order to enhance the probability of success. This can be set up with a powerful weapon (serve or forehand) or by a pattern of play that produces a weak return. It can also be from the anticipation of a weak position or a shorter return from the opponent. In these cases, it is imperative to take swift action before the tactical situation has disappeared. Being decisive and committed is the key to a good approach. There are several different types of approach shots in coming to the net:

- **Short ball situation**

  In many short ball situations, it is important to take advantage of a weaker stroke by quickly moving in to take time away from the opponent and to apply pressure by forcing them to hit a passing shot. The key here is to reach the ball on time in order to hit it at the highest point after the bounce and to take up a proper position at the net. Reaching the ball early will enhance the effectiveness of the approach shot with more power and spin and will be easier to execute with a higher impact point. The positioning at the net is dependent on the direction of the approach shot and the possible contact points of the passing shot. Whenever the opponent reaches the ball late, it is virtually impossible to hit the ball cross-court. Moving slightly over to the sideline to cut off the down-the-line passing shot is a good tactical move.

- **After opening the court**

  In opening the court with an angle shot, it is possible to apply pressure by moving in and hitting the ball early with an approach shot or volley to the open court. The key here is to move the opponent outside the court with an angle shot to create an open court and to take the ball early to take away time to recover. The opponent will have much difficulty reaching the approach shot down the line and will be forced to hit a defensive shot that will result in an easy volley. Positioning at the net will depend on the quality of the approach and the defensive stroke options.

- **Serve and volley**

  This type of approach is a classic example of applying pressure with a difficult serve and following it in with a volley. The key points in this tactical situation are to prepare the volley with a well-placed serve and to follow the serve in the proper direction. The targets can vary from wide serve, body serve, to "T" serve. Players have to be able to follow this up with a volley or half volley to keep the pressure on the opponent. The direction of the serve depends on the capabilities of the returner. The direction of the movement after the serve depends on the direction of the serve. The server should always follow the direction of the serve in order to defend the angles of the return. The direction of the volley depends on the direction of the return, the angles available, the weaknesses of the returner, and the speed of recovery of the returner. Explaining the options of the volley with each return is an important part of the training of this approach situation.

- **Approaching on the return**

  This approach is designed to take advantage of the weaker serves from the opponent by hitting the return early after the bounce and following it in to the net. The key points here are to move inside the baseline during the toss of the ball, taking the ball early after the bounce and moving into the net position in the direction of the approach. As the initial forward movement is performed, the returned steps one to two yards inside the baseline and split steps at the moment of impact of the serve. The approach can be performed with a slice or topspin stroke, according to the bounce, angle, and weaknesses of the opponent. By quickly closing the distance to the net, it is possible to defend against the angles of a passing shot from the opponent.

- **Following a high topspin to the net**

  With heavy topspin ground strokes exchanges, it is possible to follow them in to the net after the stroke or when the opponent is in a vulnerable position on the court. The key point here is to recognize when to move in and where to take position. The move forward can be realized just after the stroke, when the opponent reacts too late or at the moment you realize that he or she is off balance during the stroke. The positioning at the net needs to be in the direction of the approach.

- **After playing a lob over the net player**

  When playing a lob over the opponent at the net, it is imperative to follow it in to the net to take advantage of the tactical situation and to finish the point at the net. The key point here is to react immediately when the net player starts retrieving the lob and look for the return stroke off the lob. It is a crucial time during the rally when a defensive stroke can be turned into an offensive position at the net and no time should be wasted in taking position at the net to win the point.

- **After a drop shot**

  Whenever a drop shot is executed, it is possible to follow it in to the net to apply even more pressure on the opponent by finishing off the retrieved ball. The key here is to know when to hit a drop shot and close in quickly with a split step to finish off any balls that are retrieved from the drop shot. The split step will ensure an alertness to defend against possible passing shots. The timing of a drop shot depends on the position of both players in combination with an easy short ball from the opponent. Playing a drop shot off a short-ball situation will be much harder for the opponent to retrieve in relation to a deep ball that is longer in the air. A longer airtime will provide players more time to retrieve the drop shot. Many players stay back on the baseline after playing a drop shot and could end up in a defensive position if the opponent plays a drop shot back or a good approach shot. You can avoid having these roles reversed by moving after the drop shot and camouflaging it as if you are playing an approach shot.

All these tactical approach shot situations are different in the technical execution of each stroke and need to be practiced separately in order to master them properly. They are valuable tools to implement pressure on the opponent by taking time away and rushing them to make difficult passing shots. The recognition of each tactical situation will enhance as it is performed more often in practice and point play. The sooner a player learns how to "read" these patterns and situations, the better he or she will be able to take advantage of it with a higher success rate. Practice will enhance the results.

The Progressions of Transitions to the Net

It is very possible to follow the progressions of the transitions to the net in the same order as shown above. The short-ball and angle-shot situations are a logical first and second choice in teaching the approach shots. The serve and volley follows next as it is used more in doubles play. Try to find drills in all the transitions to the net that are designed from easy to difficult and that illustrate the tactical situations in points.

Common Mistakes in Transitions to the Net

a. Not moving in quick enough
b. Hitting the ball late
c. Incorrect footwork
d. Incorrect target choices
e. Improper positioning at the net

Martin van Daalen

Corrections

a. The recognition of the tactical situation determines the shot choice in transitioning to the net. It enables players to move with urgency in getting to the proper net position. Moving in too slow will leave too many angles and court space for the opponents to hit successful passing shots. One of the factors to make a correction is to quickly recognize the tactical situation by practicing the patterns and reactions that fit each situation. Another factor is to move the body weight through the ball and accelerate the feet as soon as the approach shot or volley is executed and take up the net position behind the direction of the approach or volley. This will make the transition to the net as smooth and quickly as possible.

b. In moving forward, players have to coordinate the forward movement of the body with the trajectory, spin, and speed of the oncoming ball in order to find the correct contact points. Most often players have trouble finding the proper contact point as they don't compensate the impact point with the forward speed of the body. The correction would be to reach further out in front in making contact with the ball whenever the body is in a forward motion.

c. The feet become important instruments in making the transition to the net. When the feet are placed in the wrong positions in the forward movement, it becomes much more difficult to move in quickly and execute approach shots. In many cases, players place their feet too much sideways before contact with the ball. This will limit the rotation of the hips and shoulders and cause players to make impact with the ball at the side of the body. It also limits the weight transfer and acceleration of the feet in the transition to the net. The correction is a simple one in turning the feet more forward just before making contact with the ball.

d. The target choices of the approach shots have big implications to the options of the net rusher and to the opponent in making passing shots. Choosing the directions and targets is dependent on the position of the opponent, the distance to the net, and the possible passing shot angles. Playing down the line or cross-court is decided by the position of the opponent being inside or outside the court. By aiming for big targets in approaching the net, the eliminated errors continue to pressure the opponent. This method will also keep the angles smaller for opponents to hit passing shots.

e. The position at the net is coordinated by the direction of the approach shot. The key here is not to try to cover the whole net but covering part of the net well. With an approach shot to one corner, the position of the net player will be on that side of the court as well in order to cover all passing shots that may pass from sideline to the middle of the court. This will cover the majority of the space available to the opponent.

Practice

- Feed short balls from the other side of the net for an approach shot down the line. The net rusher can practice approach shots, net position, and net play against the player at the baseline. Play out the points and switch around tasks.
- Play cross-court rallies and find the correct time to attack a short ball to play down the line after the opponent is moved off the court. Play out the points.
- Practice serve and volley points with a start to each exchange. Start with the return to the middle of the court and play out the point. The server can volley to the open court or back behind the return player according to the direction of the serve and the speed of recovery of the returner. Do the same for other targets on the return.
- Play points with players attacking the return off a second serve. You can start with a direction on the serve before mixing up the direction.

- Play points moving into the net position from a topspin rally exchange. Players have to choose the correct time (with opponent off balance and off the court) to move forward to a volley or volley drive. Play out the rest of the pattern.
- Start the point by feeding the baseline player a deep ball and the net player touching the net. The baseline player has to play a lob over the net player and play out the point from that situation. The baseline player follows the lob into the net and plays out the rest of the point. Exchange positions after a set amount of points.
- Play a rally exchange and a drop shot to start the point. Play out the point with a change of strategy with drop shot back or deep approach.

Del Potro (Approach Forehand)

Martin van Daalen

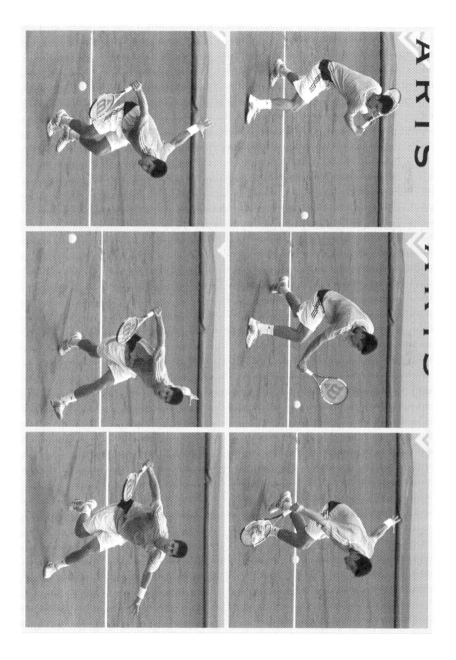

Djokavic (Approach Backhand)

Specialty Shots

There are many instances in the tennis game that you have to rely on specialty shots in certain tactical situations or to change the rhythm of the opponent. They are mainly used to disrupt the rally in various ways or to force the opponent in vulnerable positions. These specialty shots require more touch to control the ball flight than other strokes and therefore take more time to master in consistency. Learning these special skills can be a valuable addition to the arsenal of strokes and gives players more options and strategies. An important factor of teaching these specialty strokes is knowing when to introduce these to your students. You should only start teaching these strokes when the students have sound fundamentals, when they have good touch already, and when they are showing signs of trying the strokes themselves. Below, I will show you some methods on how to teach these strokes, some of the progressions, and some practice drills to enhance the use in match play.

The Slice Backhand

The slice backhand is the most versatile of all the strokes played in the tennis game. It can be used for many different purposes in playing your opponent. You can use it to slow the ball down, speed it up, or to return a wide or low ball. But you can also use it to play a lob over the opponent, to return a difficult spin serve, approach the net, or even to play a drop shot. All these tactical situations require an excellent technique and control of the stroke. There are several technical variations to hit the slice backhand that create the desired effect to the trajectory, slice rotation, depth, and speed of the ball:

1. **A low tempo slice backhand**

   This slice backhand starts with a higher backswing to generate more underspin. Most players use a continental or even continental forehand grip to open the racket angle. The swing 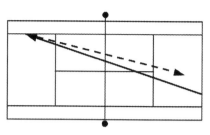 path is downward and forward. The longer follow-through is pulled underneath the ball with the racket face being flat at the end of the stroke. The amount of underspin makes the ball float through the air and slow down. After the bounce, it will skid through or sit up, depending on the height over the net. This type of slice can be used for the following tactical situations:

   - *A defensive wide ball.* This is a very common shot choice for intermediate and advanced players to neutralize the power and pressure from the opponent. Especially for players with single-handed backhands, the slice backhand can be a great defensive stroke to slow down the tempo and to reduce the attack possibility. The important tactical aspects are to play a slower slice over the net to reduce the speed of play and to place the ball closer to the middle to eliminate the angles from the opponent.

   - *A defensive low and/or short ball.* This situation requires the player to stabilize the pressure by returning the ball back low so the opponent cannot easily attack. The slice will keep the ball below the level of the net and prevent the opponent from attacking with much force. The trajectory of the return will be just above the net level and not hit too hard.

   - *A defensive deep-slice backhand.* With the ball hard and deep in the court and staying low after the bounce, it is important to have a good answer to this situation. The slice backhand absorbs the speed of the ball with sliding the racket underneath the ball to keep the trajectory slightly higher and deeper to limit the chance of attack on the return.

2. **A high tempo slice backhand**

   This stroke requires a compact backswing and a swing angle that moves more through the ball. Most players use a continental backhand grip in order to hit the ball with more force out in front of the body (backhand grip also possible in some cases). The length of the backswing depends on the speed of the oncoming ball and the speed you want to add. The backswing is slightly lower to keep the swing angle just above the line with the ball. This will keep the ball lower over the net. The speed and the swing angle will cause the ball to skid and accelerate after the bounce of the ball. This type of slice is used in the following tactical situations:

   - *To attack a high-bouncing baseline shot* downward with a penetrating slice backhand. The weight transfer will provide a lot of energy to the ball to make it bounce low and aggressively. The height of the bounce of the ball dictates the use of a slice backhand to keep the trajectory low, decrease to attack possibilities, and pressure the opponent.
   - *To attack a low ball with an approach shot.* This surprise tactic increases the pressure on the opponent by giving them less time to react and set up for the passing shot. The short ball is taken quite aggressively with a slice backhand that accelerates the tempo of play and keeps the trajectory low over the net and makes the ball skid and stay low after the bounce of the ball. Starting slightly above the ball and extending forward increases the speed and amount of slice of the stroke to apply pressure on the opponent.
   - *To attack the return.* This can be a slice backhand return or a "chip and charge." This strategy neutralizes the first-serve return or increases the pressure on the opponent's second serve by attacking it and following it into the net position. The stroke has a short backswing and a compact follow-through to keep the timing less complicated.

3. **To change the tempo, trajectory, and depth of the slice backhand**
These particular slice backhands are the touch shots of the slice backhand strokes. It adjusts the flight path of the ball with speed and elevation of the ball. The backswing is shorter to adjust to the speed of the oncoming ball, but the follow-through can be longer to control the depth and elevation. Most players use a continental forehand or backhand to execute these shots. These slice backhands are mostly used for the following tactical situations:

- *The drop shot.* The execution is easier performed on the backhand side after hitting a slice backhand on the previous shot. The stroke can then be camouflaged with an identical preparation. The backswing is short, but the follow-through can be longer to provide touch to the length of the stroke and amount of backspin to limit the forward movement after the bounce. The drop shot is most effective when hit inside the baseline, with the opponent far behind the baseline in a defensive position. This tactical position and distance will make it difficult to reach the short ball behind the net.

- *The defensive lob.* The backswing is compact with the racket angle open to allow the racket to slide underneath the ball. The follow-through is upward and longer to ensure the height of the ball and flight path over the opponent. The lob is most effective when the opponent is too close to the net and makes it easy to pass over their head.

- *A short-angle passing shot.* With the opponent attacking the net position and playing the ball outside your range to hit a topspin passing shot, you might have to resort to a short cross-court slice backhand. The ball is placed cross-court, low over the net in the service box in order to pass the opponent before they can reach it.

Practice

- One player plays an aggressive topspin-game style and with the other player only slices backhands on the backhand side of the court. This practice will teach the different types of slice and control needed to disrupt the opponent's rhythm.
- By having the server play only kick serves, it is possible to practice this slice return more easily in a point situation.
- In playing cross-court rallies to the backhand, change the direction down the line with a slice backhand and play out the point. Practice slice approach shots down the line and cross-court and anticipate the cross-court passing shots.
- Play cross-court rallies and practice the short half-court slice backhand and play out the points. Do the same for the drop shot. (Make sure to move in behind the drop shot when it is executed well to finish any possible retrieval shots.)
- Practice slice lobs and retrieve overheads in continued sequence so you can practice these shots against a net player.

After showing all the possibilities of the slice backhand, you can understand how many tactical applications exist and that it takes dedication, practice, and great skills to execute them. However, it will be a great asset to your game to practice these strokes to enhance your tactical competence. I am sure you will enjoy your newfound weapons once you start controlling them.

The "Buggy Whip" or Reverse Forehand

The reverse forehand (also called "buggy whip forehand") has become a specialty shot and adaptation to the topspin forehand. With the development of more powerful rackets and the string technology, this technique has become more popular to add topspin under extreme situations. It is most used to add extra spin when striking the ball with more power to compensate

Angelique Kerber

for the extra speed or to elevate the ball higher over the net (heavy topspin/running forehand/lob). It can also be used in some other shot choices (angle shots/passing shot) and extreme defensive positions (hard shot hit deep to baseline) to add spin when making contact next to the body (reaching wide ball). All these tactical shot choices are made in relation to the speed, spin, and trajectory of the oncoming ball and contact point, spin, and trajectory needed to execute the ball. Some players use it more than others do (see Angelique Kerber), depending on their style of play. There are some dangers in introducing this stroke to juniors too early. Their shoulders are not fully developed and injuries can occur quite easily if this is not a natural stroke for them. (Maria Sharapova also introduced this to her game early in her career, but three surgeries later, she has abandoned this technique almost completely.)

The technical execution of the stroke is not much different in preparation, but can differ in contact point and the swing angle of the forward swing and the way the follow-through ends. The contact point varies due to the depth and height of the ball and the amount of spin required to keep the ball inside the court. The arm is elevated higher and swings in a rotating motion above and over the head, to finish on the same side. This stroke is actually more suitable for advanced players and should be used for special situations, not as a regular stroke that needs to be trained on a daily basis. Anybody that has ever watched Rafael Nadal practicing will notice very quickly that he does not use this variation in his training unless he is playing points. When playing heavy topspin ground strokes, he does strike the ball out in front, but elevates the follow-through over his head, to finish with a rotating arm movement above his head (similar to picture above). Coaches should be very careful to introduce this in training. Players will usually develop this technique by themselves when they are more skilled in topspin techniques and physically ready to compete at a national or international level.

Angle Shots

Creating angle shots in tennis requires great skills in timing and racket-head control to direct the trajectory. Changing the direction, speed, and spin in the middle of the rally can be risky, and it opens the court angles for the opponent as well. When used correctly, it can place the opponent in a very vulnerable position, outside the court, leaving the whole court open to attack. The angle shot also brings the opponent forward and makes it possible to hit deeper shots behind them. This will cause the opponent to retrieve balls behind them in a defensive position. Angle shots are not about pace but about placement in combination with spin of the ball. In order to create angle shots, players have to pay attention to the following points:

1. **Adjust the contact point for direction**
   When hitting the ball cross-court with an angle, the contact point will be more in front of the body than usual. By alternating the direction of the ball between the angle stroke and a ball in the middle of the court, players will develop a feel for the contact points of both directions.

2. **Hit around the side of the ball for better angles**
   To ensure the direction of the angle, players are able to hit slightly on the side of the ball. This will steer the ball better to the target of the angle shots, but also create a slight sidespin to enhance the accuracy of the trajectory.

3. **Bend the elbow sooner for more topspin**

   In the execution of angle strokes, it is necessary to control the topspin of the ball more accurately. The ball has to dip short behind the net to fall shorter in the court. This can be arranged by bending the elbow sooner in the follow-through. The sooner you bend the elbow, after contact with the ball, the more the ball will dip down short in the trajectory.

Practice and Progressions

- Start by hitting cross-court rallies in the service box. Increase the angle more as the rally progresses and enhance consistency and spin. Try the same half-court.
- Let one player play to the middle of the cross court while the other player alternates an angle shot with a ball in the middle of the court.
- Open the court during a cross-court rally with an angle shot, hit the next one down the line, and play out the point. Alternate the exercise with both players.

The Drop Shot

This stroke is a popular shot with clay-court players in hitting the ball with underspin short behind the net. The underspin (slice) will cause the ball to check up with less forward movement and makes it harder to retrieve. In some extreme situations, the spin can cause the ball to jump back toward the net or even over the net. However, to hit good drop shots does not require players to exhibit these skills. In fact, most often, the simple execution has more consistency and eliminates unnecessary mistakes. This stroke is best used when the opponent is pushed far behind the baseline and has returned a shorter ball inside the baseline. From this position, you can make a shot choice between approaching the net and playing the drop shot. You can surprise the opponent even more by camouflaging the drop shot by using the same preparation as the slice approach shot. That is why it works so well on the backhand side since the slice backhand is much more commonly used. The forward movement to the ball will not only assist in the slice and touch of the ball, but also will close the gap toward the net and give the ball less time in the air. The shorter "airtime" will give opponents less time to retrieve the ball. Whenever the drop shot is well executed, it is advisable to follow it into the net position. In retrieving the drop shot, the opponent will be in a difficult and vulnerable position. This makes it possible to move in and finish off the point with a volley as the ball is hit upward over the net.

There are some key points to consider before hitting a drop shot:

- **Tactical position**
  Before you make a decision to hit the drop shot, you have to consider the tactical position of both players on the court. The opponent has to be pushed far behind the baseline to close the distance to the net. The position of the other player playing the drop shot should be inside the baseline to shorten the distance to the net. With a shorter distance to the net, it is easier to execute the drop shot, and the ball will be less time in the air, making it harder to retrieve.

- **The shot choice**
  The shot choice also depends on the type of ball returned from the opponent. It is advisable to choose a slower easy-bouncing ball for this touch shot. It will increase the timing and consistency of the drop shot. The timing of the shot choice during the rally is also important. A drop shot can be more successful during or after a long rally when the opponent has less energy and will to retrieve a short ball.

- **The score in the match**

  With the drop shot being a touch shot, the score can influence the performance of this stroke. There is a big difference in performing this shot when up in score than when down in score. You can also imagine that this is a bad shot choice on game point, set point, or match point. A good rule of thumb is to not hit touch shots when you are nervous or under stress of the score.

How to Hit Great Drop Shots

The key to hitting good drop shots is a simple execution. Most players apply too much backspin to the drop shot with elaborate swings or try to make the shot too good by playing it ever shorter behind the net. The backspin and shorter target behind the net are not the answer to a good drop shot. The timing of the drop shot, the tactical positions, and a simple execution are much more important. Below are some key points on how to hit great drop shots:

1. **Good preparation**

   Not unlike many other strokes, the preparation plays a large role in the success rate of the drop shot. The footwork is crucial in moving up to the shorter ball on time to have a balanced position. Players do not want to feel rushed in playing this touch shot, and you want to have ample time in setting up your feet and the backswing in executing this delicate stroke.

2. **Short and relaxed backswing**

   By keeping the backswing short and compact, it will be easier to adjust the racket-head speed, racket angle, contact point, and amount of slice for the proper distance and trajectory of the drop shot. The backswing should start higher than the ball to apply backspin to the ball on the forward swing. The arm and grip pressure should be relaxed during the backswing. Less grip pressure will enhance the consistency, control, and accuracy of the drop shot.

3. **Weight forward during the stroke**

   The weight transfer should be against the ball during and after impact to control the trajectory with the amount of speed and backspin. By keeping the weight forward, through the ball, players are able to swing slower and use the pace of the ball to apply backspin. Footwork and balance play a large role in controlling the distance of the flight path to the target area. The weight transfer also enables the player to move into the net position more efficiently.

4. **Follow-through underneath**

   The racket head has to slide underneath the ball to lift the trajectory higher and to make the ball slow down behind the net. The racket angle is open at contact as the racket swings down and underneath the ball to produce the backspin and the proper trajectory. In some cases, with low-bouncing balls, the follow-through might actually finish slightly higher than the contact point to lift the trajectory higher.

5. **Play the correct trajectory**

   In order to place the ball shorter behind the net, you have to adjust the trajectory of the drop shot stroke. By following through underneath the ball and playing the arc slightly higher at the start of the trajectory, it is possible to drop the ball shorter behind the net.

6. **Choose the correct target area**

   The target area of the drop shot is a tactical decision that is based on the distance to the target area, the positioning of the opponent, and the running direction of the opponent. Playing the drop shot in the same direction as the previous shot can camouflage the drop shot, but sometimes it is more important to choose a shorter distance to the net to create a shorter airtime of the ball. Choose the target area that is farthest from the position of the opponent to increase the distance to retrieve the drop shot. Playing behind and against the running direction of the opponent can help in winning the point outright with a drop shot.

Djokovic (Drop Shot)

The Stop or Drop Volley

Advanced net play includes the ability to play short volleys behind the net to prevent opponents from reaching the next ball. These types of strokes are called stop or drop volleys. The drop volley is a delicate stroke that is designed to reduce the speed of the ball and apply backspin to control the forward motion of the ball. Just like the drop shot, the key is to keep the execution and target choices as simple as possible to enhance consistency. Most often, players will try to apply too much backspin or play targets too close to the net or sideline, resulting into unforced errors.

How to Play Great Drop Volleys

- **Bend the knees**
  Keeping the eyes close to the level of the ball will enhance the contact, control, and consistency of the drop volley. By spreading the legs and bending the knees deeply, it is possible to get more down to the height level of the passing shots and volleys. An important factor in bending the knees is to keep the back knee at a forty-five-degree angle to maintain balance throughout the stroke. Keep this position for a while, even after the stroke has been finalized. This "freezing" in this position will enhance the consistency of the drop volley by maintaining the balance.

- **Keep the racket in the correct position**
  Positioning the racket out in front in the correct angle is imperative to control the drop volley. Contacting the ball out in front of the body makes it possible to track the ball more easily to make "clean" contact for optimal touch and control. The wrist will be in front of the body to relax the arm and produce easy power to prevent a lot of grip pressure during contact. The racket angle is at forty-five degrees with the wrist and slanted slightly back to create backspin.

- **Absorb the pace and apply backspin for control**
  In order to reduce the speed of the passing shot, the pace needs to be absorbed by the racket by applying backspin and the wrist by reducing the grip pressure. Both these factors can enhance the control of the depth and direction of the drop volley. In this case, you could call this absorption of the ball "a negative follow-through" since the racket head moves backward and underneath as the ball is struck, rather than forward through the ball, as in all other strokes.

- **Choose easy target areas**
  The shot choice of the target areas does not need to be complicated by trying to hit the ball too close to the net or the lines. Players need to learn that the opponent is already in a vulnerable position and that a well-placed drop volley to a large target will do the job in the majority of the cases. Choose easy-to-hit targets and apply the pressure on the opponent rather than on yourself in these situations.

Practice and Progressions

- Feed a ball to the net player and have them bounce the ball up once before playing it forward over the net with another volley. This drill makes students aware how to open the racket angle and soften the grip to slow down the ball.
- Feed balls to the net player and alternate the deep volley with a short volley. This can progress to different targets and alternated with forehand and backhand volleys.
- Play out a situation, starting with a feed and a deep volley, followed by a stop volley to a target short behind the net.
  Play an approach shot game with the purpose of finishing the rally with a stop volley.

The Drive Volley

This particular shot is used to attack the high balls when the opponent tries to slow the game down with high topspin shots. When this becomes a pattern, you can move inside the court and hit the ball in the air and take away the incentive to keep playing the ball in this trajectory. This obviously requires regular practice since the timing and footwork make it quite difficult to find the proper height and contact point in front of the body. You can see two good examples of these strokes on the following page.

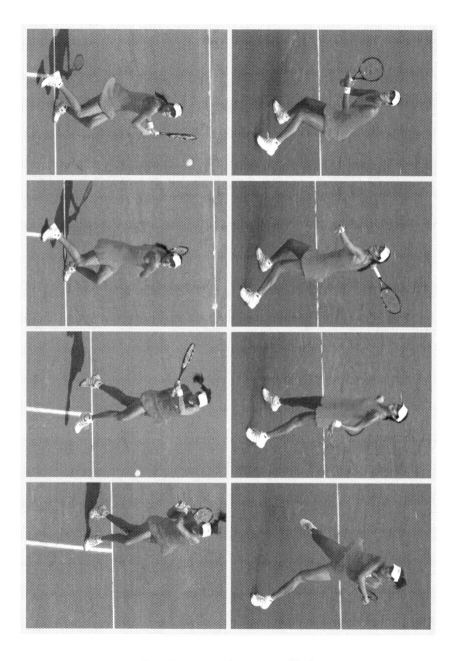

Ana Ivanovic (Drive Volley)

The Half Volley

The name of this stroke is misleading since the ball is not struck in the air, but right after the bounce on the ball. Also, the positioning is not necessarily at the net, and they can be executed from every part of the court. In most cases, it is used to approach the net when the ball is low at the feet and the player is not able to reach the ball before the bounce. It is an important skill for advanced players who play an offensive game style and attack the net more often. Some of the most important technical aspects are as follows:

- Get down low and widen your base with the feet.
- Keep a short backswing low to the ground.
- Keep the contact point out in front right after the bounce.
- Control the racket angle with a slightly closed racket face. Keep the follow-through compact to steer the ball.

Most Common Mistakes

    a. **No control of the ball as it flies in the net or out**
    b. **Missing the ball wide on a half volley**

    a. Hitting controlled half volleys is a matter of setting up well with the feet behind the ball and bending especially the back knee so you can control the ball trajectory. The contact point is in front of the body and the racket angle slightly closed to add a little spin to the ball. The closed racket angle enables you to make a slight upward swing with a short follow-through. This controls the speed of the ball since hitting it so close to the bounce creates a lot of energy.

         Martin van Daalen

b. When caught in difficult situations with a half volley, try to make things simpler rather than more complicated by aiming the half volley to the middle of the court. With this method, you keep the ball in front of you and don't open any angles. At least you won't miss it wide, your opponent has to come up with a great shot, and it will make it much tougher for them to pass you.

Practice and Progressions

- Drop the ball and try to make contact right after the bounce of the ball.
- Play mini tennis and move the feet to make half volleys on each shot.
- Feed a ball at the service line and start the rally with a half volley.
- Stand just behind the service line and practice half volley against net player.

The Chip and Charge (SABR)

The chip is a short slice motion that is executed right after the forward move, inside the court, to charge the net position. On the faster surfaces, this can be a great tactic against players that don't pass well or lack the faster footwork and reflexes to counter this surprise move. Roger Federer has taken this tactic to a whole different level since 2015 by taking the return even quicker after the bounce, closer to the service line, with a chip or half volley. It was such a successful method that it was named after him: SABR (Sneak Attack By Roger).

As you can see in the picture above, Roger Federer is far inside the baseline and about to chip this forehand return before charging the net. This positioning puts him close to the service line and provides him an opportunity to sneak in behind the return to knock off the volley, closer to the net. You can see how he keeps the stroke compact and uses his weight transfer to generate the pace of the ball. The slice effect on the ball keeps the trajectory low over the net and also makes the ball stay low to the ground after the bounce, forcing the opponent to play the ball up. This makes for an easier volley.

The Lob

This stroke is used to slow the rally down by playing the ball high in the air to gain time to recover in the court or to play over the opponent at the net position. It can therefore be used as a defensive or offensive stroke in match play. This stroke is rarely used and trained since the disappearance of the serve and volley game and with players approaching the net less than before. It is an important stroke for defensive and counterpunch players and can be a valuable weapon against net rushers and in doubles play. The differences with other baseline strokes are as follows:

- **A lower backswing**

  With the lob having a much higher trajectory, the backswing has to start lower than usual in order for the racket to swing from low to high through the ball.

- **Adjustments in contact points and racket angles**

  The tactical status in defensive, neutralizing, and offensive situation dictates the contact points and racket angles necessary to produce the different types of lobs.

- **A higher follow-through**

  The follow-through and finish of the stroke is higher than usual to direct the flight path and to control the depth and spin of the ball.

- **Open the racket face with a lob volley**

  The racket angle should be opened up for a higher trajectory, and the follow-through is extended upward to steer the ball farther over the head of the net player.

The lob can be executed in many different tactical ways. It can be a defensive lob when retrieving a ball out of a corner to gain time to recover, but at the same time can be a defensive slice lob over the net player. It can also be an offensive lob hit with topspin over the net player to then take over the net position.

Practice and Progressions

- The student has to hit lobs after the approach shot to the net. The object of this exercise is to push the opponent back to the baseline with a defense slice lob.
- Execute the same drill as above, but this time, first play a topspin ball low to draw the net player closer to the net, followed by an offensive topspin lob over the net player.

- The player has to retrieve overheads after hitting the overheads. The object is to anticipate and retrieve as many overheads as possible to practice the defensive lob.
- Play out the situation in doubles by playing the return with a lob over the net player and playing out the point.
- In playing a volley rally at the net, have players alternate playing a volley lob and playing out the point.

The "Jump-Kick" Backhand

This special shot is used to get higher off the ground to gain leverage and strike through the ball forcefully. It is a relative new technique that has been developed over the past fifteen years. You will see it used with double-handed backhands on high-kicking second serves and in high topspin rallies to change the tempo and gain initiative. The stroke is best executed by jumping off the front leg and then kicking back with the other leg to create a reactive force to accelerate the racket head. This technique requires excellent timing and great athletic ability to perform and can be very effective to surprise an opponent. Marcello Rios was one of those players in the past that used it quite often and with great skill, but it is seen more often in today's advanced players as well. Technically, you don't have to strike it by jumping up and could easily step forward and take the ball earlier, but the strategic value can be high if used correctly to create confusion. This specialty shot is not for everyone, and unless you are very confident and skilled, it is better left for others.

Footwork

One of the major factors in playing a high level of advanced tennis is the quality of the footwork. The differences of good and bad footwork are clearly visible in the many small adjustments that are made to balance the body before, during, and after the stroke. The development of the game requires more speed, balance, and recovery in order to cover the whole court. The technique of the footwork needs to be precise and efficient to play faster and to last in long matches. Some of the advantages of good footwork are as follows:

• Better balance before, during, and after the shot
• Improved control of the ball during the rallies
• Faster recovery after the shot to cover the court
• Better court coverage and allowing player to reach more balls
• More aggressive strokes with better preparation and loading
• Efficiency of movement and preservation of energy

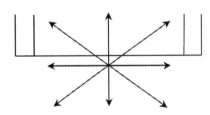 You need to be able to move in all directions to place your body in the right position behind the ball. The sideways movement are certainly most common, but advanced players are able to move in all combinations of directions, whether it be to the forehand or to the backhand. In the graph below, you can clearly see the movement needed to cover all possiblities and directions. Practice should replicate these movements as much as possible in order to get used to these types of shots and footwork.

Types of Footwork

The most common forms of footwork and movement are the following:

- Running (fastest form of movement)
- Stepping in or forward (used for weight transfer against the ball)
- Side steps (sideways movement)
- Overstep (used as a first recovery step and to turn the body)
- Back shuffle (when positioning behind the ball)
- Recover step (squaring off body for balance)
- Skip (used to recover the balance)
- Split step (starting action before movement)

All these types of footwork and movement have the sole purpose of maintaining the balance before, during, and after the stroke. These different types of movement are necesarry in order for the player to adjust to the speed, spin, and trajectory of the ball. It is important to teach these at the appropriate time in sequence with the strokes, the pattern development, and the tactical situations. Try to incorporate these in a competitive setting in point and match play whenever possible.

Players have to adjust their footwork to the surface they are playing on. There are distinct differences in playing on green clay (Har-Tru), red clay, hard court, indoor, and grass courts. For each surface, there are specific movements that require specific footwork. These specifics can be in the preparation, the movement to the ball, the hitting phase, or the recovery of the stroke. The specifics of the footwork are as follows:

Positioning

A player's positioning on the court is defined by the starting position, at the beginning of every rally, and the recovery position after every following stroke. They are both tactical positions to cover the possible hitting directions of the opponent. In the case of the starting position, players try to find the best place to start the rally with a return of serve. Players will try to cover this position by setting up in the middle between the angles of a possible forehand or backhand return. For the recovery position, the positioning of a player will constantly differ according to the angles and court space available to the opponent. Players will set up along the dissecting line of the angles available (see graphic page 201). Here are some of the details of the starting and recovery positioning:

- **The serve**
  The serve position is different for singles and doubles, but can also vary from player to player. This position for singles play is usually one yard from the center in order to cover the court. In doubles, this might be two to three yards from the center. It is possible to change this position to create more angles or to pretend hitting to a certain direction and camouflaging the real direction. It is also possible to take a certain serve position to seduce the opponent into changing their return direction or to take advantage of this serve position on the return (standing more to the backhand side in order to leave forehand side open).

- **The return**
  The positioning of the return position is more similar to defend against service directions. The position of the return might change to move around the forehand or backhand for a better recovery to the center of the court or to hit a stronger return with a better stroke. Most players choose a position of one yard behind the baseline with the outer foot inside the single line. The depth of the position can also vary by stepping inside the baseline to attack the opponent or to step farther back with heavy kick serves and to return them with a higher topspin trajectory. These choices need to be made going by the knowledge of the opponent or the experience gained during the match, but they are usually made before the execution of the return. In some cases, it can be more advantageous, with heavy spin serves, to step forward to cut off the angle of wide serves, before they bounce outside of the returner's reach.

- **After the recovery**

   The positioning of the body after the recovery is probably the most important factor in tactical positioning. After every stroke, a player has to recover and reposition the body to cover the next shot. In general, this would be to the dissecting line of the possible return angles of the ball, but you also have to keep the specific tactics and patterns of the opponent in mind. Every time you have to anticipate the possibilities of opponents, go by the following information: (1) the positions of the players on the court, (2) the possible angles of the stroke, (3) prior tactical experience in this situation, and (4) tactical information and experience of the opponent. This information can give you valuable feedback in making decisions on the court positioning.

Movement

The movement of tennis players is quite specific to the sport because of the different strokes, stances, and recovery footwork that is involved. The movement always has to be coordinated to the speed, spin, and trajectory of the oncoming ball in order to properly take up a balanced position behind the ball. If the movement is inappropriate to any of these factors, most often the position to the ball will be incorrect. This will be visible by players reaching for the ball or overrunning the position. In many cases, this will cause unforced errors through unbalanced strokes.

Movement in any sport has similar fundamental concepts that define the quality of the action. Movement consists of several different phases in order to travel from point A to point B. These phases can be compared to tennis specific movements:

Fundamental actions Tennis specific actions

- Initial action   Split step
- Acceleration   Speeding up of the footwork
- Momentum   Continuous running speed
- Deceleration   Slowing down of the footwork
- Stance   Set up and load for the strike
- Strike   Unloading and stroke production
- Recovery   Recovery

Movement on a tennis court can be broken up into several factors. These factors of movement are in a specific sequence that repeats itself every time a player hits the ball. After this sequence of movement and footwork, the player ends up a new starting position to await the next stroke from the opponent, and the whole sequence starts again.

The sequence of movement is as follows:

1. **Split step**

   The split step is crucial to any type of movement since it creates a balanced athletic position to start the movement. The split step is created with a little hop off both feet followed by a wide stance and the knees slightly bent to push off fast with power. The reaction time to start the movement will be shortened with the body already being active. The timing of the split step is the most critical part and always needs to be coordinated with the strike of the opponent's ball and the split step being at the highest point of the hop or jump. This precise timing of the split step will enable the player to move immediately after the strike as soon as the feet hit the ground. The height of the hop or jump needs to be kept low to increase the reaction time.

Practice

• You are able to practice the timing of the split step by counting out loud (1) when the ball is struck by the opponent and making a split step at the same time. Coaches are able to hear if players are seeing the contact with the ball and timing it well.

2. **Moving behind the ball**

   The movement behind the ball starts with the initial step toward the direction of the ball. The first few steps should be executed with a sense of urgency and acceleration, to be followed by a deceleration and setup of the stroke. This movement can be in all different directions and needs to be adjusted to the speed, spin, trajectory, and distance to the ball. If the ball is closer in distance to a player, the movement will be totally different than when the ball is farther away. The initial movement will also differ when moving sideways

Andy Murray

or moving forward or backward. With the sideways movements, this is initiated with the outer foot turning and stepping in the direction of the ball. The sideways movement consist of sidesteps and/or running to reach the ball with time to spare to set up for the ball. With a forward movement, one of the feet will step back and the other foot forward to push off the back foot. The movement is directed to set up the body to one side of the short ball in order to strike the ball. With moving back, one of the feet will step forward and the other foot will step back. The body turns sideways to the forehand or backhand side to move with more speed and set up for the stroke. The speed and distance of the movement determines the type of strokes that can be played. These four types of balls will all require a specific movement behind the ball.

- **Stepping in stroke**
  In stepping in to strike the ball, the back foot sets up first to "anchor" the body before transferring the weight forward with the step in toward the ball.

- **Open-stance stroke**
  With this stroke, the back foot is placed behind and on the outside of the ball to provide balance and rotation to the body during the stroke. In this case, the body stays mainly above the outside leg until the strike of the ball.

- **Running stroke**
  In running toward the ball, the back foot provides the acceleration by pushing off forward and upward. The feet are accelerated at the moment just before impact with the front foot landing just after impact with the ball.

Martin van Daalen

- **Running-around stroke**
  The movement of the feet is accelerated by cross-over steps to quickly run around to strike the ball. The back foot is placed behind the ball and the front foot is placed diagonally in front, on the outside of the ball (semiopen stance).

Practice

- Train the speed of the movement by feeding the ball to predetermined spots on the court. Players have to learn to split step and accelerate the first three steps, to then slow down to organize the feet. You can first start by catching the ball with both hands. This will organize your feet to set up for a catch between hips and shoulder.
- After this method, you can switch to hitting the ball at the same height. The focus is still on the movement (first three steps) behind the ball. With this approach, you will move with urgency, set up early, slow down the backswing, and load the legs and arms before every shot.
- Train the movement behind the ball with different trajectories. You can feed the ball left and right, but also change the depth to make players aware what height and distance they need to achieve for best results.

3. **The setup**
   The setup of the stroke is organized by the footwork and early preparation of the backswing with the arms. This movement will balance the body and provide time to execute the stroke with consistency and control. Finding the proper setup behind the ball will definitely have a large effect on the quality and fine-tuning of the stroke. The distance and height of the body, in relationship to the ball, becomes crucial in order to strike the ball with power, spin, and direction.

Practice

- Finding the proper starting position (stance, body, and arm position) to strike the ball is crucial for ball control and power. Moving quicker behind the ball will create more time to set up. The footwork needs to be quick and precise. (See "moving behind the ball" drills above.)

4. **The hitting zone**
   During the hitting zone, the body movements rotate forward toward the ball as the knees are extended. The feet will rotate as the stroke is completed and in some cases swing around to assist in the stroke and to maintain the balance.

5. **Recovery**
   The recovery of each stroke is initiated by the momentum of the movement and the stroke against the ball, in combination with the unloading of the legs, hips, and shoulders. The energy of the linear movement toward the ball can be transferred to a rotational force. As the feet leave the ground, they adjust to the direction of the ball by swinging them around. The heel on the outer foot turns slightly outside in order to use more force from the thigh and calf muscles. This method ensures a forceful push back to recover more quickly and efficiently.

6. **Moving to a tactical position**
   The movement back to a dissecting angle position needs to be swift and smooth in order to cover the court angles and space more easily. All these factors of movement need to be coordinated with each other through specific footwork training and footwork drills. This can be conducted on and off court with both having a positive effect on each other. Coaches and players need to realize that without proper attention to footwork and movement, it will be difficult to play points. Match play requires an automated functioning of the footwork and movement in order to compete with the mind (strategy).

> ## Technique and strategy become useless
> ## if you can't reach the ball!

Movement on Different Surfaces

Parts of the movement are specific to certain surfaces. The surface demands different footwork when playing on clay, a hard court or indoor surface, or a grass court. The clay and grass courts are much more slippery, and sliding is a requirement in order to move well on those surfaces. Hard and indoor surfaces provide much more grip, and recovery is less of a problem.

Clay-court movement. The grip of the shoes is limited on clay court when you are not used to it, but for experienced players, it can be advantageous once they learn how to move on it. Footwork practice is key on this surface, a necessity in order to gain any sort of feel and balance. Special shoes are available to increase the grip on clay courts. The type of clay courts determines the type of shoes. Clay courts with large granular clay require less profile on the shoe than fine granular clay courts (French Open). The sliding can help in making small adjustments to the distance and positioning of the body to the ball. It is possible to increase or decrease the grip of the feet with the surface by the weight distribution on the feet and the flexion or extension of the knees. Using small fast steps right after the recovery helps the player to maintain balance in case the shoe slips.

Grass-court movement. The grip is also limited on grass courts. This can be even more accentuated when they have not been used much, the grass is still dark green and filled with moisture. Grass courts require special shoes. They have many small protruding flat spikes that provide the grip on the grass courts. The split step becomes very important, and the timing of it imperative in order to keep your footing. In both accelerating and decelerating, it is necessary to use many more steps in order not to slip. It is possible to slide on grass, but it is not recommended for everyone. The uneven grass-court surface can be slippery in some spots and dry in others and easily cause serious injuries to the ankles. With this in mind, many players choose to take initiative early on in the rally to get players out of position or in a defensive position. Another strategy is to hit in the center of the court where the grass is worn down and bounces are very unreliable. Wrong-footing the opponent can be a very good strategy on this surface.

Hard and indoor court movement. The movement and footwork can be much more abrupt on hard and indoor courts since there is much less sliding due to the grip of the shoes on these surfaces. Players are able to accelerate, decelerate, and recover much quicker and play a faster game style. There is less of a demand on specific footwork, and balance is less of a problem. With the increased speeds of the ball, it is possible, and often necessary, to hit open stances and running forehands and backhands to cover the court adequately. The shoes and soles can be adjusted to even slide on indoor hard courts and carpet if the player so desires with their footwork.

Stances

In setting up for the strokes, players have to take a balanced, athletic position with a certain stance that creates the proper distance to the ball for stability and consistency. These stances can vary to the tactical status, the tactical situation, and the shot choice of the player. For the baseline strokes, there are several different stances possible:

Closed stance. With the feet in this position, it is easier to load the hips and shoulders but more difficult to square the racket at impact with the ball on the forehand side. It blocks the stroke production of the forward swing and is not recommended on that side. For the double-handed backhand, it can provide better stability, if the player has good flexibility and recovery footwork.

Square stance. This stance will provide the best weight transfer to the strokes with good rotation of the body. The hips and shoulders are able to open up toward the target to square the racket head at impact with the ball. This stance teaches proper technique for the rotation, balance, and weight transfer.

Semi-open stance. This stance can be introduced to intermediate and more advanced players to enhance the forward rotation of the shoulders and the hips. It should also be used to move out of the way of the ball when the ball is too close to the body.

Open stance. This stance is not suitable for beginning players and should be reserved for intermediate and advanced players. Students first need to learn the basic footwork and the proper weight transfer before trying to accelerate the strokes. Introducing these types of stances too early often leads to balance and recovery issues and sloppy and inconsistent stroke production.

Some stances are more suitable for specific strokes than others. This will mainly depend on the amount of available preparation time; the incoming angle, spin, and speed of the ball; and the shot choices. With more time available, you will see more closed and straight stances to produce more weight transfer. As the exchange of the balls speeds up, you will see more semiopen and open stances. (The use of stances will not be possible when players have to hit balls on the run). Some stances are more efficient than others in producing consistency, depth, direction, spin, power, and tempo. This can be important when utilizing them in offensive, neutralizing, and defensive positions. In the list below, you can see what stances work best and most efficient for all of these technical, tactical, and physical aspects.

Martin van Daalen

Closed stance - Consistency, depth, spin and slice, double-handed backhand
Square stance - Weight transfer (power), consistency, depth, direction, and tempo
Semiopen stance - Consistency, depth, topspin, power, and tempo
Open stance - Topspin, court coverage, defensive, neutral

As you can see, not all stances are most efficient for all aspects. This does not mean that it is not possible to produce these aspects well; it only means that other stances can be more efficient in many stroke situations. It is up to each player to become as comfortable as possible with each of the stances to use them at the appropriate time.

Recovery

The recovery footwork has become one of the most important factors in today's tennis game with the increased speed, spin, and tempo of play. With players playing ever faster and taking the ball earlier on the rise, there is less time available to set up and recover for the next shot. Speed and efficiency of movement has become a very important commodity in advanced tennis, and players would be well advised to learn this special skill. The recovery footwork is very specific to the shot choices, court surface, stances, and balance of the body.

The shot choice can influence the recovery of a player by how and where they place the ball in the court. The speed, spin, and direction of the ball determine the best recovery position in order to retrieve the next ball. The direction and targets of the ball will initially determine the recovery point of each player. The recovery point varies with each direction due to the return angles that are possible from each target. The correct recovery point will be on the dissecting line between those angles. See the picture below and look at the differences of the recovery point A and B with a cross court target and a down the line target.

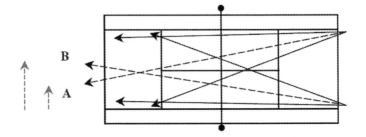

The surface has a great influence on the recovery footwork in the amount of grip and friction of the surface. The recovery on clay can be different than on hard or indoor courts. On clay and grass, the feet can slide out from under the body when pushing off to recover. This is caused by shifting the weight distribution to the inside foot too early and not keeping enough weight on the outside foot. On hard and indoor courts, it is possible to shift the weight much more and earlier since the friction with the ground is much higher. With slippery surfaces, make smaller and more frequent steps to maintain the balance in the recovery. If you slip with one foot, the other foot will restore the contact with the surface and restore the friction.

The stances influence the recovery footwork in execution. A closed or straight stance has a different recovery than open stances. With a square or closed stance, the back has to swing around and placed in a wide stance to push off. (See the figure below on the left. The feet end up pointing in the direction of ball.) With open stances, this push off occurs after the strike of the ball and the feet have been placed back down on the surface. The forward momentum of the strike and the push upward from the load of the legs will cause the body to leave the ground and rotate forward in the direction of the ball. See below two forehand examples:

Square stance　　　　　　**Open stance**

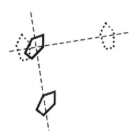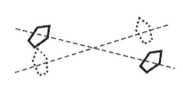

The balance of the body plays a role in the recovery footwork when shifting the body weight from the outside to the inside. The balance of the body is maintained when this shifting of the body weight is performed smoothly during the stroke and with the correct amount of body weight distribution on both feet to recover without the feet slipping. If the shift of the body weight is performed too early, you might see the outer foot start slipping away from underneath the body. Whenever the feet slip suddenly, without warning, it will create an unbalanced recovery that will affect the stroke in trajectory and consistency.

The Recovery Steps

The method of recovery will vary to the distance a player has to move away from the starting position. As the distance increases, the speed of the movement will increase accordingly. This increase in movement demands an adjustment in the recovery steps. To illustrate how this affects the recovery of a baseline stroke (forehand), we can observe four different recovery methods.

1. **Stepping forward**

   In stepping forward to strike the ball, the back foot swings around with the feet facing the target area. The placement of the outside foot is crucial in keeping the grip with the surface. As the outer foot makes contact with the surface, the whole foot needs to be planted on the ground with the weight on the inside edge of the shoe. Using the whole foot surface on the ground will provide more grip to the surface and will decrease the chances of ankle injuries. The weight distribution will increase the grip on the surface and prevent ankle injuries. The heel is slightly turned outside to increase the power to the outside of the knee and the thigh. The outside foot pushes off toward the middle of the court. The recovery steps consist of side steps with a shorter distance to the recovery point. (See figure on the right.)

Practice

- The first drill should be to step through forward at the completion of the follow-through. The timing and the placement of the step are important here.
- The step back to the recovery point is the next step after the step through has been mastered (sidestep or overstep).
- Adjust the recovery and push back by using sidesteps or oversteps according to the distance that needs to be covered to the recovery point.

Martin van Daalen

2. **Open stance**

   With longer distances to the corner, the open stances will be more favorable to recover from the corners. The outer foot pushes off upward and rotates till the toe points in the hitting direction. As the speed of the stroke increases, it will rotate the body to the point that the outside foot moves forward, and the inward foot moves backward in an "X" shape. (See figure above of open stance.) After completion of the stroke, the outside foot pushes off and steps across one step (crossover step) to then either run or use side steps to recover. The wider the distance from the middle, the more a player needs to use running steps to recover. If the speed of the movement to the corner increases, there will be an additional movement shift to the outside before the push of the recovery step commences. This shift to the outside helps players get the racket around the outside of the ball and to maintain balance through and after impact with the ball. A common mistake with these wide balls is to reach and lean over to hit the ball. The players will lose balance and fall outward and lose control of the stroke. The heel of the outer foot is turned slightly outside to provide more power from the knee and thigh. In this position, it is easier to maintain the knee flex. Below, you can see the recovery of a forehand open stance with the rotation of the feet on the left and the crossover step after the push off.

Practice

- The first progression should be the placement of the outside foot. This can also be executed with a slide when playing on clay courts. Focus on the setup.
- The next phase is the rotation and replacement of the feet at the completion of the follow-through (X shape).
- Practice the skip with the outside foot after the unloading of the legs. The foot is rotated and replaced to push back to the recovery point. Stop right after the skip to practice this part of the movement first (freeze movement).
- Add several side steps to the outside after the skip of the foot. This particular practice will enhance the commitment of the weight transfer to the outside of the court.
- Add the recovery footwork and the weight shift after the skip with the outside foot. The key here is to find the timing of the weight shift and to use the outside foot to recover. Keep the heel outside after the rotation of the body.
- Use different types of recovery steps with side steps or over steps, according to the distance to the recovery point.

3. **Running forehand**

As the speed and distance of movement increases, it will be necessary in some cases to use running forehands to reach the ball. The speed of the movement is high, and players will have to slide or use small steps to slow down and recover after the stroke has been executed. The feet turn more sideways to decelerate the movement by creating more friction from the edges and the larger bottom surface of the

shoes. The last step of the deceleration is made with the outer foot placement. The heel of the shoe is down on the ground and turned slightly outside to quicken the push off and "crossover step" to accelerate back to the recovery point. (See graph below.)

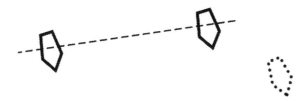

Practice

- Accelerate through the ball without any recovery. This is to make sure that players don't slow down during the stroke.
- Use small steps to slow down on hard court or use the slide on clay courts. The turning of the heel on the outside foot will accelerate the recovery.
- Use the over step to increase the running speed. Slow down the movement as the recovery point gets closer by using side steps and split steps.

Grigor Dimitrov

Martin van Daalen

4. **Running around forehand**

In order to apply more pressure on the opponent, players often run around the backhand to use their stronger forehand. This particular shot requires great footwork and should not be attempted without mastering the running forehand. (By running around the backhand, it will leave two-thirds, or more, of the court open.) The movement to the outside of the court will push the momentum of the body to the outside foot. The outer foot will also be the one to push off back to the recovery point. If the speed of the movement is too high, it can cause the outside foot to skip outside before pushing off and stepping back toward the recovery point. (See graph below.)

Practice

- Run around and take position with the weight distribution toward the outside foot. Freeze this position when the stroke is completed.
- Add the skip forward and to the side to accelerate the stroke. This footwork will also accelerate the rotation of the hips and shoulders. The feet should be open up forward.
- Add several side steps to the outside or approach the ball to enhance the weight distribution into the ball.
- After these skills are mastered, it is time to recover to the middle of the court. It is possible to do this with side steps or with over steps.

Fernando Gonzalez

After all these different types of footwork have been trained separately, it is important to start working on using them all together and at the appropriate times in the rally. The best way to do this is by playing points and making corrections whenever the wrong type of footwork has been used.

Another method of improving the footwork is with specific footwork training that mimics the movements during point play. You can see practice and drills of this type of training in the physical training chapter.

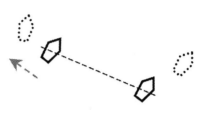

STRATEGY AND TACTICS

In order for the strokes (read technique) to have any benefit and/or impact on your game, it is important to know how to apply them. Having good strokes is not enough. A player also needs to possess the tactical, physical, and mental skills in order for the technique to have impact on their game. Every stroke production should have a general tactic and the proper shot choice (speed, spin, trajectory) for it to be effective. The player has to be fit, strong, flexible, and fast enough in order to keep up with the tempo of play. And the player has to be mentally tough and stay competitive in order to deal with the ever-changing situations, especially when things are not always going your way in a match.

The Difference between Strategy and Tactics

Strategy is a plan to use your own strengths to attack your opponent and prevent them from attacking your weaknesses while exploiting your opponent's weaknesses. **Tactics** is the method of execution of a plan. An example of a strategy is to attack the weaker side of the opponent. A strategy can be executed with several different tactics:

Tactic A. Play long rallies to the weakness of the opponent. This will increase the pressure on the weakness of the opponent through consistency of the rally.

Tactic B. Use your stronger stroke against the weaker stroke of the opponent. The pace and pressure of the stronger stroke will apply mental pressure on the opponent.

Tactic C. Serve and return to the weaker side of the opponent. This will immediately apply pressure to the opponent to take advantage and initiative in the rally.

Tactic D. Play the ball to the weaker side with topspin or slice. This will keep the ball out of the comfort level of the opponent and apply more pressure on that side.

Tactic E. Play out wide to the stronger side of the opponent to open up the weaker side. This will increase the pressure on the weakness of the opponent.

As you can see demonstrated with the examples above, the strategy forms the concept of the plan while the tactics contain the detailed execution plans of the strategy. There are many tactics available for each strategy, and players need to be made aware of the many possibilities to combat their opponents. Besides the tactical aspects, players can combat their opponents with technical, physical, and mental capabilities. Some players are very talented with their technical capabilities, and others might be more physically and mentally gifted or a combination thereof. Whatever their strengths might be, in today's game, advanced players need to be well rounded to be successful.

Tactical

In order for your strokes to have any benefit and/or impact to your game, it is important to know how to apply them. Having good strokes is not enough. A player also needs to possess the tactical, physical, and mental skills in order for the technique to have impact on their game. Every stroke production should have a general tactic, and the proper shot choice (speed, spin, trajectory) for it to be effective. The player has to be fit, strong, flexible, and fast enough in order to keep up with the tempo of play. And the player has to be mentally tough and stay competitive in order to deal with the ever-changing situations, especially when things are not always going your way in a match. Many of the methods and progressions with technical subjects also apply in learning tactical applications. These basic progressions form the foundation for strategy and tactics in the tennis game. In order for players to get a proper understanding on how to combat their opponents, they should be taught in the following sequence:

1. Consistency   Shot tolerance
2. Depth   Pressure
3. Direction   Change of direction
4. Spin   Topspin, slice, sidespin
5. Power   Speed of the ball
6. Tempo   Speed of play

Consistency is one of the most important tools of a strategy. Without this skill, it is not possible to complete any strategy or tactic. Many juniors, and even advanced players, bypass this progression in strategy, and you can often find them only using the last two on this list: power and tempo. This means they often try to hit too hard and/or play too fast. Consistency of play is one of the most important tools in applying pressure on the opponent. As mentioned before earlier in this book, consistency isn't only created by your technical skills. Having a strategy (basic plan) and a tactic how to execute them will often create consistency merely through the process and completion of the tactic. But besides this, the physical and mental factors play a contributing role in executing the technical and tactical skills in an efficient and effective way.

Shot tolerance is the amount of shots a player usually hits before making an error. We have to think in terms of average amounts when looking at this number. It will vary in different age groups, gender, and competence levels. It can also be very important to understand this concept when playing different opponents in finding out their number (shot tolerance) when they miss. Just playing one more shot would be a good strategy to start with. As play improves with depth, direction, spin, power, and tempo, judgments need to be made on how much pressure can be applied before unforced errors are made. A certain risk-reward balance needs to be maintained to ensure consistency in the rally. This judgment of the other factors will influence the trajectory and speed of play and is described as shot choices.

Tactical routines are automated patterns and actions with a tactical purpose. The best players in the world follow a routine to start matches that follow the list above while lesser players choose a much more risky approach. An example to this would be to watch top players in playing the first strokes of each rally and the first three games of each set. You will find that they all have a certain routine to start points, games, and sets. They play to big targets and don't open any angles early on. This method gives them the opportunity to improve the rhythm and timing before playing close to the lines. These routines can only be established if there is a plan or strategy. It is very important to give players a basic strategy to work from so they can start building a way to play through automated routines. As they progress further in their routines, you can introduce more complicated strategies with patterns, different shot choices, different styles of play, and weapon development.

The Basic Strategy

All good players follow a basic plan to play points and compete in tournaments. This basic plan should be founded on very simple principles to construct a point and apply pressure on the weakness of the opponent. Especially when players don't have so much power yet (younger players); this basic strategy is an important game plan for their tactical development. The basic strategy is as follows:

1. Know the strengths and weaknesses of your opponent.
2. Keep a high first-serve percentage.
3. Hit the return to the middle, preferably to the weakness.
4. Play the second ball after serve and return to the weakness.
5. Play to the open court and then attack the weakness again.
6. Engineer the patterns of play to use your strongest shots as a weapon.
7. Knowledge of percentage play will influence your game strategy.

1. Exploiting the weaknesses and strengths of players and opponents requires reading these well and recognizing them. Scouting your

opponent in other matches will give you valuable information on their strengths and weaknesses and style of play. It takes focus and experience to learn these skills in order to make a plan for a strategy and tactic, the ultimate goal to combat your opponent! (Practice scouting players by looking at matches together with your coach and discussing styles of play, strength and weaknesses, strategies and tactics, shot choices, etc.)

2. The first-serve percentage should be high in consistency and aimed at the weaker side to apply pressure. Ideally, the serve percentage will be 7 out of 10 or above in order to set up the second shot. Obviously, this also will assist in avoiding double faults and taking the pressure off the serve, especially on crucial points in the game. (You can practice this by setting up target areas and counting how many you can make out of ten serves or tracking some of your matches and looking at serve percentage.)

3. The return should be close to the middle (preferably on the weaker side) and deep in the court to increase the consistency and pressure on the opponent. Big targets on the return will also relieve pressure on the return player and prevent unforced errors early in the rally. I will also decrease the angles on the second shot of the opponent to attack you right away and can also be used when in trouble on a wide shot in the rally. (Practice returns to target areas in point play and what shots to expect next.)

4. Players should be looking to position themselves quickly after the serve or return to hit their best strokes on their second shot. Ideally, this should be targeted to the weakness of the opponent to keep applying pressure. Many times, less-experienced players are not ready after the first shot and end up playing a defensive shot on their second exchange. Maintaining controlled pressure is the ultimate goal to keep the opponent in a neutral or defensive position with less opportunity to strike back. It is important to practice this second-ball situation in order to read the trajectory and establish a routine for the different options. (This type of practice can be executed with the coach feeding you a certain return to improve the next shot.

As you make improvements, it is possible to mix them up and play out the point.)

5. At the start of the match and each point, rallies should be initiated to big targets of the court before venturing out closer to the lines. However, as soon as the player is more comfortable, and pressure is established on the weaker side, the open court should be used to make the opponent run and then apply pressure back to the weaker side. This method will keep the opponent in a neutral or defensive style of play and not allow them to attack you as often. Pay attention next time you see the top players start matches and how they construct point with the targets they use and shot choices in the rally. (Practice the pattern of seeking the weaker side first and then open court and back to weaker side and vice versa. Play out the point.)

6. You can set up your strongest weapon on the second shot by using the patterns and targets. It will provide you with more chances to win the rally and give confidence to your plan. This can mean that you have to use your legs more in order to use your weapon more often. A good example of this is the inside-out forehand. Advanced players frequently use this shot. They are able to use part of the backhand area, closest to them in the middle, to dominate with their stronger forehand shot. By pressuring the opponent, they are able to control the middle of the court and put the opponent in a defensive position. Once your opponent plays to your weaker side, play down the line so they play back to you stronger stroke or weapon.

7. The knowledge of basic percentage play will influence your way of playing in match play. Some examples of percentage play in match play are as follows:

- The person who wins the first set wins about 70 percent of all matches. Knowing this stat should increase the focus on the preparation and intensity at the start of the match and first set.
- The person who wins the first set and is up a break in the second has an 85 percent chance of winning the match. This brings the focus

not only on the first set but also on creating an early break in the second. Many players tend to slow down in the second set and lose intensity in their play.

- Keeping the focus and intensity on certain points in the game and set can help you win much easier (first point of the game, 30-15 and 30-30 points, game points, the first three games of the set, the seventh game of the set, how to take initiative in tie breaks, and closing out sets and matches).

These simple rules in competition are used on a daily basis by the best players in the world, and it would serve you well to follow these first before trying more complicated methods. Having a method and a game plan will always increase your chances of success. I have taught these rules to many students in the past, and all of them have dramatically increased their consistency and results. After learning the basic strategies, you can make the next step by learning the patterns of play, improving and applying different shot choices, learning to master different styles of play to enhance your skills, and work on weapon development of your strokes. The possibilities in learning new strategies and tactics are limitless, but learning the basics and a method to apply them will always help you to improve your confidence in your game and have fun in competition.

Tactical Fundamentals

The basic strategies and tactics are the fundamental concepts and requirements that are needed to execute a chosen plan. These tactical fundamentals are listed below in order of importance:

1. Consistency
2. Depth
3. Direction
4. Spin
5. Power
6. Tempo

The tactical fundamentals are the same as the technical teaching order. The order of teaching tactical subjects is therefore connected to the technical development of the players. These tactical fundamentals alone provide many subjects for practice and point play for advanced players.

Consistency. This is the first tactic every player should use as a game plan to combat an opponent. Consistency is the first element to break down when a player becomes nervous. In playing longer rallies, the pressure builds up and mistakes are more likely to happen. Consistency is used as a weapon at any level of play and is the basis of any game plan.

Depth (change of depth). This tactical fundamental can be used in the offensive, defensive, and as a neutralizing weapon. When used appropriately, it is possible to force mistakes from your opponent, but also accomplishes four important factors in defending yourself. It provides you with extra time with a longer ball flight. It assists you in covering the court more easily, with the opponent having fewer angles available. It often generates short balls from the opponent with the opportunity to attack and use the wider angles against them. And finally, better depth generates opportunities to move the general position of a player closer to the baseline. This is a good position for defense, offense, or neutralizing play. Depth can also be used by changing the length of the trajectory to move the opponent forward and backward. Some players move well from side to side but don't handle the short- and deep-ball situations very well.

Direction (change of direction). The accuracy of direction is a powerful weapon and tactical skill. This can be performed by returning the ball in the same direction or by changing the direction. Changing the direction of the ball requires more skill due to the adjustments needed for the trajectory and racket angle. Understanding when and when not to make direction changes takes experience and practice. Advanced players rely heavily on the ability to control the direction in order to maintain consistency in the rallies.

Spin. The rotation of the ball will influence the trajectory and bounce of the ball. Rotations are useful to control the ball flight and increasing consistency and speed of rally. Players are able to hit the ball harder and higher over the net with the use of topspin. The topspin will also increase the speed and height of the ball after the bounce, increasing

Martin van Daalen

the pressure on the opponent. With slice strokes, it is possible to slow the ball down and keep the ball below the net and decrease the chance of winning from the opponent. Sidespin, or combinations thereof, is a common rotation with the service action and controls the trajectory and bounce of the ball. These rotations are a valuable tool for advanced players to increase consistency, speed, and ball flight before and after the bounce. This makes it a powerful weapon to pressure the opponent and to attack their weaknesses.

Power. This component can be measured by the speed alone or by the speed in combination with the rotation of the ball (also named "heavy ball"). It is possible to use power to the strokes by speeding up the ball to outpace the opponent. In this case, the speed of the ball will be faster than the opponent can run and/or react to the ball. However, power can also be used by combining speed with spin or slice to maintain the control of the ball. Players will experience the pressure with the uncertainty of where and how the ball bounces and how the ball flight will be after the bounce. (Nadal is a good example of a player that uses this component well.) Players have to make split-second decisions on how to handle each situation separately.

Tempo. Speeding up or slowing down the tempo of play will disrupt the rhythm of the opponent. This powerful weapon is used by many advanced and top players but is also the most difficult tactical skill to master. Tempo is determined by the timing of the strike of the ball. This can be achieved by taking the ball earlier or later after the bounce and in some cases even in the air before the bounce of the ball (volley, volley drive). The tempo change will pressure the opponent to feel rushed (speed up) or lose rhythm (slow down) in their play. Opponents will be pressured into making many adjustments that will often lead to confusion and more errors.

Strategies in Progression

After mastering the basic strategy and execution becomes routine, players can progress to more challenging strategies and tactics. Phase 2 in the progression should consist of tactical skills to outmaneuver your opponent. The skills and methods needed for this task require a lot of repetition and should be practiced frequently by more advanced players. As coaches, we can assist the player by taking one subject at a time, introducing the topic with explanation and examples, and practicing it separately in point situations.

Patterns of Play

Patterns are repetitive designs of play. They are used to move the opponent around the court to gain a positional or tactical advantage to win the point. You might think there are endless amounts of patterns until you start writing them down and find out there are only a few basic ones. Coaches and players need to be aware of these in order to train them in an organized fashion. Understanding the possibilities will make it much more obvious what to do and to play with a purpose and a plan.

The Center Pattern

This pattern of play will neutralize the opponent. The shots in the corners of the court are returned deep to the center or slightly to the weaker side of the opponent. This neutralizing strategy will limit the angles of attack. It can also be used 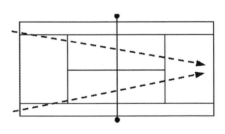 as a defensive strategy as long as the player is able to return the ball with depth and height over the net. You can also see this pattern used against a stronger opponent and when returning the serve.

The Open Court Pattern

The purpose of this pattern is to keep the opponent on the run. This can be accomplished by aiming the ball wide and playing the following strokes to the open court. This design should be used with opponents that don't move well or 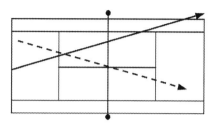 have less defensive skills. It can also be initiated by a serve or return. No matter if the ball is returned cross-court or down the line, players should proceed to play the following ball to the open court.

Playing Behind the Opponent

This pattern is used as a variation to the "open court pattern." While starting with an open-court pattern and playing the ball from side to side, a variation can be introduced by playing the ball back behind the 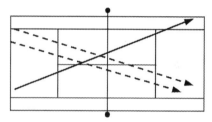 opponent. This method will wrong-foot the opponent and/or cause a loss of balance and rhythm. This will often lead to unforced errors.

Opening Up Down the Line

After a cross-court rally, players can redirect the ball down the line. This pattern is often used to surprise the opponent with a sudden change of direction. This direction change needs to be organized at the 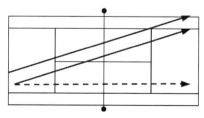 appropriate time, keeping in mind the position of both players on the court and the difficulty of the stroke when changing direction. A

good rule of thumb is to not be outside the sideline and closer or just inside the baseline when changing directions while having time to execute the ball down the line in a balanced and controlled fashion. If the player is too far outside the sideline, it will be difficult to cover the court on the following return from the opponent. The targets should be well inside the sideline to reduce unnecessary errors. It requires discipline and experience to execute this stroke with consistency and confidence, but it can be very effective when executed well.

Playing Short and Long

Another pattern is to combine an angle shot with a deep shot behind the opponent. The angle shot will draw the opponent inside the court and create an opportunity for a defensive return if a deep shot is hit 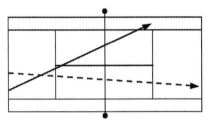 behind the opponent. This pattern is also very effective against high topspin players (moonball players) to force them to lower the trajectories. These short-angle strokes can either be performed with topspin or slice strokes. Either way, this pattern is effective against different styles of players as long as you are alert and prepared to strike with commitment, control, and confidence on the following shot. Be aware to use big targets on these particular strokes so you can speed up and swing more freely.

The Inside-Out Pattern

By running around the backhand and using a forceful forehand, it is possible to pressure the opponent (possible the backhand) even more with the angles and speed of the ball. This pattern is a favorite shot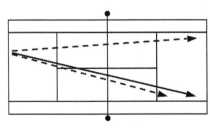

Martin van Daalen

in today's aggressive baseline game. This pressure shot will open up opportunities to either hit the ball again inside out or change direction to inside in. This shot will largely be determined by positions of the opponent.

Changing the Pattern

It is often necessary to change a pattern when the pressure during the rally increases. This is possible in many different ways by hitting the ball in a different direction or by changing the spin or trajectory. 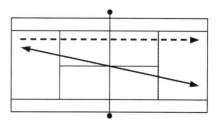 An obvious example is a backhand-to-backhand rally that is changed by hitting up the middle or down the line. Hitting up the middle of the court can make the opponent change direction, but also make it easier to run around the backhand. Sometimes you will see players use a slice down the line to make it even more difficult for the opponent to go back down the line with such a low shot, increasing the probability for a cross-court shot.

Starting the Point

Starting the point. Starting play happens either with the serve or with the return. Having a plan and a pattern will increase the amount of success in each point. In playing the first shot, it is important to understand the strength and weaknesses of the opponent. In general, the forehand is the strongest and often a weapon in the arsenal of strokes. The first shot can set up a neutral or defensive stroke from the opponent and increase the chances of winning the point. With this in mind, it pays to apply pressure as soon as possible to the weakness of the opponent. Serve and return strategies can vary from men and women's tennis at each level so it is imperative to know when to introduce these strategies. (Example: Many young inexperienced female players often serve to the forehand even though this is the stronger side. The slice, which is naturally created on the right-handed serve, curves the ball to the forehand side of a right-handed opponent. As players progress, there is more variety and placement to the body and backhand side. On the pro side, you will see a dramatic change with players attacking the return since the pace is less and in having a first-strike strategy, especially in woman's pro tennis.)

Serving Patterns

There are several options available in opening the pattern with the different targets of the serve. The targets can give the server a large indication where the return might go so they can plan the second shot. The return will usually be in 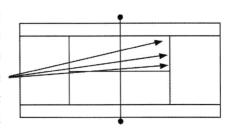 the opposite direction of the serve or in the middle of the court. This gives the server the option to choose for the weaker return or play the serve that will most likely provide the return they want. It also sets up the pattern to play the open court or play behind the opponent.

Return Patterns

In order to start the rally with the return, you first have to get the ball in play. With the stronger serves today, this is not always an easy task. The return player has to make quick judgments on 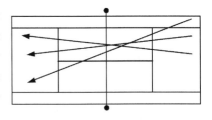 the type of return, trajectory, spin, and direction to start a preferred pattern. In general, it is most simple to return to the middle of the court on first serves, especially if it is a difficult serve to return. On second serves, the player can have the option to attack other targets, as long as consistency is maintained to start the rally. The second objective is to neutralize the opponent or even put them in defensive position, if possible. Return players need to plan ahead where to hit the return so they can start the pattern that provides the most chance to pressure the opponent on the return or second shot.

Tactical Positioning

In order to cover the court in a tactical way, we have to understand the patterns of play and anticipate (read) the most likely options to take up a position to act from. We call this tactical positioning. These locations on the court should give you the optimal position to reach the next ball or to take action and take control of the point. Keep in mind that positioning on the court is organized to the tactical situation during that point. The tactical situations are defensive, neutral, and offensive. You can imagine how players might go from a defensive position to a neutral and offensive position to win the point. Learning this skill takes practice and lots of point play to gain experience. Even experienced players have to play points to maintain the feel of timing and footwork to position themselves for a tactical advantage. The sooner you reach the proper positions to strike the ball, the more it will increase the amount of shot choices.

Shot Choices

Once the basic strokes and strategies are mastered, advanced skills are required to progress to a higher tactical level. Changing the speed, trajectory, spin, and tempo of the ball will increase the shot choices and tactical options to combat opponents. The added skills can be used in every tactical status: offensive, defensive, and neutralizing. It also plays a large role in all the tactical situations:

- Serve and return
- Baseline play
- Approaching the net
- Net play
- Playing against the net player

All these tactical situations require much more footwork and ball control in order to execute them correctly. The proper shot choices in these situations are crucial to the tactic, execution, and consistency. You have to practice them each regularly to maintain and/or improve these tactical situations for match play.

Weapon Development

Every good player has several weapons to their disposal when playing matches. On the men's side, it is usually the serve and the forehand. On the women's side, it is usually the baseline strokes and returns of second serves. Of course, these are general trends that are very much visible on the pro tour. However, these individual weapons that players might possess are not just limited to strokes. Their weapons could be physical with speed and stamina or strategic or mental in the way they play points and matches. In developing junior players, we need to help them develop their weapons that fit their style of play.

Trying to develop weapons outside a style of play can be disastrous for the development of a player. Players have to feel comfortable with the style, but also show some ability at a younger age to develop this into a weapon. This process can commence when players physically mature with the first signs becoming visible in practice and matches. In learning these weapons, juniors sometimes try to use these weapons all the time. This can lead to many unforced errors when not building the rally first and waiting for the correct time to use their weapon (shot choice). Weapon developments are part of the advanced skills needed to become a competent national or international player. (You can find more on tactical and strategy development in *Teaching Tennis Volume 3*.)

Styles of Play

There are several different styles of play when playing the game. They represent a basic method and structure in executing the points during play. Here are some of the different styles of play:

- Aggressive baseline player
- The all-court player
- The defensive player
- Serve-and-volley player
- The counterpuncher

Many players are not just one style, but a mix or combination of the styles above. The style of a player is determined by the method and consistent reproduction of the strokes and patterns. Every player eventually chooses a certain style of play they feel comfortable with. A style of play has to mature over time. It is not something that is often found in beginning tennis players. They might have either an aggressive, neutral, or defensive style of play. It is the task of the coach to assist the player in finding a style that suits their strokes to make them feel comfortable during play and to suit their character and expression of the game.

The aggressive baseliner. This player tries to dominate from the baseline with aggressive baseline strokes in order to get the opponent off balance. They move the opponent around the court using the speed, spin, and angles of the ball to draw mistakes from their opponent. They play aggressive in every way: physical, mental, technical, and tactical. The player is quick to move around the court and has a first-strike mentality. The qualifications to become an aggressive baseliner are as follows: (1) aggressive nature of play, (2) mental and physical strength, (3) speed in arms and legs, and (4) first-strike mentality.

Training: The coach will try to assist this player by teaching the basics of "the third-ball strategy," "open-court strategy," and "midcourt strategy." The "third-ball strategy" is the tactic and technical execution of how to play the ball that returns from the opponent after the serve. This first-strike strategy is based on taking advantage of the return by taking time away from the opponent and applying pressure. The "open-court strategy" is the tactic and execution in keeping the opponent running to draw errors and to not allow them to apply pressure on you. Note: Once this open-court pattern is established, you will have an opportunity to play behind a player and wrong-foot the opponent.

The all-court player. The player tries to mix up baseline and net play in order to disrupt the rhythm of the opponent. The all-court player is comfortable at the baseline as well as playing serve and volley or approaching the net. A player can mix up spin and slice and accelerate at any time. The footwork needs to be very adaptable to the situations in playing either offensive or defensive tennis. The qualifications for an all-court player are the following: (1) technical development in all strokes, (2) good footwork in offensive and defensive situations, (3) good strategic and tactical insight, and (4) creative and adaptable mindset.

Training: The coach will stimulate this creative player in learning all the different strokes and footwork in feeling comfortable all over the court. The player will have to spend time practicing offense and defense but also in practicing serve and volley and approaching the net in different situations. The coach has to be very supportive and instill patience since the development of an all-court player takes more time.

The defensive player. The player plays very consistently and tries to run down and return as many balls as possible in order to draw mistakes from the opponent. Often these players will try to slow down the rallies by playing higher over the net and adding spin. The defensive player has very good footwork and relies much on their speed to track down every ball. They can play topspin as well as slice on their ground strokes. They have a high first-serve percentage to apply pressure. The qualifications for this player are as follows: (1) well-developed ground strokes with topspin and slice, (2) great speed on their footwork, (3) great stamina, and (4) mental endurance.

Training: The coach will support the player by practicing consistency in the execution of the defensive ground strokes. As the player becomes more proficient, you can add more topspin and slice. Footwork and fitness are key elements to play this game style. Practice matches are focused on playing defensive and neutralizing patterns.

The serve-and-volley player. This player seeks to go forward behind the serve and volley the ball in order to apply pressure by taking time away from the opponent. The serve-and-volley player has an aggressive playing style and likes to play fast points. The player has strong legs and great balance and likes to use the volley and speed of the footwork to dominate the opponent. The first and second serves are a key element in supporting this style of play. Most often the player will have the same aggressive nature in the return games and try to seek the net position. The qualifications for this particular player are (1) good serve and volley development, (2) fast footwork, (3) aggressive ground strokes to force a short return, and (4) aggressive nature in playing the game.

Training: The coach will assist in the practice of the serve-and-volley techniques and aggressive ground strokes. This style of play takes a lot of time to develop and is not suitable for beginners. It is possible to practice a lot of approach games to hone the skills for later in their development.

The counterpuncher. This style of play is for players that like targets to pass the player at the net or to lure them into certain positions and then accelerate. The counterpuncher has fast and agile footwork and is handy and crafty in creating shots to maneuver the opponent. The qualifications for this player are (1) fast and agile footwork, (2) topspin and slice ground strokes, (3) creative mentality, and (4) good touch.

Training: The coach will try to create practice sessions where the player has to defend either at the baseline or create a passing shot or lob over the opponent.

As juniors progress to intermediate or advanced players, it is important for coaches to introduce all styles of play over time. This will give students an opportunity to make an informed decision on the style of play that suits them best. A coach can assist in this by pointing out the strengths of each individual player to fit a certain game style.

How to Win Points

It is important to understand how points are won and lost. With inexperienced players, most points are won by errors of the opponent since the players are not good enough to hit outright winning shots yet. As players progress and become more accomplished, they learn how to accelerate the ball to a speed that is not retrievable anymore. Advanced players are able to hit more outright winners and create forced errors from the opponent. However, this process can also bring along some unforced errors as well. The ways to win points are the following:

- Unforced errors from the opponent
- Forced errors from the opponent
- Winners

Winners. These points can be won without the opponent having a chance to touch the ball or barely touching it (think of the serve). It is important to learn the mental commitment and shot choice needed to produce these shots with consistency and confidence.

Forced and unforced errors. Consistency in your ground strokes is one of the most important factors to build confidence for your game. Players will try to eliminate errors as much as possible to increase consistency. In playing different opponents, however, errors can be affected by the playing style and pressure applied by the opponent. There are two types of errors:

Forced errors are errors that can occur with increased pressure from the opponent. The direction of the ball, the pace and spin of the ball, and the patterns of play can force the player into compromising positions. The contact points of the strokes and the balance of the body can be adversely affected and result in poor control of the ball.

Unforced errors are errors that occur without an apparent reason. The player is not pressured in off-balance strokes or increased speed or spin from the ball. The unforced errors result from improperly executed strokes or misjudgment of the timing.

To produce a quality match, unforced errors should be kept to a minimum at all times during matches. However, there are some elements that can influence the amount of unforced errors with the way the game is played: the physical and mental state of the player, the surface it is played on, and the conditions of the match.

Playing against Opposite-Handed Player

When you are a right-handed player, it can be quite difficult to play left-handed players. This is mostly complicated by the fact that you don't encounter it every day and might not have your strategy ready and/or cannot act with automated strategic reflexes. You have to think about it and lose time and efficiency in your response. On the other hand, the left-handed players are used to playing mostly right-handed players and can react quicker to strategic situations. Points to focus on:

1. Play to weaker side with your serve and return.
2. Use your strongest weapon against their weakest.
3. Open up aggressively to their stronger side to get them on the run to weaker side.
4. When approaching the net, attack to the weaker side.
5. When in doubt, play up the middle.

Playing against One-Handed or Double-Handed Backhand

There are some differences in playing an opponent with a one-handed backhand or a two-handed backhand. The one-handed backhand has more reach on that side and usually has a better slice backhand as well. The mobility and flexibility is easier on that side, but two-handed backhands usually have better returns, especially on the high backhands.

Against one-handed players, focus on the following:

1. Getting the ball high on their backhand
2. Serve to the backhand (kick) or slice to inside body/backhand

Against two-handed players, focus on the following:

1. Getting the ball out wide to the backhand
2. Serve out wide to backhand
3. Open up to forehand to make opponent run to backhand and hit slice

PHYSICAL DEVELOPMENT

The speed and tempo of today's game requires players to be much more fit and faster than before. The physical part of the game can be trained and improved without a practice partner, or coach for that matter. It is the one component that you can train on your own to make significant impact on your game. Of course, you can get some advice to train the proper way and with more efficiency to get the desired results. This segment can give you some guidance to your physical development for advanced play.

The physical training of tennis players is very diverse since the skills of a tennis player are multifaceted. The footwork used in tennis is very specific and involves not only endurance in the length of the matches, but also speed, strength, coordination, balance, and flexibility with the many sprints, change of direction, and recovery footwork. The strokes will rely heavily on the coordination with the timing of the ball, but strength, flexibility, and balance play a role in the quality of the execution. The style of play will influence these aspects as well. The makeup of each tennis player is unique in the amounts of these components. You can compare it to slices of a pie (see graph below). Some players will rely more on their stamina, whereas others might use their strength and speed. One of the most important components in the tennis game is the coordination of the strokes and footwork to synchronize the contact points. This is what we call the timing of the ball. The physical components are the following:

- **Endurance (stamina)**
- **Strength**
- **Flexibility**
- **Coordination**
- **Speed**
- **Balance**

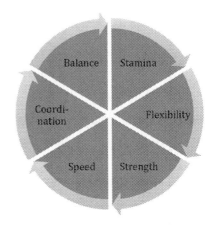

Endurance (or stamina) comes into play when matches start lasting longer than one hour. Since the best out of three set matches can sometimes last up to three hours or more, it becomes more important to train this component well. The training of endurance for advanced tennis players needs to be diverse and specific in order to train all the muscle groups used in the movements and strokes during match play. This can be performed on court with continuous life-ball drills, but should also be supported with off-court training. The intensity of the rallies in advanced tennis is much higher, and the physical training should be performed accordingly. There are many different ways to train the endurance of tennis players. Here are some methods commonly used for advanced tennis players to improve endurance:

A. Using continuous life-ball drills will lengthen the rallies.
B. Lengthening the time of the practice.
C. Having a sensible off-court training program (weight training, running program, movement program, stretching, or yoga program).

A. Using continuous life-ball drills will lengthen the rallies as if no mistakes are made. The lengthening of the rallies will put much more pressure on the stamina of a player since there is no break in the rally. The coach keeps feeding in the next ball as soon as a mistake is made to continue the pattern. Players have to react to the speed, direction, and spin of the feed and continue longer with the same drill.

B. By lengthening the time of the practice, it is possible to improve the endurance. This can be achieved by lengthening the practice unit time or by adding a second practice in the day. (As the practice time is increased, it is necessary to also increase the amount of breaks and the break time to maintain quality and intensity.) As long as a decent quality is maintained during practice, it can be beneficial for the enhancement of endurance. Make sure to shorten the practice sessions again when the quality is not maintained in the execution of the drill.

C. There are many factors that can help to improve endurance, and some of these can come from the way players train off court. Having a sensible off-court training program with weight training, running and movement program, and a stretching or yoga program can be very beneficial and stimulating. All these will improve the endurance by improving the muscle structure in its own specific way. Knowing how much you need to do is the key so that it helps you to improve rather than tire you to the point that improvements stall. Watch for telltale signs of the body language in players to know how much workload they can take. The mix of exercise is also important to keep players mentally fresh and keen to learn and improve. Adopting a running and movement program will greatly improve the stamina of a player. The endurance of the muscles will be improved over time, and the movement will become more efficient during point and match play. Running is an excellent way to improve rhythm and focus and also, indirectly, will have an effect on the mental toughness and confidence of a player. (See running and movement programs.)

Coordination is the most important physical component in synchronizing the strokes and footwork together. It involves the flexing and extending of the muscles to move the body in a smooth and timely fashion. The coordination, needed to strike the ball with the racket, at the correct impact point, is called "timing." Proper coordination and timing not only controls the correct contact points, but also the direction, spin, and trajectories of the ball. The other physical components have an influence on the quality, consistency, and endurance of the coordination. In long matches, you can imagine that the strength and stamina will affect the coordination and performance of a tennis player. Note: When practicing with excessive power, the coordination will be negatively affected. Testing players has proven that with around 60 percent of the maximum power, the coordination of the strokes will decrease (see technique instruction). Knowing this fact is very important for the improvement of coordination. There are two ways to look at this: Either improve coordination by using less than 60 percent of the maximum power or try to improve the strength so that the maximum power is at a higher level. Therefore the coordination can be trained in the following ways:

- Practice long rallies while using a medium pace and focusing solely on the contact points of the ball. Improving the timing will relax the muscles even more and will improve the coordination with less use of strength.
- While maintaining good timing, slowly increase the pace of the ball over time. As the maximum power of over 60 percent is reached, gradually increase the pace until the coordination breaks down. Keep going back and forth in increasing and decreasing the pace of the ball while maintaining quality of coordination. This will lift the level of coordination by using consistency and timing.
- By introducing strength training, it is possible to raise the maximum power level and indirectly improving the coordination by increasing the strength. This will increase the point where the coordination decreases or breaks down.

Strength is the force or power available in the muscles to execute the strokes and footwork in the tennis game. The flexing and extending of the muscles in the movement and strokes is created with a certain power and speed. It takes time to develop strength in any tennis player, and well-defined improvements are usually made in increments of six months. With tennis being a repetitive sport and the matches lasting quite long, the strength in a player is defined by endurance as well. The strength of a player can be improved on and off the court. Here are some examples of strength training:

- The drills on court can be adjusted to simulate strength training by speeding up the footwork and the strokes. By playing two-on-one drills, players will feel the urgency to speed up the motions of the strokes and footwork in order to keep up with the timing of the ball. Especially with players in the net position, the reaction time will be cut in half and stress the muscles to a much higher level.
- A weight-training program in the gym is highly recommended to improve strength of all the basic muscle groups. There are many good weight-training programs for tennis players, but try to use free weights, bands, or multidirectional machines as much as possible to enhance the balance in the joints while working out.
- A plyometrics program will enhance the explosive strength of a player. These skips and jumps can be performed using benches or ladders to increase the intensity and speed of the acceleration and deceleration footwork.

Speed is defined by how fast the movement is performed within a certain time frame. With a tennis court having the same constant dimension, it is possible to train the players to cover specific distances. Speed is made up of several components that determine how fast a player can move. They can be trained separately or in combination with each other. Some players may not be able to attain a high quality in every type of speed, but they can all be trained to a certain degree. The different types of speed are as follows:

- *Velocity of movement* is the speed of a player in running from point A to point B. This particular speed is easily tested by timing the running speed on and off the court. The common distances on a track or grass field are easily trained and tested.
- *Quickness of action* refers to how fast the body parts move during the hitting phase with the ball (fast body action). This speed is measurable by the racket-head speed and how fast the player hits the ball from baseline to baseline.
- *Change of direction* is the speed of deceleration and acceleration of a player in changing direction. This can be measured in the

time it takes to run a course where players have to slow down the movement, turn, and run in a different direction. A good example is the spider run (see movement training).

Flexibility is defined by the range of motion in the joints, in combination with the elasticity of the muscles and ligaments. This range of motion in the joints is different for every player, but can be improved over time. It is a component that needs to be trained on a regular basis to maintain a fluidity of motion. Good flexibility comes with some added benefits to a tennis player. It provides less friction in the joints and therefore less effort in performing the motion. With good flexibility, the strokes have more efficiency and endurance. It can also be very beneficial to the speed of movement and racket-head speed. By increasing and maintaining the range of motion in the joints, players will have a high level of flexibility with less chance of injuries. The following are methods of improvement:

- A stretching program before and after practice sessions can assist in improving the flexibility. A combination of a dynamic (in motion) warm-up routine and static stretches will help to maintain the range of motion before the start of the practice and prevent injuries. Stretching (static) after practice (cooldown) will ensure a relaxation in the muscles and help to maintain the range of motion.
- Weight training can serve as a stretching program if performed properly. The dynamic action and range of motion of the weight training will stretch the muscles, ligaments, and tendons (see weight training).
- Yoga is an excellent way to improve and maintain the flexibility, range of motion, and balance in the joints. I used to use yoga myself when still playing competitively and experienced many benefits from this type of training. It helped me in stretched- out situations, in the corner of the court, to recover while maintaining my balance.

Balance is part of every stroke in tennis and provides the stability in motion. Without balance, it would be very hard to coordinate strokes and footwork to hit the ball with any kind of smooth action. It is a necessity to uphold the balance before, during, and after the stroke in order to maintain control of the ball. If any of these three components is out of sync, it will immediately have a negative result in the execution of the stroke and movement. Coaches should look for these signs during practice and matches since they often indicate a problem that needs attention. This could be the balance of the stroke itself or it could be a deeper-lying technical, physical, or even a mental issue. Methods of improvement are as follows:

- The two-on-one drills increase the speed of movement and recovery and will stress the balance of the stroke even more. It is also possible for the coach to take one side of the net position to speed up the rallies.
- Balance drills are easily trained by using movement drills that simulate the strokes in motion. By training the action with the racket, players are able to pay attention to the balance of the body throughout the motion.

Strength Training

Strength training has become an essential element of tennis fitness for junior and pro players. Formerly, coaches believed that resistance exercises only added unnecessary bulk to an athlete, hindering their ability to execute their strokes. With the modern-day technology of rackets and strings, the ball speeds have increased, making the movement and endurance even more important. Here is where the benefits of strength training are enormous. However, sport-specific resistance training, like in the tennis sport, requires a more refined approach than simply lifting heavy weights to complete exhaustion. A physiological analysis of the game will confirm that most players require explosive power, muscular endurance, maximal strength, or some combination of all three in order to excel.

Elements of Strength Training for Tennis Players

There are several elements of strength training to consider when training advanced tennis players. These elements are as follows:

Maximum Strength

The maximum strength is the highest level of power an athlete can generate. This is trained by using maximum weight possible with very few repetitions (3–5 reps). For tennis players, this particular form of training is less valuable on a regular basis but can be used in a training program to increase strength. The greater an athlete's basic maximum strength is, the more it can be converted into sport-specific strength-endurance or explosive power. Maximum-strength training can improve exercise efficiency and endurance performance over time.

Explosive Power

The tennis sport requires rapid movements that demand a high explosive power output that is generated with plyometric training. An athlete can be exceptionally strong but still lack the ability to contract the muscle groups quickly enough. Plyometrics can be employed to convert maximal strength into explosive power. The training consists of rapid movements that demand maximum strength over a short period of time. A good example is jumping on and off an elevated bench. The muscles are quickly accelerated and extended when jumping on the bench and quickly decelerated and flexed when jumping off the bench (5–10 reps).

Strength Endurance

Explosive power is not always the predominant goal of a strength-training program. You only have to watch the developments on the professional tour to realize how much the strength endurance has become a major factor in the tennis sport (especially for men at the Grand Slam events where it is the best of five sets). A higher starting level of maximum strength can influence the strength to be maintained for a prolonged period of time. Strength endurance can be developed through circuit training or with the use of low weights and high repetitions (15–20 reps).

Strength Training and Periodization

The method of periodization is key to sport-specific strength training. It is important to divide the training plan into phases or periods, each with a specific purpose in mind to allow the specific strength training to peak at the right times whilst minimizing the risk of overtraining. This also makes it possible to work more diligently on the specific strength training in parts. It is not possible to work at maximum capacity week in and week out without the chance of overtraining. Having a good plan that regulates the different types of training and the intensity is the key here. Periodization permits athletes to progress indefinitely through variations in intensity and volume to promote performance enhancements for as long as possible.

Weight-Training Program

With younger kids, it is important to understand where they are in their development before attempting to start a weight-training program. This is why it is difficult to train them as a group when they are in the growing phase since they are all at a different stage of development. Individualizing the programs is the key here unless they are at the same level. As players mature, it is possible to start a more serious weight-training program, but there are still several ground rules to consider:

1. Use your own body weight as much as possible.
2. When using weights, use free weights (not machines) with many reps (15–20).
3. Make use of rubber bands and/or light medicine ball as resistance training.
4. Train both the sides (extension and flexion) to properly stabilize the muscles.
5. Train the muscle groups every other day: arms, legs, chest, and back.
6. Keep a record of your training with intensity, weight, and reps.

As player reach the puberty stage, they are able to adopt a much more serious weight- training program. Below is a simple program for junior tennis players:

Exercise	Muscles	Sets x Reps
Squat or lunges	Hip and thigh	3 × 10 - 15
Bench press (dumbbell or barbell)	Chest	3 × 10 - 15
Seated row or lat pull down	Upper back	3 × 10 - 15
RDL or leg curl	Hamstrings	3 × 10 - 15
Shoulder front/lateral raise	Shoulders	3 × 10 (front raise ×6; lateral raise ×6)
Biceps curls	Biceps	2 × 10 - 15
Triceps extension	Triceps	2 × 10 - 15
Core (abdominal and lower back)		3–5 different exercises; total reps = about 100
Shoulder rehab		1-2 × 10 - 15

Make sure to use the proper weights that make the number of reps and execution of the exercise possible. I have witnessed many juniors either starting too early with heavy weight training or using improper weights that distort the technique and execution of the exercise. These training situations can lead to burnout and injuries that are limiting to their progress. In some cases, they can become permanent injuries.

As players advance, it is possible to slowly increase the weights as long as technique and reps are maintained. There are some things to watch while players are learning to train with weights. Below are some technical points to monitor while players are performing the exercises:

• Breathing
  Make sure that students are breathing properly while performing the exercises. Students need to learn to breathe out during the heaviest part of the exercise so they stay in control of the motion.

- Exercise speed
  Train the extension of the muscle three times faster than the flexion. This can be done with a counting method. The slower action during this motion increases the power more efficiently.

- Balanced approach
  Train the muscles more that are used less during tennis. Think of the back muscles, hamstrings, and rotator cuff. This method will balance the muscle groups around the joints and will prevent against injuries.

Plyometric Training

This type of training is designed to build power into explosive speed and agility. This is achieved by firing the fast twitching fibers in the muscles by flexing and extending the muscles as fast as possible. Low-impact jumps are slowly increased to high-impact jumps with increasing heights. The intensity in a tennis match varies with the level of play. However, advanced players have a high intensity of explosive movement in each rally of about six to ten seconds. This intensity is even higher for pro players with the ever-increasing tempo of play. Training the explosive power and speed can be accomplished with plyometric training. Some of the exercises of a plyometric program are illustrated below:

- Fast footwork training: the use of a rope ladder on the ground, movement drills with the use of one or more balls, reaction drills with a reaction ball
- Lower-body plyometrics: jump training (squat jumps, box jumps, lateral jumps, split squat jumps, tuck jumps, lateral push offs, bounding, hurdle jumps, depth jumps)

- Upper-body plyometrics: overhead throws, sideway throws, over-back toss, slams, explosive start throws, squat throws, single arm overhead throws, plyo push-ups.

This type of training needs to done progressively by starting out with lower intensity and impact before moving up to higher intensity and impact. The technique of the bounce and/or jumps needs to be monitored to ensure students are performing the exercises properly in order to prevent injuries. All of these plyometric exercises are designed to create more explosive power in the lower and upper body. This form of training has become a valuable tool to develop the speed and agility in tennis players. Many top players have this form of training as part of their fitness routine, and they often use it to warm up before they go out to hit balls.

Movement and Speed Training

The movement and speed training of tennis players is one of the most important parts of the fitness routine and is often overlooked. Weight training alone, although very important to improve power, will not make you a better mover on the court. The weight training is the basis to prevent injuries and to improve speed of movement of the legs, the hips, the trunk area, the shoulders, and the arms (preferably in that order). Players need to use the power from the ground up (kinetic chain) to produce power rather than trying to muscle with the shoulders and the arms. This is why movement and speed training is so important, the speed training to get there on time to hit the ball and the movement training to set up, recover, and change direction with ease. There are a few factors that will positively influence the movement and speed training for tennis:

1. Make the movement and speed training exercises tennis specific.
2. Time them to monitor and stimulate progression.
3. Use the racket as much as possible.

There are some tennis specific movement and speed tests you can perform to provide feedback to students. This feedback is important for students to gauge improvements.

It will not only provide a continuous stimulating effect for players to keep improving but will also give them goals to work for. Goals will set a target to work toward, and testing the tennis-specific exercises regularly shows the progressions made over time. Some of the tennis-specific movement and speed tests are listed below:

- **Spider run**

  This movement drill mimics the movement of tennis players during points. The students start in the middle of the baseline and run as fast as possible to the five points in the corners that connect the sidelines and the middle of the service line. By using opposite feet in changing direction in the corners, you can practice the recovery footwork during rallies. It is possible to time this movement and speed test, but be aware of the results on different surfaces (clay - hard). This test represents very closely the level of play of a competitor.

- **Twenty-yard dash**

  This is a straightforward sprint from behind the baseline to the service line on the other side of the net. This test is to see the maximum speed a player can reach. The type of surface will have little effect on the results of this test.

- **Service box movement**

  By standing in the middle of the service box, you can test the foot speed of the side steps and oversteps by touching the middle line and the sideline of the service box with the top of the racket. The object is to do this as many times as possible within thirty seconds.

- **Sideline movement**

  A. The speed of the side steps can be tested by making side steps over the singles and doubles line. This speed drill starts with the feet in between both lines. Count the number of times you can cross past the lines in thirty seconds. Try to keep the feet in a wider position while doing this drill. Use a racket while doing this test.

  B. You can perform the same drill as above by moving forward and backward over the singles and doubles sideline. Use a racket in hand while performing the test.

  C. You can test speed endurance with the eleven-line drill. Students have to touch the sidelines of the court eleven times as fast as possible. This test will give you a quick look at where the players are with their fitness level in general. The test does have different results when performed on clay or hard courts. Use a racket in hand.

- **One-mile run**

  This test is best performed on a track when doing some running training. It will give you a very clear picture of the endurance level of a player. Especially for more serious tennis players, this test can be a valuable tool to show the necessity of a running program to increase the endurance level.

Advanced Boys (Average)

Exercise\Age	12–14	14–16	16–18	18–23
Spider run (sec)	16.85–15.50	15.60–14.50	14.60–13.80	14.15–13.35
20-yard dash (sec)	3.40–3.15	3.30–2.95	3.05–2.85	2.95–2.65
Service box (30 sec)	25–28	26–30	28–32	30–35
Side A (30 sec)	26–29	28–32	29–33	31–35
Side B (30 sec)	27–30	29–33	30–34	32–36
Side C (sec)	34.0–31.0	32.0–30.0	30.0–28.0	29.0–27.0
One mile (min. sec)	6.00–5.15	5.30–4.50	4.50–4.20	4.30–4.10

Advanced Girls (Average)

Exercise\Age	12–14	14–16	16–18	18–23
Spider run (sec)	16.95–15.65	15.85–14.65	14.95–13.95	14.30–13.85
20 m dash (sec)	3.50–3.20	3.35–3.00	3.15–2.95	3.05–2.85
Service box (30 sec)	25–28	26–29	27–30	29–33
Side A (30 sec)	26–29	27–31	28–32	30–34
Side B (30 sec)	27–30	28–32	29–33	31–35
Side C (sec)	34.0–31.0	32.0–30.0	31.0–29.0	30.0–28.0
One mile (mins)	6.10–5.45	5.30–5.00	5.10–4.40	4.50–4.30

All the results above are measured and performed by elite top juniors and professional players. They should be seen as a goal to work toward if you are not accomplished yet with the movements. These results are from life measurements in the field and should be tested on a hard court to have a baseline for comparison. By training and testing on a regular basis, you will get immediate feedback to your performance. Timing yourself as often as possible and using the racket in hand makes the training of the movement all the more realistic and will mimic competitive play.

Running Program

Advanced tennis players will benefit from incorporating a running program in their fitness routine. Tennis has become an increasingly faster sport where movement is key to the success of competitive tennis players. You can observe the top players and notice the difference in speed and movement. They all have made great strides in their speed and movement with a running program. A track is a great place to train since most tracks have the same dimensions. Tennis players should train mostly two-hundred-yard and four-hundred-yard distances and time them continuously. The rest time in between can be as long as it takes to run that distance. Eventually, you can bring the rest time down to twenty-five seconds (the same rest time when playing points). Below is a chart with some test results.

Advanced Boys (good - excellent)

Distance\Age	12–14	14–16	16–18	18–23
20 m (sec)	3.40–3.15	3.30–2.95	3.05–2.85	2.95–2.65
50 m (sec)	7.50–6.70	7.00–6.00	6.30–5.40	5.52–5.05
100 m (sec)	14.2–12.5	12.7–11.0	12.0–10.8	11.0–10.4
200 m (sec)	29.0–24.5	25.0–22.9	23.2–21.5	21.9–19.5
400 m (sec)	58–53	56–51	54–48	51–47
1 mile (mins)	6.10–5.45	5.30–5.00	5.10–4.40	4.50–4.05
3 mile (mins)	14.45–13.45	13.50–13.20	13.40–12.50	13.20–12.40

Advanced Girls (good – excellent)

Distance\Age	12–14	14–16	16–18	18–23
20 m (sec)	3.50–3.20	3.35–3.00	3.15–2.95	3.05–2.85
50 m (sec)	7.64–6.80	7.15–6.20	6.50–5.80	5.68–5.13
100 m (sec)	14.8–12.8	13.2–11.4	12.4–11.2	11.5–10.8
200 m (sec)	29.5–24.9	25.5–23.4	23.7–22.0	22.4–19.9
400 m (sec)	59–54	57–52	55–49	52–48
1 mile (mins)	6.30–5.30	5.40–5.20	5.30–4.50	5.10–4.20
3 mile (mins)	15.00–14.15	14.30–13.50	14.0–13.10	13.30–12.50

Keeping Track of Results

By tracking the results over time, you can observe the progress of the movement and running program of each individual player. Below, I will show you an example (spider run) shown in a graph. It is clearly visible how much this player has improved.

Flexibility Training

The elasticity in the muscles and joints of an athlete will have a large effect on the performance and execution of the movements. In general terms, flexibility has been defined as *the range of motion* from a joint and its surrounding muscles during a passive movement. Passive in this context simply means that no active muscle involvement is required to hold the stretch. Instead, gravity or a partner provides the force for the stretch. A better flexibility will improve the speed of recovery of the footwork movement and enhances the release of the racket head to speed up the ball and/or to provide spin. Especially when in difficult positions (think low shots up front or wide shots outside the court), it is easier to recover from those positions when the flexibility is optimal. Some players are gifted with natural flexibility, but it is also possible to train this physical aspect. There are several different types of flexibility training:

- **Dynamic flexibility training**

  This type of stretching is the ability to perform dynamic movements within the full range of motion of the joint. Common examples are low squat steps or high kicks of the foot to shoulder level. The dynamic flexibility is generally more sport specific than other forms of stretching.

- **Static active flexibility training**

  This type refers to the ability to stretch an antagonist muscle using only the tension in the agonist muscle. An example is holding one leg out in front of you as high as possible. The hamstring (antagonist) is being stretched while the quadriceps and hip flexors (agonists) are holding the leg up.

- **Static passive flexibility training**

  This is the ability to hold a stretch using body weight or some other external force. To use the example above, hold your leg out in front of you and rest it on a chair. The quadriceps are not holding the leg up in this extended position.

After extensive studies with top athletes, they have concluded that for a warm-up, it is better to use dynamic stretching rather than static stretching. The static stretching can actually have a detrimental effect on the performance and may offer no protection against injuries although there is no conclusive evidence on this method.

There are definite benefits from stretching when increasing this joint range of motion. The performance may be enhanced, and the risk of injury will be reduced. The rationale behind this is that there is less friction in the joint and that a limb can move with a larger range of motion before an injury occurs.

Yoga can be a great form of flexibility training for tennis players. With all the combination of stretching exercises and the focus that is required to perform the execution, it is an excellent way to increase the range of motion, strengthen the muscles, and prevent injuries. It also will increase the focus on the movement and flexibility.

Diet for Advanced Players

In order to play highly competitive tennis, it is necessary to fuel the body properly. You can compare a diet from a competitive player with the fuel of a racecar. You always have to make sure you have the best fuel to make the car run fast and last as long as possible. The same goes for an advanced tennis player. What you eat makes a difference to your performance on the court. Eating a balanced diet is obviously important to maintain all levels of nutrients, vitamins, and minerals for the body to function properly. But there are certain food groups that are healthier than others and improve the energy needed for practice and matches. You can find some more information on this in my first book *Teaching Tennis Volume 1*.

The Influence of Diet on Conditioning and Competitive Play

A proper diet can have a big influence on the performance of a player. It can affect the endurance and energy level of a player, but also influence the function and performance of the body in general. Over time, a proper diet can also affect weight and efficiency of athletes through a better weight to energy output ratio. Here are some diet aspects that can enhance competitive play:

- **Have a balanced diet**

  A balanced diet will help you maintain all the levels of nutrients, vitamins, and minerals you need to perform on a daily basis and stay healthy over time. A good ratio of carbohydrates, protein, and fat can be found in whole grains, meat, fish, vegetables, fruit, nuts, milk, etc. It is important to choose food groups that contain many vitamins and minerals that are easily digestible. Having excessive amounts of one or two of these food groups or limiting one food group can have a negative effect on the performance. Every person is different, and it can be helpful to find what ratio works well for him or her.

- **Use a relatively low-fat diet**

  Although every competitive player needs some fat in their diet, having too much fat can make them feel sluggish and slow down the performance. Many fats also have an important role in providing other beneficial nutrients. An example is omega-3 oil in fish. However, by limiting the intake of fats, you can maintain or decrease the overall weight of the athlete and influence the performance of their speed and endurance indirectly. You can imagine how much faster a tennis player will be able to move and change direction with ten pounds less weight to carry around. Also, think how this might help endurance with playing a three- or four-hour match.

- **Eat more vegetables and fruit**

  These types of foods not only have a high level of fiber, but also contain high levels of vitamins and minerals. They are an excellent source of antioxidants that protect the cells in the body, stimulate the digestive system, and maintain a healthy and energetic lifestyle. They are also very useful as snacks when you feel hungry. Try to eat more vegetables and fruit in your diet whenever possible.

- **Use less sugar to maintain glucose balance**

  By not adding extra sugar in the diet, you can prevent a spike in the glucose levels. Maintaining a balance in the glucose levels is important for a consistent energy level when performing in practice and matches. There are many natural foods available that already have sugars in them. (Note: many processed foods have added sugars in them.) If extra sugar is added, it will often produce a temporary increase (spike) in energy levels, followed by a decrease (crash) in energy levels. To avoid these drastic changes in energy levels, it is better not to add extra sugar and get used to absorbing the sugars from the nutrients. Natural products have already plenty of sugars in them without the need to add extra sugars.

- **Eat more frequently but with smaller portions**

  Smaller meals are more easily and better digested than larger meals. It takes a lot of energy for the body to digest nutrients. So it makes sense to eat smaller portions so that energy can be used for the performance of athletes. Smaller portions also don't make you feel full and sluggish. To keep fueling the body, it is necessary to eat more frequently, especially during long matches. Bananas have been a popular snack during matches and usually don't upset the stomach. There are many energy bars on the market today that have taken the place of this commonly used nutrient. The trick is to find the one that agrees with you and that provides the most energy through nutrient replacement.

- **Drink plenty of fluids and add sports drinks when needed**

  Competitive players need to hydrate on a regular basis during practice and matches. By keeping the body balanced and hydrated, it is easier to keep performance high. It is imperative to hydrate from the start of the match. Don't wait until you feel thirsty. Once the fluids become depleted in the body, it is very difficult to restore a proper balance. In some cases, this can lead to cramping. In long matches and during tournaments, it is advisable to use some form of sports drink that not only replenish the fluids but also replaces the vitamins and minerals that are lost through sweating.

- **Add extra salt during extreme heat and humidity**

  You need to be prepared when playing in extreme hot and humid weather. In these conditions, players lose a lot more fluids and minerals, especially salt. By adding a little packet of extra salt to a sports drink, you can prevent excessive losses during competition and maintain performance as much as possible.

Recap

By adding all these physical factors into your training, it is not always necessary to add the separate physical workout sessions. You will soon find that your physical ability will be enhanced and that you are able to use your physical skills as an added weapon in combating opponents (more on physical development in *Teaching Tennis Volume 3*).

Eating to Win

Whenever I was coaching players on the road, I always tried to improve their diets and eating habits. Many of the kids that were used to eating the proper foods at home usually had fewer problems on the road. The development of top juniors or young pros requires the best of anything you can provide. The fuel intake of a tennis player can be complex when playing multiple matches, long matches, hot weather conditions, or playing at times you usually have your meals. It takes some experimenting and experience to organize this well.

Ryan Harrison was only twelve years old when he started traveling with me on the road. One of his first international tournaments was "Les petite ass" in France. It is the world championships fourteen and under that is played indoors in February. I noticed right away that his eating habits were bad. He was the youngest one on the USTA team and was in a phase where he was not eating enough and only would eat limited food groups. Not enough to keep up his energy, if you are playing tennis all day. On top of that, he also did not like the food there in France. I had trouble getting him to eat his dinner, and he would mostly stick to eating too much bread. Eating some vegetables or fruit was out of the question. So I made a point to slowly get him used to eating certain portions and the vegetables he liked. By the second week, he ran out of steam, got a little sick, and started losing energy during the day and finally lost in the quarterfinals. That summer, we went to Holland and France for international junior events and he started to get used to eating more different foods and some vegetables. The weeks in Holland were the best with a wide variety of foods available. He ended up winning the tournament, beating a fellow team member in the final.

Years later (age eighteen), we met at the Eddie Herr tournament and laughed about many of the struggles back then, and he proudly mentioned, "You know, Martin, I am eating much better!"

Since that time, Ryan has turned pro and has fought his way up to the top echelon of young and upcoming players. A while ago he was a valuable addition to the Davis Cup team that beat France in Monaco. I hope he liked the food there.

**Winner Ryan Harrison (left) and Devin Britton (right)
Final 14's boys Tennis Europe in The Netherlands**

Martin van Daalen

MENTAL DEVELOPMENT

During competition, the mental aspects become increasingly more important as players progress. Some players already possess the mental toughness and perseverance to compete and succeed. But for others, it does not come easy and is usually a learned behavior. For many athletes in any top sport, the mental aspects can be the most difficult to master. Most players don't knowingly work on their mental ability, but every game will intrinsically introduce a mental aspect to it. Competition requires players to push themselves to find an answer to every problem they encounter in the game, may it be a technical, tactical, physical, or mental obstacle. The manner and forcefulness of their pursuit determines the strength of their mental skills. It is possible to observe the differences in mental attitude from a young age. Mental training for beginning tennis players is best trained without the knowledge of the player by introducing it as a tactical part of a game in order to play better. With older players, you can discuss the subject more easily and make them aware what mental aspect they need to work on during practice matches.

> **The mental aspects of the game are dominating factors to win matches.**
>
> **At the same time, it is one of the least-trained aspects of the game!**

You can learn some mental aspects through habits and routines, but they are difficult to obtain when complementing parts are not inherently available. The determination or passion has to drive the person to acquire these mental traits. If however bad mental attitudes and routines are already ingrained in the character of a person, they are hard to shake, unless they themselves make the effort to change. Therefore it is much better and easier to learn mental skills at a young age, especially when teaching them in a playful and competitive structure. Parental guidance and education is an important factor in the mental development of tennis players as well. When looking at mental aspects, we started originally with three main aspects, but I would like you to consider these below:

- **Parental guidance and education** (trainable aspects)
  How young athletes are raised by their parents and family impacts in a large way how they will behave and perform in any given sport. Parents and their immediate family shape the mental development over time in how to handle difficult situations, how to behave, to show respect to others, to follow rules of sportsmanship, learning how to work hard to get ahead, learning discipline in performance, creating good habits and routines in life and in sports, having good eating habits, doing well in school, etc. In short, parents help train and shape the mental aspects from a very young age and are the gatekeepers to the social development throughout the lives of their children. The education in school should also be stimulated as much as possible to help train their brain and mental aspects to the fullest capacity. (Especially if you decide on homeschooling your kids, this should be maintained. If school becomes an afterthought in developing a tennis player, you are not helping them as a parent; you could be stunting their mental development as a person and limiting their chances in being successful in college.)

- **Emotional mental aspects** (trainable aspects)
  The emotional parts are trainable aspects with the cooperation of the student. They include aspects like nervousness and excitement, fear, pressure, and aggression. The feelings of the player are very much involved in playing tennis, and coaches should be aware of these. With training, guidance, and experience, it is possible to steer these emotions in a direction that can stimulate the energy and intensity of a player in a positive way. On the other hand, when the emotions become too high, they will use up the energy much faster

than most anticipate and will negatively affect the physical energy reserves as well. Staying calm under pressure, while maintaining intensity and controlled aggression, is the ultimate goal of a great competitor.

- **Intrinsic mental aspects** (less trainable aspects)
  The intrinsic or natural mental aspects are less trainable since they are mostly driven by the character traits of a player in combination with accomplishments and results. These intrinsic aspects include motivation, drive, determination, willpower, discipline, and confidence. These mental aspects can be stimulated and shaped by their upbringing, social surroundings, and education and improved over time with positive feedback from parents and coaches and mentors in life.

- **Reasonable mental aspects** (trainable aspects)
  The reasonable mental aspects come from the thought processes that guide and stimulate the decision making of a player. The player can make decisions on many aspects of the game (technical, tactical, physical, and mental), but also on the intensity and method of thinking that enhances the toughness in match play. Some of these reasonable aspects include concentration, discipline, routines and habits, problem solving, and stress management. They are all trainable mental skills that are needed to succeed at an advanced level of play.

Trainable Aspects

So let us focus on the trainable aspects of mental development. There are many things you are able to train, but oddly enough, very few coaches and players seem to focus much on this area of development. As mentioned before, it is the least-trained area of most athletes in any sport although it is getting more attention lately and there are many more mental trainers popping up. It is possible to have a problem in one or some of the mental aspects, but mostly these have been created at a younger age or have not been trained or addressed on a daily basis in your regular tennis training. Here are some of the things you can add to your mental training:

Practice with purpose. Mental training should be part of every practice by making students aware to practice with purpose. Just like the technical, tactical, and physical skills, the mental skills need constant attention. Choose a topic to work on every practice session. By giving purpose to the training, students have goals and direction and will develop their mental skills: focus, composure, intensity, habits, and rituals. As soon as this diminishes during practice, coaches can assist and remind players to train and improve these skills. Having goals and an overall plan on what to work on every training session will greatly impact improvements.

Keep a training log. When keeping a training log of topics, it is possible to keep track of details of problem areas and improvements made and, most importantly, how they were achieved! This is not only important for technical, tactical, and physical improvements, but most of all it is important for mental aspects of development. It documents how you have trained, what and how much you have worked on certain areas, and how you have fixed them. This log will eventually provide great feedback and mental stimulation to your confidence, as it will show you how far you have come in your development and push you to higher accomplishments.

Channel your emotions. Playing tennis requires highly developed skills in many areas and is a difficult sport to master. The emotions can be positive or negative. Positive emotions are demonstrated in the way the competitor moves and acts on court (composure), maybe a short fist pump when successful. Negative emotions are often voiced and acted out with frustration. Keeping both of them in check is beneficial to the stability during practice and match play. When successful, it provides a lot of joy, but it can also be very frustrating and bring out some disappointment and anger. It can even lead to fear of losing and attitude problems that don't help the progress at all. Controlling and channeling these emotions to renewed competitiveness and intensity is the key to mental development and growth. The habits and rituals are one method to stay mentally stable and keep the focus. Another method is to focus on the strategy at all times so that negative thoughts don't creep in. To use this method requires you not to stand still too long after winning or losing a point, but to turn around and walk to your towel and be busy with how to play the next point. This method is very evident in watching pro players in match play.

Conquer any Fear

Whoever has played this game has gone through some fears. There are different types of fears. There are fears of losing, which are probably more familiar. But there are also fears possible when players are winning and being afraid of finishing the task. Staying calm and maintaining belief in your abilities is obviously something that every player strives for. The score in the game, set, and match are powerful stimuli to either help your confidence when leading in score or lose confidence and have doubts creep in when down in score. So how do we become the calm and fearless competitor we so admire in big tennis events? There are several things you can do and focus on:

- Accept that everyone has fears and doubts to a certain degree. The better players are just better at focusing on the factors that help them be positive and competitive: strategy, intensity, and the will to always want to improve their game.
- Copy the mental attributes from the best players. Don't copy only the parts you want, copy the parts you need the most to help your weaknesses and your game. If you still have trouble keeping your composure, at least fake it and be a good actor!
- Never quiet! You never are defeated when you keep trying 100 percent; you lose when you keep quiet or give up on what you need to do to compete.

- Accepting that perfection is not obtainable and that there are only a few matches a year you will be completely satisfied with your performance. That doesn't mean you can't win, it just means there will be room for improvement.
- Having realistic and reachable mini goals for each match or tournament keeps you focused on improvements and gives you positive feedback of the successes and in moving forward with your game.
- Having a big picture view of your development as a player that is not connected to wins and losses of that moment. Your improvements should be a fun challenge instead of a grade of success.
- Having a winning attitude and great composure. The opponents will get energy or confidence from any bad attitude or frustration showed. Don't help your opponent!

Attitude and Composure

The way you behave and control your demeanor in point play and matches influences your competitiveness and shapes your reputation as a player. Your attitude also influences your confidence. Most players don't realize this until you make them aware. For instance, if you always get mad and lose your composure when you are down in score, all an opponent needs to do is to make sure to get ahead in score and keep you there. Your reputation will precede you since players and coaches will ask how you play. Now, of course, it would be beneficial if you already have a good attitude and stay calm during matches, but it is another weapon that is often overlooked. There are examples enough to watch of players with positive and negative attitudes. Just make sure you help yourself and be one of the players you admire in this aspect. There is nothing wrong with looking cool and collected. No matter what your level of play, always strive to have a professional attitude at all times.

Adopting a Winning Attitude

Every player experiences some doubts or negative thoughts during competition. Those usually creep in when you don't have a game plan and a winning attitude. The game plan is your tactical purpose for the match and keeps your mind focused on ways to beat your opponent. The winning attitude is the confident manner of a player. A positive attitude helps you to believe in yourself in order to succeed, but a winning attitude takes it a step further in adopting all the traits of a winner. A player with a winning attitude will act with determination, purpose, and confidence. They will control their emotions at all times to maintain focus on their game plan and to enhance their execution.

As a spectator, you can detect the players that have a winning attitude fairly easy. The character traits of players can influence this aspect during training and competition. To give you a few examples, being a perfectionist can help you to develop as a player, but it can also hurt you when the learning process takes too long. Patience is important to stay calm and to keep working on your game in a positive and constructive way. In some cases, the player has their expectation too high or less understanding of the process of learning. As a coach and/or parent, it can be helpful to know the character traits of a player so they can explain and assist where needed. As a player, the focus should be on the process during practice or the strategy during match play. This will keep the mind occupied to eliminate negative thoughts creeping in and to stay focused on the task at hand.

Confidence

The level of confidence is defined by how you feel about yourself (self-esteem) and your performance. It is a very subjective part of your emotions. Sometimes your feelings are correct, but more often they are misleading and not realistic. Obviously, the results in practice and competitions can improve your confidence, but you can also use some methods to enhance it with visualization and by adopting a professional attitude and composure. Using imagery (visualization) can improve a stroke, strategy, or physical performance by inwardly thinking of the action. It is like preprogramming your brain to act automatically without hesitation. You can imagine how this could improve your confidence when confirmed in results. A positive and professional attitude will have an inward effect on how you feel about yourself and as a tennis player. Acting the part is half the work by walking and talking like a champion. Winning and losing are part of any sport, but not everybody deals with it in a professional and positive way. The moment you can be proud of yourself, no matter if you win or lose, you are already on the right track to enhancing your confidence, and improved performance are soon to follow. Some tips to improve your confidence:

- **Prepare for maximum performance.** There is no substitute for hard work. Confidence is largely built through physical training and knowing you've trained longer and harder than your competitors. Having a physical edge also gives you the advantage to dig deep in beating your opponent in more than one way.

- **Have obtainable mini goals.** By making reachable goals for the near future, you will feel successful and gratified at making progress and improving your game. This method will improve your confidence in yourself and your performance.

- **Don't compare yourself to others.** If you always feel that others are better, it is almost impossible to beat them. Don't look at their size, skills, or record. Focus on your own game and strategy and find weaknesses in their game to attack.

- **Only focus on what you can control.** There are many factors you cannot control, like the weather, the time you play, opponents, referees, etc. Focus instead on you and your game so you can keep your concentration and intensity high to compete.

- **Stay positive and never give up.** Being negative always kills your confidence and also will affect your energy and attitude. Always try to find an advantage in every situation and challenge yourself to solve it.

- **Keep a training and match log.** By making notes of your training and competition, it will provide feedback of your accomplishments and things to improve. It will remind you of what you are doing right and will inspire you to work harder.
- **Be a good coach to yourself.** Negative self-talk is pretty obvious in sports, and tennis players are no exception to this. Change your habits in being positive and encouraging by telling yourself what specifically to do or to improve instead of dwelling on the mistakes and chastising yourself.
- **Play within your comfort level.** Don't play above your means in trying to hit too hard or playing too risky. You know the level you can play that still gives you consistency in most rallies and provides you confidence in your game. Taking some risk is okay, but don't beat yourself in the process—beat your opponent.
- **Play high-percentage tennis.** Help your confidence by playing less risky. Some examples are to organize a high first-serve percentage by using a little spin (less pressure on your second serve), using large targets and slightly higher trajectory in aiming your strokes, and playing your returns deep up the middle. This method will make you feel free to swing faster. As you become more comfortable, you can venture out to the sidelines.
- **Be brave.** Believing in your skills and being courageous to execute them is another step to becoming more confident. If you have fears or are scared to execute, you cannot get the most out of your game.
- **Have a game plan.** Always have a direction and method in how to beat your opponent. Stepping on the court without a game plan is competitive suicide. Have an idea of their strengths and weaknesses and formulate several tactics how to deal with those. There is no better feeling when a plan is successful, and it will increase your confidence immensely.

Fun

When improving as tournament players, it is often overlooked why we started this game. It started with fun and games. No matter what level you play, may it be beginner or pro player, you will never reach your full potential without letting go, enjoying the path of development, and having fun in competition. Fun is an essential aspect to improvement and excellence! The opposite will be very visible when pressuring yourself too much or if coaches or parents are adding too much pressure. Training and competition should be a fun and enjoyable experience.

Intensity

This aspect of mental development is one that is often overlooked, but actually solves a lot of other mental problems that might occur. Intensity in tennis is the amount of speed, concentration, power, and accuracy of execution that is exerted in each point, game, sets, and the match. The level of intensity is driven by the mental and physical energy. Some have a natural tendency to play at a high intensity, but most students need to learn that level of intensity through practice and competition. There can be several causes of lower intensity. If players are nervous or too emotional, they will often not be able to play with intensity for very long. It affects the footwork speed and stamina considerably, limiting players to play freely and to reach their potential in match play. But it can also be a fitness problem that limits players to practice or play matches with higher intensity. Preferably, you want the intensity to be high during the point, low in between, and to bring it up again just before starting the next point. Nervousness, attitude, or being overly emotional will keep energy usage high in between points and limit the use of energy during points over time. (See the graphs on next page.)

As you can see in this first graph, the intensity will be building up as the nervousness of the start of the match reduces and players get down to business. If players stay calm, they can be efficient with their energy and reach a high level of intensity during the points. When the intensity is limited in between points, and heart rate can be reduced, they will be able to sustain their intensity to the max for a certain period of time.

In this case, I took a set (nine games) with a score of 6–3 as an example to show.

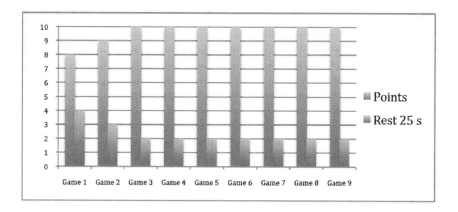

In the next graph, you can see what happens when players become frustrated or angry. Usually, you will also see these players not being able to keep their composure well as the match progresses. The heart rate will stay at a high level in between points. The energy output will not be efficient and will "eat up" the energy needed to reach a high intensity.

Compare both graphs and see how the energy-level usage stays high in bottom one when the heart rate stays high due to agitation or frustration. Over the course of a set or match, players will continually start losing energy during the points.

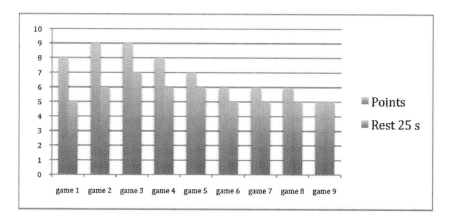

When competitors feel their energy fading under these circumstances, another mental aspect of panic creeps in to lose even more energy in the process. That is why it is almost impossible for players that struggle with this problem to be competitive and to come back from behind. It is possible to change all these negative effects by making players aware of their intensity level during practice, points, and practice matches. You can introduce a number system from 1 to 10, with 10 being the highest level. Focus on intensity during points and in between points.

Habits

As players progress and become more competitive, mental training should become a part of practice. Starting young players with "good habits" can have a long-lasting effect on the success of a player. Creating good habits in dealing with playing under pressure and having the proper competitive response to situations has to be taught at an early age. Players usually pick up improper mental responses by copying them from others. These responses, if not corrected immediately, are very hard to change later on as they become a customary response or a ritual of the player. Good habits help you in focusing during your match and having more consistent results.

Good habits of players:

- Preparing properly with training, equipment, and rest
- Being on time to warm up physically and hitting balls
- Having drinks and nutritious snacks for on court
- Being tactically prepared with info on opponent
- Cool down and ask feedback after the match

The following example is common in prepubescent and pubescent kids due to the peer pressure of trying to fit in with everyone else.

Example: Many juniors don't start throwing their racket or having extreme vocal outbursts until they start playing competitively and observe other juniors doing this. The same goes for girls that grunt excessively during play and copy this from each other.

Rituals or Routines

Many rituals are part of the learning process of mental training. They help to maintain focus to stay on track with the game plan and execution of the strokes during play. It stimulates the thought patterns to stay calm but alert. When you are distracted or agitated, it adversely affects the quality of play. As a coach, it can be very beneficial to teach these rituals to your players to enhance their focus and demeanor on court. As a player, you would do wise to learn these rituals and find out which ones fit with you.

Note: When a player constantly looks to the side for reassurance from the coach or the parents, it will have a negative effect in maintaining the rituals. The same goes for too much attention or coaching from the side. Rituals maintain focus within and maintain the thoughts on the strategy of the match instead of the distracting factors outside of the court.

Some rituals for players:

- After finalizing the point, hold racket in the nondominant hand.
- After points are played, walk back to the fence, towel off, and get ready for the next point.
- Take your time (25 sec.) in between points. Don't rush.
- Maintain focus by looking at the strings of your racket, not at surroundings.
- Think of your strategy in preparation for the next point.
- Organize a good start with preparation of the serve and return.
- Maintain a good attitude and demeanor throughout the match.

Focus and Concentration

Tennis is not an easy sport to play considering all the different strokes, possibilities of patterns, strategies, and the mental aspects involved. To play tennis well takes great concentration and discipline. It also requires great mental and physical stamina to endure in long matches and tournaments. To consistently perform well, you have to train the brain as well as the body. The importance of education cannot be underestimated when it comes to focus, mental stamina, and discipline.

Exercise: One experiment you can do with your student is to see how long they can focus on a ball held at arm's length. The object of this exercise is to see how long they can focus on one spot on the ball before the eyes stray or other thoughts creep in. You can use a stopwatch and let the player indicate when the eyes wandered or when they lost focus with their thoughts.

Mental Training in Progression

1. Play as many games as possible with young players. They love to compete with their peers and will try harder in a game. Use games with and without points to see if players show a difference in mental attitude. (This will be a good indication of the mental ability of a player.)
2. Play actual matches with normal scoring to see how the player responds to the pressure of a match and competition against their peers. Ask them what strategy they intend to use.
3. Practice playing with different tactical or mental subjects in mind. You can do this for one or both players. This trains the focus and problem-solving aspects.
4. Practice playing under pressure by shortening the game. Starting at 30 all, the intensity will increase considerably!
5. Play points when down in score and up in score. By starting the game score at 0–15, 15–0, 15–30, and 30–15, players can train the

focus of playing one point at a time instead of focusing too much on the score.

6. Play matches with the sets starting at 3 all in game score. It will shorten the sets and increase the intensity and pressure. Players will feel the urgency to play more tactically and physically and automatically increase the mental aspects.

7. Play points with tie breaks. Not only does it teach students to play these better, but will also train their mental capabilities as well.

8. Play three sets to see how the physical stress will influence the mental aspects of their game. The endurance of a player will have a large impact on the mental stability over time. Playing longer matches will teach them how to cope with the added physical stress and enhance the mental toughness.

Playing points and practice matches will enhance your competitive skills tremendously, but there is no substitute for playing matches in tournaments. Make sure to compete in tournament play as often as possible to enhance your mental skills. (You can find more on mental development in *Teach Tennis Volume 3*.)

TIPS FOR ADVANCED PLAYER DEVELOPMENT

Whenever we are involved in developing tennis players, we always have to keep in mind the basic and fundamental reasons we wanted them to start playing this sport. When we get started, it is not because we ever think it will be their profession, but more about the other factors: basic health, social development, fun and games, competition, etc. But all this can change in a drastic way when we get carried away by results in tournaments, with players becoming successful in sectional and national/international events. The individuals who are responsible to guide this in the proper direction are parents, coaches, national federations, management companies, and players themselves. There have been many examples in the past where talented players have failed to progress in the proper direction due to many different mistakes in guidance and development. I have personally witnessed many players losing their way, falling back, or completely giving up the sport. There is no shortcut to becoming an advanced player, and every person has his or her own timeline in development that cannot be forced. As parents and coaches, we can at least make sure our juniors enjoy the sport as much as possible and make it a sport for life. (Seventy percent of kids quit their sport before age thirteen because of losing interest or fun due to pressure or burnout.) So what are the dangers to watch for in development of tennis players? Obviously, there are factors that play a large role and can be used as guidelines of development:

- **Always keep in mind why you started playing the sport.** Fundamental reasons for playing the sport will keep you grounded. They will provide a healthy attitude of your accomplishments and help in preventing stress and burnout. A good example of this is easy to see in some top players who obviously don't need to play anymore for an income, but clearly enjoy the competition and fun in playing the game.

- **Every junior player has their own talent level and development timeline.** Not every tennis player can become a professional. So it is unwise to give young juniors the notion this is a possible future job for everyone. It is just not something you can study for in college and start it as a profession. It is totally dependent on results in professional events and the talent level and timeline of development. You can create all the perfect circumstances of training and coaching, but not everyone has the skills to succeed. Also, there have been many cases in players developing at a young age or even after college. So there is no "cookie-cutter" method to develop tennis players. The best advice you can give to young players is to strive for college first. This way, they always have a backup plan and don't neglect studies, will keep training their brain besides their bodies, and increase their options of going to a good school and a career for the future.

- **Don't make predictions based on their talent and results as a junior.** The worst thing you can do as a parent or coach is talking about a pro career or their talent. In the first case, it makes no sense to talk about a pro career unless you are a top 20 ITF player or ranked 300 to 400 on the ATP or WTA tour. Talking about it before you reach this level is only distracting. Telling players they are talented only can create problems in feeling they don't need to learn or work that hard to reach their goals. This can also limit the players reaching their maximum potential over time.

- **Have a development plan and stick to it!** This plan should include a short- and long-term plan with a yearly tournament schedule. This way you prevent rushing or skipping developmental phases of technical, tactical, physical, or mental aspects of the game. The tournament schedule is important to competitors so they don't play too many events and prevent overtraining and burnout. So request a developmental plan from your coach that includes a tournament schedule and have input to both.

- **Play the correct number and level of tournaments.** Competition provides feedback to specific training needed and the level of events you are playing. If you analyze your matches, you can make conclusions on your technical, tactical, physical, and the mental aspects and what to improve. Match play can be your best instructor when you use it in a positive way. Very young players can play two to three events per month, as long as they are weekend events and have a day of rest afterward. With age, players can play several events after another. This is where a yearly schedule becomes important to limit the amount of tournaments per year (20–30). The amount of tournaments depends on the total amount of matches played. The level of the tournaments should be suitable to your skill level. As you become accomplished and more experienced in one level, you can venture out in the next level or age group. Try to find levels that give the player a 2 to 1 win ratio. Also a mix of levels that provides tournaments they can win, reach the quarter finals, and high-level events that challenge them to win against stronger opponents.

- **Have a good balance in the amount of training and rest.** The amount of training can vary due to the age, strength, other sports activity, their passion for tennis and their skill level. Young players can thrive in after-school programs as their bodies are still growing and so they can attend regular school. Continued training without proper rest will cause overtraining and burnout. To get optimal results, schedule time off to stay motivated and eager to train and play with energy and a competitive attitude.

- **Focus on development versus results and rankings.** Competition is a great tool to provide feedback on development and will point clearly to topics needed for improvement. But keep the focus on improving their game instead of results in tournaments or their ranking. I have seen many parents look up rankings or results and make comparisons with other players. This information will distract them from staying on track and possibly cause added anxiety and mental pressure to winning matches or losing to certain players.

Martin van Daalen

Chasing results or ranking never has a positive result on developing players. It makes it almost impossible for young players to keep their focus on improving aspects of their game; they will always be thinking of the consequences in the future instead of staying in the present.

- **Find the proper coach and program that suits your needs.** It takes some research to find the appropriate coach with the knowledge and reputation of developing advanced players. A player has to be inspired by their coach so they can believe and trust their guidance. The program should have the different levels of players and contain group and private instruction. As players become more physically mature, they should also have a fitness component or another sport that supplements this. If you as a parent are acting as the coach, be sure this is what your child wishes as well and is the best solution above an experienced developmental coach.

- **Let them play the sports they want.** Playing other sports than tennis (called cross-training) can be a great tool to practice all the different physical and mental skills in a fun way. Some young tennis players play other sports and some don't. There is not one way to improve the most in a certain sport. Cross-training can be advantages to improving coordination and movement, but there are also many examples of juniors that have had specific skill training early on without cross-training and went on to be very successful.

- **Make sure it is their sport and passion to progress.** It is so easy as parents, family members, and coaches to get carried away by results from the player and live vicariously through their success. We always have to remember it is their sport and their results. You can see this happen all the time at tournaments where parents start copying remarks of coaches or have their own opinions/ideas of what their child should do in matches and training. There is nothing wrong with guiding and supporting your child; however, this is possible without making coaching remarks. The remarks/ suggestions can become confusing or even contradictory. It can diminish their trust and belief in their coach and then you don't really need to hire a coach. Pushing them too hard in training or results shows your passion, not theirs. By letting the player choose their direction, they feel empowered in their sport. Confidence will grow and fuel their drive and passion even more.

- **Never change a winning formula.** Not unlike in a tennis match, never change a winning strategy when things are going well and you are improving. This counts for players, parents, and coaches and even for most things in life. Why make a change if it is working for you personally. This could be the case in the way you hit the ball (technical), the way you play (tactical, physical, mental). But it could also apply to what equipment you use and who you choose as your coach, especially as you are making some transitions from one level to another. This is where you are most vulnerable and need to count on what you know instead of the unknown. This is very much the case when juniors are turning pro and often change coaching, rackets, and equipment. It is also the period in their development where they need continuity and stability rather than changes that can severely undermine their confidence.

DRILLS FOR ADVANCED PLAYERS

Drills are exercises to enhance automatic responses in tactical situations. The coach feeds balls to his students in order to initiate movement and patterns of play.

The drills need to be organized to facilitate tactical practice while improving reaction, movement, and ball control under pressure. After sufficient repetition, players will start to execute better and react automatically to similar situations during competitive play. There are several things to consider before introducing drills:

Level of Play

The players need sufficient repetition of the technique, and consistency needs to be established in order to avoid an early breakdown in the stroke production. They need to be somewhat close in level to have the best results with all players.

Proper Subject

The drills need to be coordinated with the subject matter and the technical, tactical, physical, or mental development of the player. They need to feel a connection with the subject matter and their proficiency level before raising intensity.

Progression of Drills

There should always be a progression in the drills from easy to more difficult. Make sure the students have a positive experience to build their confidence before making the drills more complex.

Feeding

The coach can adjust the feed of the ball with speed, trajectory, spin, and tempo. This will directly influence the response from the player. Adjusting the feed to the level of competency of the player is a matter of practice and experience.

Work and Rest

Drills can be much more strenuous on the players than hitting with each other. It becomes an art form for the coach to correlate the right speed and tempo of the feed, with the movement capabilities of each player. As the intensity increases, during the drills, it is important to provide the players with short breaks to recover. Coordinate the intensity of the drill with the effort level of the players by having the drill last for 2–5 minutes followed each time with a short break. Another good way to include breaks is to have one player pick up balls while the others are practicing, to later rotate back into the exercise.

Key to Court Diagram

●   Player position

▯   Coach position

○   Target

⟶   Coach feed

- - →   Hitting direction

· - ·→   Player movement

← - →   Rally direction

Drill 1: Baseline Direction and Recover Drill

The coach feeds balls to the corners of the court. Players move to return the balls to alternate targets. The students recover to the middle of the court.

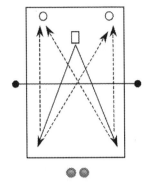

Practice: The purpose is to practice the recovery and movement of the players back to the middle of the court. The combination of movement and accuracy of the strokes is important to construct a point.

Drill 2: Baseline Movement and Rhythm Drill

The coach feeds 6–10 balls to the corners of the court. Each student then retrieves the balls and plays two balls cross and two balls down the line.

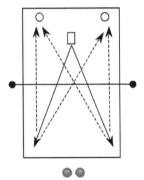

Practice: The purpose is to give the students a rhythm and feel for the rally by running them side to side. The coach can observe movement, balance, ball control, and recovery footwork.

Drill 3: Inside out and Wide Forehand

The coach feeds balls to two targets on the baseline. The object is to control the court with the forehand stroke and footwork. After 3–5 repetitions, switch players.

Practice: The coach adjusts the speed, spin, and trajectory of the balls. Students focus on the different footwork and direction control from both sides of the court.

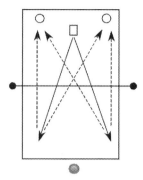

Drill 4: Inside out and Running Forehand

The coach feeds the first ball inside out, followed by a wide ball for a running forehand along the baseline. Afterward, they run around and join at the back.

Practice: The coach adjusts the speed, the frequency, the height, and spin of the ball. Players need to learn how to prepare quickly and play the different targets on the court.

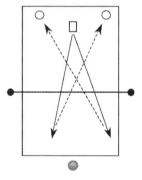

Same drill in reverse with forehand and running backhand.

Drill 5: Running Forehand and Backhand

The coach feeds several (6–10) balls wide to forehand and backhand. The players try to neutralize the opponent with the target in the middle of the court. Afterward, they run and join at the back. Practice control, spin, and trajectory.

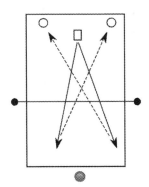

Practice: The purpose is to get players accustomed to running down the ball and returning it in the right direction. The coach can gauge the speed and the direction of the feed to the capabilities of the player.

Drill 6: Baseline Consistency during the Rally

The coach feeds the balls to the players on the baseline. They can only play to one side of the court. The one player can play anywhere. Make the rallies as long as possible. This drill is also possible with points.

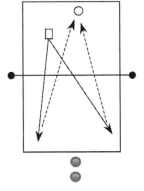

Practice: The purpose is to improve directional control from the two players and to improve consistency with the change of direction from the one player.

Drill 7: Baseline Consistency Two-on-One Play

The coach feeds from the side of the court to the players on the baseline. The players can play freely to each direction. This drill is also possible with points.

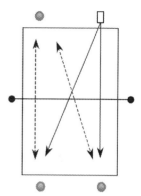

Practice: The purpose is to simulate play against a strong opponent. The coach has influence of speed and angle of the feed in moving the players around the court. As errors occur, the coach feeds in the next ball.

Drill 8: Volley Movement and Direction Drill

The coach feeds to the players at the net. Players step forward to volley. Alternate directions to the targets. The coach can adjust the speed and angle of the feed.

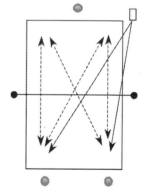

Practice: The purpose is to train movement and direction of the volley. Players should train both forehand and backhand. Recovery footwork becomes essential to the volley.

Drill 9: Volley Direction and Movement

The coach feeds the balls across the court to the net players. They will move continually closer to the net position. The coach can vary the speed and interval of the balls. Practice in both direction.

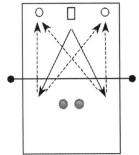

Practice: The purpose is to train "closing the net" with the volley. As players progress, they learn how to close more rapidly in approaching the net.

Drill 10: Volley "Poaching" Drill

The coach feeds one ball at a time through the middle of the court. Players intercept (poach) the ball as they move across the net. The coach can vary the speed and direction of the feed.

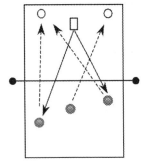

Practice: The purpose is to learn to intercept the ball for doubles play. The players move around and repeat the action from both sides.

Drill 11: Combination Approach Drill

The coach feeds three balls in sequence. Start with a baseline stroke then an approach shot and a volley to finish. Practice this drill from both sides. The coach can adjust speed, spin, and intensity.

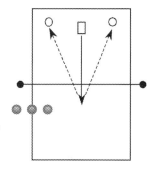

Practice: The purpose is to hit a variety of shots to mimic a match situation or rally in approaching the net.

Coaches need to watch for recovery and balance during the execution of this drill.

Drill 12: Approach Shots and Passing Drill

The coach feeds short balls so players can approach the ball down the line. The passing shot can go cross-court or down the line. Coaches can adjust speed, spin, and height of the ball. Play out the point.

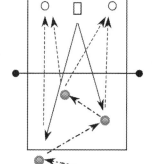

Practice: The purpose is to increase the control and consistency of approaches and passing shots under pressure. Make sure the players maintain consistency.

Drill 13: Two-on-One Volley and Baseline Drill

To start the rally, the coach feeds the ball to the net players. They only return the volley to one side of the court. Coaches can vary speed, angles, and overheads.

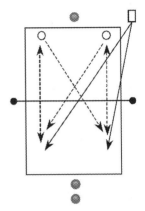

Practice: The purpose of the drill is to train automated responses from the players to rally under pressure. The coach should provide a wide variety of shots and keep the students adjusting to different situation

Drill 14: Two-on-One Volley and Baseline Drill

To start the rally, the coach feeds the ball to the players on the baseline. They only play to one side at the net player. Coaches can vary speed, spin, and direction with the players adjusting to point situations.

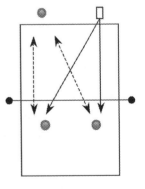

Practice: The purpose of the drill is to train automated responses from the players to rally under pressure. The corrections are made to stroke production and footwork.

Martin van Daalen

Drill 15: Two-on-One Volley and Baseline Drill

To start the rally, the coach feeds the ball to the net player. Players can rally the ball around the whole court. Coaches can adjust speed, spin with lobs to create match situations for the students.

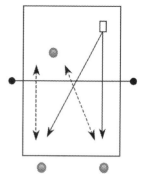

Practice: The purpose of the drill is to train automated responses and movements from the players under pressure. Coaches should watch to see if the players demonstrate recovery, balance, and control.

Drill 16: Two-on-One Volley and Baseline Drill

To start the rally, the coach feeds in the ball to the player at the baseline. The players can play the ball around the whole court. Coaches can vary speed, spin, and depth of the ball.

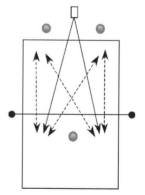

Practice: The purpose of the drill is to train automated responses and movement from players under pressure. Coaches should watch for recovery and control.

REFERENCES

- Successful Coaching (Tennis Edition 1990)
  Rainer Martens

- Guideline and Training Book for Coaches KNLTB Part A and B (1995)
  Editor: Frank van Fraayenhoven

- USA Tennis Parents' Guide (2001)
  USTA

- Coaching Different Gender (2002)
  David C. Gosselin

- The Power of Concentration
  Remez Sasson

- Basic Nutrition for Tennis
  High Performance Coaching Program Study Guide

- Playing Tennis in the Heat
  Dr. Michael Bergeron

- Nutrition
  Page Love

- Sports Psychology Guidebook for Coaches
  USTA

- Periodization for Tennis Players (2008)
  Anne Pankhurst

- Tennis Recovery (2010)
  Mark S. Kovacs, Todd S. Ellenbecker, W. Ben Kibler

ACKNOWLEDGEMENTS

Foremost, I have to thank my parents for introducing me to this wonderful sport. They have always tried to guide me and encourage me to be the best I can be in whatever I attempted to do.

TAcknowledgement and thanks go out to my two sons, John and Tom, for being my biggest supporters in my career and in writing these books.

I am grateful for all the wonderful coaches that taught me the game. Their teaching has brought out my passion for tennis and instructing others to enjoy the game as much as I have. My thanks go to Mr. van der Berg, Jan Hordijk, and Eric van der Pols for being patient and diligent in teaching me the intricate parts of the tennis game.

In my playing days, there was one person who took an interest in teaching me the tactical and mental aspects of the game. Henk Korteling was a mentor to me, and he was instrumental in teaching me how to control the mind and enjoy the game.

As a student coach, I went through several teaching courses in the Netherlands. There are, however, some coaches that take a special interest in stimulating you to reach a higher level of coaching. Tom de Goede was one of those coaches, and my thanks go to him for pushing me to excel.

Lynne Rolley has been a friend and colleague in coaching and guiding players. She always has been a great support in helping me with players and difficult situations. Her clear vision and experience in management of players, coaches, and parents has been instrumental to me and taught me to look at many different perspectives of coaching and teaching. Thanks, Lynne, for all your advice over the years.

Rodney Harmon has always supported me in many ventures and ideas as a coach. He has become a close friend and advisor over the years of working together. I have to thank him for stimulating me to write and create these books of teaching tennis. His passion for tennis instruction combined with his insight for the game and his positive attitude have been an inspiration to me. Thanks, Rodney, for the advice, many suggestions, and with the help in editing this book.

Magnus Norman has become a close friend and colleague while working as director of player development in Finland. He used to help me with the top juniors and and pro players in providing advise, training, and camps. Thanks for your support, your professional example and in writing a foreword for this book.

Many thanks have to go to David Kenas to create the sequences of the strokes. They certainly make it much more visual in showing the key positions and specifics of the fundamentals.

INDEX

A

acceleration, 144, 151, 198, 201–2, 207–8, 215, 224, 228, 231, 236, 248, 251–52, 324–25
accuracy, 140, 182, 194–95, 223–24, 232, 241, 247, 266, 269
Agassi, Andre, 11
ATP (Association of Tennis Professionals), 11, 33, 203, 407
  ranking, 19, 203

B

backhand, 27, 76, 79, 162, 164–65, 170–71, 257, 273, 301, 354–55, 364, 416
backspin, 300, 306–7, 309–10
backswing, 107–10, 124, 135, 142–46, 155, 157, 161–62, 181, 185–86, 204, 208, 210–11, 214–15, 217, 219, 222–26, 239, 250, 253, 255–56, 258, 261–63, 265, 268–71, 273, 277, 298–300, 306, 316, 326
  height of, 262, 265
  length of, 262, 268, 299
  long, 208, 215
  speed of, 253
  tempo of, 224
balance, 30–31, 45, 82–83, 107–8, 116, 118–19, 134–37, 176–77, 180, 184, 190–91, 194–95, 209–10, 212–14, 217, 219, 222–31, 235, 240, 250, 268–70, 281–82, 284, 309, 319–20, 325–34, 336, 366–67, 372, 387–88

loss of, 180, 353
balls
  angle of, 140, 181, 186, 194, 199, 264
  deep, 290, 294
  direction of, 140, 194, 327, 333
  elevation of, 140, 186
  flight of, 27, 117, 186–87, 191, 197–200, 212, 265, 297, 350–51
  heavy, 172, 351
  high, 28, 146, 280, 285, 311
  high-bouncing, 200, 212, 215
  low, 297, 299
  low-bouncing, 199, 212, 215, 307
  short, 26, 146, 203, 286, 293, 298–300, 305, 325, 350, 419
Berdych, Tomáš, 226
Boca Raton, Florida, 132
body language, 14, 57–58, 60–62, 65, 130, 368
Buchanan, Chase, 153

C

camouflage, 172, 242, 247
Capriati, Jennifer, 11
centrifugal force, 144, 207–8
Clijsters, Kim, 11
coaches, vii, ix–xi, xiii–xvii, xxi–xxii, 3, 6, 9–10, 18, 37, 48, 52–55, 57–58, 61–63, 69–70, 79, 83–84, 105–6, 121, 133–34, 179, 210–11, 233, 240–41, 351–52, 372–73, 393–94, 406, 410, 419–21, 423–26
  demeanor of, 6, 39
  national, xv–xvi, 100–101
  novice, 1

energy, 34, 96, 142, 208–9, 218, 299, 313, 327, 387, 389, 393, 399, 401–2
  aerobic, 117
  anaerobic, 117
  channeling, 120–21
  levels of, 96, 98–99, 385, 387
  preservation of, 319
  storage of, 208
  transfer of, 218
errors, 135
  forced, 363
  primary, 129
execution, xxi, 3–4, 8, 22–25, 27–28, 40, 44–45, 54, 57–58, 63, 65, 72, 78–79, 87–89, 103–7, 110, 115–16, 119, 121, 125–29, 150–51, 189, 230, 244–45, 272–73, 304, 306, 342–43, 360–61, 376
  accuracy of, 400
  problems of, 24, 88, 125, 182
exercises, xxi, 63, 67, 104, 126

F

Federer, Roger, 11, 110, 123, 221–22, 225, 314–15
feedback, 1, 128
fitness routines, 378, 382
flexibility, 28, 50, 117–18, 143, 148, 185, 207, 364, 371–72, 383, 385
footwork, 7, 13, 15, 22, 27–28, 31, 86–87, 118–19, 133–35, 137, 168, 170–72, 176–78, 180–82, 184–85, 190–91, 196–97, 211–12, 215–16, 229, 286, 319–20, 322–23, 326–34, 340–41, 357–58, 360–62, 366, 369–70, 414–15
  recovery, 28, 45, 118, 137, 162, 165, 177, 182, 191, 212, 215, 322,

330, 332–34, 337, 366, 379, 414, 417
forehands, 20, 22, 27–29, 75–76, 79, 82, 85–86, 110, 131, 133, 136, 153, 157–58, 170–72, 180, 182, 187, 197, 199–200, 234, 244, 273–74, 302, 321, 333–34, 336–37, 340, 348, 354–55, 415–17
  running, 22, 111, 136–37, 171, 199, 329, 337, 340, 415
  topspin, 20, 47, 85–86, 92, 157, 187, 302
  wide, 153, 415
friction, 141, 187, 197, 264, 333, 337
fundamentals, 4–5, 8, 105, 123, 133
  tactical, 349

G

game styles, xxii, 13, 77, 257, 361–62
Gasquet, Richard, 11
gender, 5, 37–38, 81, 129, 345, 423
goals
  long-term, 9, 70, 73, 78–79
  performance, 72, 84, 93
  process, 72, 84
  short-term, 9, 73, 78–79, 354
grip, 5, 8, 108–9, 135, 140, 155, 193, 195, 200, 202, 242, 245, 248, 253, 274, 284
  analysis of, 108
  backhand, 200, 299
  forehand, 110, 234
  incorrect, 235, 240
  pressure of, 143, 209–10, 223, 252, 306, 309–10

H

habits, 31–32, 76, 392–95, 399, 402
Harkleroad, Ashley, xvi, 50–51
Harrison, Ryan, 389

Hingis, Martina, 11
hitting zone, 158, 162, 165, 190–93,
    205, 278, 327

I

impact, 124, 142, 144–45, 172, 191–
    93, 215, 239–40, 248–49, 251,
    258, 285, 292, 307, 325, 330,
    336, 378
improvements, 8–9, 25, 80, 82, 89,
    102, 104, 125–26, 174, 178,
    233, 347, 369, 371–72, 396, 409
  methods of, 371–72
injuries, 81, 90, 98–99, 117, 211, 226,
    232, 239, 302, 329, 335, 371,
    376–78, 384–85
Isner, John, 226

K

Key Biscayne, Florida, 148
Kuznetsov, Alex, xvi, 128

L

learning process, 1, 20, 43, 45, 69, 91,
    100, 127, 130–31, 133, 397
lessons, 21, 84, 152–53
  group, 7, 68, 88, 162, 205
  organization of, 55, 66
  private, 7, 21, 68, 88
  progression of, 4
level
  entry, 17, 95
  international, x, xxi, 17, 100, 303
  national, 5, 16, 80
  of play, 66
  pro, 5, 16, 100–101, 209

M

Match Play, 13–14, 23, 28, 30, 32,
    62–63, 68–69, 89, 95–97, 104,

    115, 134, 179–80, 189, 223,
    229, 231, 280, 297, 315, 320,
    327, 348, 358, 367–68, 393,
    395, 397, 400, 408
mental skills, vii, 31–32, 174, 342, 344,
    391–94, 405, 409
motivation, 9, 32, 37, 53, 81–84, 393
movement program, 8, 367–68

N

Nadal, Rafael, 11, 110, 170
National Training Center, 132

O

opponents, 8, 12–14, 27–29, 76–77,
    112, 135–36, 138–39, 150–53,
    170–72, 179, 186, 188–90,
    211–14, 216, 233–34, 241–42,
    254–55, 261–62, 266–68, 275–
    76, 288–94, 297–301, 303–5,
    307, 309–11, 314–17, 320–24,
    342–57, 360–65, 396–400
  weaknesses of, 12–13, 28, 152, 177,
    289, 343, 346–47, 355
overhead, 26–27, 137, 280–86, 317,
    377, 420
  common mistakes of, 284
overtraining, 18, 82, 96–99, 374, 408

P

plan
  basic, 344, 346
  game, 3, 400
  periodization, 74, 96
  tournament, 4, 74, 83
players, xxii, 5–6, 125–26, 168, 174
  age of, 125
  all-court, 360–61
  best, 345, 348, 396
  clay-court, 304
  competitive, 93, 263, 385–86, 388

listening, 55–56

organizational, 54

spin, 131, 141–42, 145, 170–72, 183, 186–87, 197–98, 200, 212–13, 215–16, 218, 223–24, 227, 229, 232, 234–35, 237, 239, 242–48, 251, 253–58, 261, 264–66, 270–72, 275, 288, 292, 302–4, 331–32, 344–45

amount of, 141, 151, 186–87, 201, 230, 243, 302

split step, 135, 157, 161, 164, 204, 214, 261, 263, 265, 268–71, 273, 275–77, 289–90, 320, 323–24, 326, 328, 338

sports, ix, xiii, 7, 30, 35–37, 48, 52, 61, 68, 97–99, 120–21, 322, 384, 392, 394, 398–99, 406–7, 409–10

stability, 10, 106, 119, 158, 162, 165, 191, 205, 220, 230, 238, 240, 278, 330, 372, 395, 410

stamina, 7, 15, 87, 116–17, 151, 257, 359, 361, 366–69, 400, 404

stances, 144, 178, 185, 190, 217, 222–23, 327, 330–32

closed, 159, 166, 330, 332–33

foot, 107, 192, 194–95

open, 137, 330–32, 336

semiopen, 181, 326, 332

status, tactical, 114–15, 316, 330, 357

Stosur, Sam, 226

strategies, 2, 14, 96, 127, 147, 172, 342, 345, 349, 355

basic, 96, 177, 234, 345–46, 349, 351

strengths, 7, 9, 28, 30–31, 34–35, 70, 73, 75–77, 81–82, 91, 96, 98–99, 103, 115–17, 134, 142–43, 152, 168, 172, 177, 207, 210, 222, 247, 342–43, 346, 355, 366–67, 369–70, 373–74

stress management, 32, 393

strings, 50, 140–42, 144, 176, 187, 190, 197, 207, 211, 243, 247, 257, 272, 274–75, 373

flexibility of, 50, 207, 272

strokes, 8, 14, 79, 83, 107, 123, 134, 137, 143, 151, 155, 162, 170, 176, 180, 185, 197, 201, 208–9, 258, 267–69, 285, 297, 302, 304, 320, 340, 366, 370–72, 398

analysis of, 107, 156

arsenal of, 297, 355

baseline, 47, 131, 150, 152, 174, 186, 198, 315, 330, 334, 359–60, 419

basic, 26, 123, 133

coordinate, 119, 369, 372

corrections in, 6

cross-court, 180, 189

defensive, 290, 355

delicate, 306, 309

depth of, 139

detecting errors in, 129

down-the-line, 182

drop shot, 307

forehand, 22, 26–28, 47, 75–76, 79, 110–11, 131, 153, 158, 170–73, 182, 197, 200, 246, 257, 271, 273, 288, 310, 319, 321, 325, 334, 336, 340, 348, 355, 359, 365, 415–17

fundamentals of, 13, 96, 124

ground, 12, 22, 26, 131, 199, 207, 238, 257, 262, 290, 303, 361–63

key positions of, 155

lob, 315

off-balance, 191, 363

offensive, 153, 315

open-stance, 325

overhead, 280

visual, 69

weight, 8, 117, 171, 207, 367–68, 372, 378

training plan, 4, 74, 81, 84, 86–87, 125

trajectory, 13, 27, 45, 103, 107–10, 115, 136, 138–39, 141–42, 151, 170, 172, 183–84, 211–12, 214–15, 232–33, 235–36, 239–40, 262–66, 274–75, 280, 297–300, 302–4, 306–7, 315–16, 320–22, 344–45, 350, 355–57, 415–16

Tsonga, Jo-Wilfried, 226

V

van Daalen, Tom, 21–22

vision, 3, 10, 37, 49, 52, 85, 180, 426

volleys, 11, 26–27, 87, 111–13, 142, 145–46, 213–14, 216, 226, 229, 257, 263, 265–66, 271–78, 288–89, 291–94, 305, 309–11, 313–17, 351, 360–62, 417–21

common mistakes of, 273

drive, 213, 216, 311–12

half, 145, 289, 313–14

poach, 276

W

weaknesses, 9, 12–14, 18, 28, 70, 73, 75–77, 80–82, 103, 115–16, 152, 172, 177, 289, 342–43, 346–47, 350, 355, 396, 398, 400

weapon development, 8–9, 12, 14, 76, 345, 349, 359

weight-training program, 177, 370, 375

weight transfer, 136, 142, 144, 158, 162, 165, 179–80, 190–91, 194, 205, 207, 209, 211–12, 225–26, 249, 278, 285, 292, 299, 307, 315, 320, 330–32, 337

Williams, Rhyne, 148

Williams, Venus, 11

Wimbledon, 101, 112, 174

winners, 79, 112, 170, 203, 261–62, 267, 363, 397

work ethic, 15, 120

WTA (Women's Tennis Association), xvi, 11

Y

Yeager, Andrea, 11

Printed in the United States
By Bookmasters